Praise for Democracy at the Crossroads

"Craig Barnes has compiled nothing less than a narrative history of the rule of law, a highly accessible, sweeping, historical panoply that represents jurisprudence for everyday citizens. Once again, the Great Writ that protects the rights of all of us has found its champion."

—Gary Hart, author of *Under the Eagle's Wing*

"*Democracy at the Crossroads* is a timely reminder of our forefathers hard-fought struggle for the rule of law and an inspiring call to arms to all Americans to work together to make our nation one of laws and essential democratic values once again."

—Bob Edgar, president, Common Cause

"Where did our governmental institutions come from? A fascinating and readable genealogy of Democracy."

—Richard D. Lamm, former Colorado governor

"Like a mariner taking back bearings with his compass as he navigates a narrow passage in cross currents, Barnes's book provides the historical perspective of key transitions in the history of democracy—a perspective, if heeded, sufficient to keep this democratic republic off the shoals of apathy and the rocks of excess as we transit the epochal changes of the twenty-first century."

—Buie Seawell, Professor of Business Law and Ethics,
University of Denver

DEMOCRACY
AT THE CROSSROADS

DEMOCRACY
AT THE CROSSROADS
PRINCES, PEASANTS, POETS, AND PRESIDENTS
IN THE STRUGGLE FOR (AND AGAINST)
THE RULE OF LAW

CRAIG S. BARNES

FULCRUM

GOLDEN, COLORADO

Library of Congress Cataloging-in-Publication Data

Barnes, Craig S.
  Democracy at the crossroads : princes, peasants, poets, and presidents in the struggle for (and against) the rule of law / Craig S. Barnes.
      p. cm. -- (Speaker's corner)
  Includes bibliographical references and index.
  ISBN 978-1-55591-726-5 (pbk.)
  1. Democracy--History. 2. Rule of law--History. 3. Civil rights--History. I. Title.
  JC423.B26119 2009
  321.8--dc22
                              2009030656

Printed on recycled paper in the United States of America by Malloy, Inc.
0 9 8 7 6 5 4 3 2 1

Fulcrum Publishing
4690 Table Mountain Drive, Suite 100
Golden, Colorado 80403
800-992-2908 • 303-277-1623
www.fulcrumbooks.com

To the memory of Donald Barnes,
whose sense of fairness and integrity framed a life
of quiet commitment to the public good,

and

to the memory of those heroes and heroines
whose lives, recounted here,
tell the tale of the remarkable emergence
of the rule of law.

Contents

III: American Values Deeper than Capitalism, Deeper than Law

IV: An Age Ends

Preface

In the 1940s, when I was a small boy growing up under cotton-woods amid the wheat fields of eastern Colorado, we did not have work to do in the evenings. There was no TV at that time, and we were too far out of town—and often could not afford—to go to the movies, so mostly we stayed at home. On special occasions my father would pick up Robert Louis Stevenson or *Black Bartlemy's Treasure* and read to us of pirates and kings and grand frigates on heaving seas. Some winter nights he would read Babe and Little Joe stories from *The Saturday Evening Post*. Then my mother would find a place on the big couch by the fire and pick up her knitting. As we three boys grew older and larger she would have to make new wool sweaters for us each year, so she was always knitting a great deal. Sometimes, while my father read out loud and assisted Babe and Little Joe into—and then out of—great trouble, I helped wind my mother's yarn into tight balls while my two brothers lay sprawled on the floor at my father's feet.

During those years, although we were growing up rural, my father was apt to draw attention to grand issues like slavery in ancient Athens or the extraordinary tradition of American support of public education. He was proud of the labor movement, which had made a place for working people in the United States, and was fully aware that, but for very good fortune, he would still be working in the logging camps of Oregon. He was an escapee from backbreaking labor by reason of his own effort to get an engineering education that he eventually turned into a career in international development, building dams and roads to villages with names that traced all the way back to Nebuchadnezzar. He liked to think of the world as progressing toward some better place and the United States as having an important role. In that way he was a direct descendant of Thomas Jefferson and John Adams, for, as I was later to learn, they too saw the United States as pioneering a new order for the ages. At home, my father was inclined to praise neighbors who were honest when it came to sharing irrigation water or hay, and he was proud of the US government and its assistance to those less fortunate than we. He was a civil servant and often told us that it was the highest duty of a civil servant to look out for the public interest. He knew many men in government, he said, who were honestly devoted to doing the best that they could, and we should never accept this idea that government was by nature bad for the American people. What I remember most was his emphasis on good and honorable men, some of whom he knew and some of whom he had read about, who had made this country decent and generous. (He did not speak of good and honorable women in public life because at that time there were very few women in politics and very little had been written of their contributions through the centuries.) He was not a pacifist, though. He did not ignore men in history who had pioneered diplomatic or legislative or legal solutions to great crises, but he had fought in World War II and was proud of that service. On the other hand, he might have said that the law to restrain kings was the thin line that marked our new civilization from the old world of czars and tyrants. He would point out during dinner table conversations that in those places where kings were above the law, common people invariably suffered.

Study history, he said, and you will see.

And so I did.

What I found was of two parts. The first was that Western ideals of liberty and equality had evolved through a long and extremely dramatic series of confrontations over centuries. The second was that the architects of these ideals had been men and women of extraordinary courage and substantial education. Some were warriors, but some were lawyers or historians, some moved by an inner passion so great that they moved against kingly power, were drawn to that danger like moths to the flame, risking, and often giving, their lives. They wrote, cajoled, and sometimes cried out for all to hear that the law is above the king. Not only that, perhaps even unknown to themselves they birthed the foundational idea that in an urban society, the law is also the enforcer of decency, compassion, honesty, and something we call fairness.

As my life and personal exploration unfolded, and after eighteen years of practicing law in Colorado courts, I was caught up in informal negotiations on issues of nuclear weapons in the Soviet Union. These negotiations in the 1980s were between members of the Soviet Academy of Sciences and Western scientists who had raised issues concerning the probabilities of nuclear war. On the Soviet side—and my most prominent bargaining opponent—was Anatoly Gromyko, son of the president of the USSR. At the table with him was an array of Soviet academicians, some at the very highest levels of Soviet science. On our side was a team consisting of US scientists, editors, businessmen, and a prominent Stanford professor, Martin Hellman. Hellman was a world-renowned cryptologist whom the Kremlin wanted very much to subvert. They did not succeed. Hellman and I worked side by side to pursue his thesis that if the mind-set did not change, nuclear war was certain. For two years he and I traveled back and forth between the United States and the USSR debating, squeezing out language from Soviet scientists and compromises from their US counterparts. These negotiations finally produced a joint volume of essays entitled *Breakthrough: Emerging New Thinking*, which was published by Progress Press in Moscow (in Russian) and Walker Publishing in New York. It turned out to be the first such joint production since the Bolshevik revolution of 1917 and was eventually endorsed by both General Secretary Mikhail Gorbachev and US Secretary of State George Shultz. My job had been to edit the manuscripts of the two sides. Through the years of these editing negotiations, which took place in the Santa Cruz mountains of California, in Kiev, Leningrad, and predominantly in Moscow, I gradually found that I was engaging a cultural history that used the same words as my own but operated with vastly different assumptions. We said the same things but didn't mean the same things.

After the fall of the Berlin Wall in 1989 our contact continued, and Soviet legal experts would say to me, "We just want a *normal* society." Conversations among us at Soviet institutes of law and policy then became discussions about what was "normal." The Russians argued that if they were given an appropriate constitution or codes, they would be on their way. Most Americans believed the same thing. But during the *Breakthrough* negotiations, I had become convinced that other values were operating under the surface that were not so clear and were a distinct barrier to becoming if not normal, at least democratic. At the time I still did not know what those assumptions were.

All told, I spent twenty years going back and forth to the former Soviet Union negotiating and debating issues of corruption, ethnic cleansing, water and power, law and commerce, and the psychology of civil society. Over these years it became abundantly clear that my first impressions from the *Breakthrough* negotiations had been correct. US assumptions about power and competence and equality, to name a few, were not the same as Russian or Armenian or Azerbaijani or Kazakh or Tajik assumptions. We used the same words, but often expectations concerning honesty, contract, or imponderables such as fairness or justice were vastly different. Beneath the patina of civil codes were centuries of accommodation to power and privilege that an American could hardly comprehend.

As these negotiations were winding down I began, at home, to look for answers in that history of the Western world that my father had loved so much. Something else then became clear: democracy is not a given of social evolution. Many people will hold on to family and clan, loyalty to persons or leaders, corruption and privilege rather than to the ideals of Thomas Paine or Thomas Jefferson. Not just elsewhere. Even in our own country, many politicians and commentators do not believe that the law should be above the king or the oligarchs or above the interests of the vastly propertied.

It became apparent, finally, that this noble inheritance, the rule of law and a civil society bound by conventions of justice and fairness, is today under challenge. The United States is once again engaged in a great struggle for its civic soul, and once again we are called upon to ensure, in the words of Abraham Lincoln, that those few who have already given their lives for these civic ideals shall not have done so in vain.

The tale does not, however, begin with Gettysburg or Lincoln. Nor does the struggle for human dignity and freedom begin with the American Republic. The longer story is a tale of courage and blood, ideals and desperate risk that goes further back than 1776. I think my father would be pleased if we took time to explore themes marking the birth of the rule of law, and also the despair in the lives of those who believed in it. They thought the law should be above the king, or, as the case may be, the president.

Acknowledgments

In the earliest years of Moscow negotiations over the issues raised in the nuclear arms race and eventually the issues raised in this book, I was repeatedly hosted with consideration and great kindness by Andrei Melville and Alexander Nikitin, who miraculously opened doors at the Soviet Academy of Sciences. Detailed and intense discussions of the differences between Western and Soviet culture then ensued over a two-year period with Sergei Kapitza at the Institute of Physics and Roald Sagdeev at the Space Research Institute, who was in turn tirelessly assisted by Elena Loschenkova, herself a physicist and a driving force behind our joint work. Anatoly Gromyko opened doors at the Central Committee of the Communist Party of the Soviet Union and at Progress Publishing, and together he and I engaged in months-long debates over the content of the Western and Soviet thinking. It is from the sum of these conversations at the Academy of Sciences that I first gleaned a profound appreciation of the nuances of a culture based upon personal relationships, which is the subject of part three of this book. My American colleagues who were engaged in this project are far too numerous to name, but special recognition must be given to Martin Hellman of Stanford University and to my colleagues at the Beyond War Foundation: Bill McGlashan, Don Fitton, Bill Busse, Richard Rathbun, and Rick Roney. No team could have been more profoundly enriching.

After the collapse of the Soviet Union, my participation in talks between Azerbaijan and Armenia would have been impossible without the devoted weeks and months of conversations with Arzu Abdulaeva, Zardusht Ali Zadeh, Anahit Bayandour, and Hasmik Chutilian. Bill Busse again assisted in these conversations, together with Libby Traubman and Samantha Schoenfeld from the Beyond War Foundation. Lee Ross at Stanford guided us into the intricacies of mediation. Subsequent talks over the years concerning civil society and the nature of the rule of law that were held in Baku, Azerbaijan, would have been entirely impossible without the aid of Alexander Chernyumurkin and Laura Dodson. The pursuit of such projects independent of dictatorial government requires Herculean stamina that most Westerners can little imagine.

I am deeply indebted to Bob Baron and Sam Scinta at Fulcrum Publishing who, at an early stage in the contemplation of this book, encouraged thoughtful rumination about what an American learns from years of negotiating within the former Soviet Union. Without Haley Berry, my editor, it is unlikely that this book would ever have come to any kind of coherent whole, and I am grateful for her thoughtful redirection of my multiple diversions.

Librarians at the Stanford University Law Library were especially gracious, and John Sturgeon's assistance to gain entry into the Huntington Library in Pasadena was invaluable. Without the Huntington and therefore Catharine Macaulay's contribution to my knowledge of the seventeenth century, I would have been dependent largely upon David Hume, who was in no sense a democrat. Finally, my wife Mikaela's tolerance for late-night reading of endless volumes of dusty history has sustained me throughout, and without her encouragement I should have long ago turned to dust myself.

Prologue

JOHN COOKE INDICTS HIS MAJESTY THE KING

On a cold January day in the year 1649, a perfectly ordinary lawyer stood in the vastness of Westminster Hall in London to read a charge of treason against Charles Stuart, king of England. Beside that lawyer, in the equivalent of the prisoner's dock, sat His Royal Majesty. Before this most unlikely pair was arrayed a jury of sixty of England's most wealthy and prestigious landowners, burghers, lawyers, and military men. The jurors had been assembled by Parliament, and not one of them was glad to be there. To try a king for any reason was unheard of. To try a king for treason was to link him to an offense that presented a contradiction in terms. The king *was* the state, *embodied* the state, and could not therefore *act against* the state. Such a trial had never before occurred anywhere in the Western world.

Like other monarchs of his time, King Charles I was accustomed to making the law, not being governed by it. He derived his authority, he said, directly from God and claimed divine sanction to determine matters that might arise under the traditional common law. In the king's chambers, any man who entered the presence was expected to kneel silently and await the king's nod so that he might speak. In the exercise of his absolute authority, Charles had a habit of rounding up troublesome subjects and throwing them into prison for not paying him "loans" to conduct his wars. He scorned the ancient writ of habeas corpus that maintained that a subject could be jailed only for a crime. In Charles's mind, royal power was close to absolute. Parliament had begun to discuss the idea that power came not from God or the king, but from the people. That would be a source of contention for many years after this.

On this day in January 1649, however, England had long been involved in a desperate and bloody civil war, a war that Charles had finally lost. As a result, the man now stood trial in Westminster Hall. This was a great oaken chamber built by his ancestor Richard II; here common law courts had been held for hundreds of years. On this day there would be only one court. All the rest had been cleared out for a case certain to make history.

The lawyer chosen to read the charge against the king was one John Cooke. He had been born to a simple rural family and was one of a rare few who without status or privilege had still managed to obtain training in the law. Cooke had, during the course of his career, even championed certain legal reforms. The death penalty for stealing a loaf of bread, he argued, was too harsh. To limit access to the law to the wealthy and privileged, he argued, was too narrow. During the course of Cooke's career, other lawyers of nobler lineage had thought him a troublesome outsider. But in the 1640s, the king and Parliament had fallen into all-out war. After seven years, the king lost a pivotal battle and was captured. Parliament thereupon confined him to a castle, not sure what to do with him. Some legal remedy had to be found to dispose of him, but no man of aristocratic descent could be found to do this job. The legal problem was this: how could an inferior body, Parliament, judge the superior part, the sovereign of them all? Still, the man had made war upon his own people, had imprisoned his own people, had denounced and attacked the whole idea of a parliament, had suspended Parliament and attempted to govern alone. Was this not tyranny?

Then, while the king was still in captivity and while the leaders of Parliament were pondering his fate, spies determined that Charles had been sending secret messages attempting to rouse loyalist troops from Scotland. He would have them reinvade

England on his behalf. These troops might, in turn, be eventually supported by soldiers from France. The Stuart dynasty had long enjoyed close ties to the Catholic monarchy in Paris. If Catholics reinvaded, Anglican England would again be at war with the papist continent. On the basis of all this evidence, the leaders of Parliament concluded that as long as Charles Stuart lived, the portent of war would forever hang over England. Their lives and properties were at risk and would remain so as long as the king was alive to scheme and conspire. Something drastic had to be done to bring the matter to an end.

War against Parliament must surely qualify as treason, but how could a king commit treason if his actions were those of the state itself? No one was sure. They called upon John Cooke, the commoner's lawyer, the outsider. Cooke accepted their invitation and studiously set to prepare a charge. Finding that he was willing, Parliament now was in a great hurry to get the business over with. Cooke had only to give them the legal justification. They would allow Cooke a few days to prepare, perhaps over the weekend, but all England was unsafe as long as the king was plotting and scheming to start up the war again.

So Cooke got to work. He wrote in the charge that a sovereign was trusted with a *limited* power to govern *for the benefit and good of the people*. And, said Cooke, for a sovereign to attack his own parliament and thus attack his own people, to ignore the long tradition of habeas corpus, and to deny the even older tradition of due process was to violate the very principles of law at the foundation of the realm. This was not only treason, this was the crime of *tyranny*. He wrote it all out on paper and went to court.

The king was duly brought to Westminster Hall, surrounded by soldiers and before a huge crowd of curious onlookers. Probably more than two thousand people were crammed into that hall that day. The king was dressed in silks and finery, his garments themselves emblems of unimpeachable authority. Cooke, by contrast, was in legal black.

Cooke arose and stood before the hushed assembly. "My Lord President…," he began.

"Hold!" cried the king, who would now challenge the very jurisdiction of the assembled parliamentarians.

The two men were so close that the king could reach out with his silver-tipped cane and touch the lawyer. As he cried, "Hold!" he tapped Cooke sharply upon the shoulder.

"I do, in the name and on behalf of the people of England…," Cooke went on reading.

"Hold!" cried the king a second time, and this time the monarch jabbed the commoner wickedly in the ribs.

"…according to an order of this High Court to me directed…," Cooke went on reading.

"Hold!" cried the king a third time, and now he struck Cooke upon the shoulder with a blow of such violence that the silver tip of his cane broke off and rolled down Cooke's considerable chest, over his stomach, and onto the floor. An astonished hush fell upon the assembled thousands. The king motioned to the broken silver tip of his cane. From the look on his face, no one could doubt his royal command: Pick it up!

"…do bring into this court a charge of high treason, whereof I do accuse Charles Stuart, King of England, here present…," Cooke went on reading.[1]

The king of England, lord of the English, Irish, Scotch, and all their dominions, protector of the faith, first among the lords of the realm, now bent down to the feet of John Cooke the lawyer to pick up the broken tip of his own cane. The son of the son of the daughter of kings, inheritor of the crown of Tudors, Lancasters, Yorks, and Plantagenets, bowed down beneath the law.

The age of democracy had begun.

A POCKET HISTORY
OF THE RULE OF LAW

1

THE LONG LIFE OF LYING

I announce that my origin is from Crete.

—Odysseus, deceiving the swineherd upon his return to Ithaca,
from Homer's *The Odyssey*

Cretans always lie.

—Epimenides, sixth-century BC Cretan philosopher

It had taken almost thirty years for Charles Stuart to work him-self into that chair in Westminster Hall. England had not gotten to that historic turning point in one lifetime, or, truly, in a dozen lifetimes. No king could be brought to trial without the force of history heaving against him like some great wave pushing the royal craft onto the rocks. No one in Parliament really wanted democracy. But the umbrage, insult, hurt, and sorrow that led the parliamentarians to that day had become an irresistible emo-tional force. Parliament wanted relief from chaos and anguish and confusion of loyalties and, in its way, the trial of Charles Stuart would justify and resolve their pain.

The English struggle, however—and later the American tri-umph—cannot be understood in terms of one incident or one man. They are more than the story of John Cooke or Thomas Paine. The progress is not a straight line. The move toward democracy is some-times reversed. It may be, ironically, that free societies are much easier to lose than to create. Reverting to tyranny is quicker. "Time is the enemy of republics," said former US senator Gary Hart. The senator may have been thinking that it did not take thirty years to get from Pericles to the death of Socrates, put to death by nameless elites. Caesar effectively did away with the Roman Republic in one lifetime. Whatever there was of German democracy was done away with by Hitler in less than a decade. Whatever strides Mikhail Gorbachev and Boris Yeltsin made toward the rule of law in Russia were done away with by Vladimir Putin in less than five years. Whatever was built by Americans over three hundred years was threatened by George W. Bush and Dick Cheney within the first four years of their term. It was clear during the years 2001 to 2009 that some deeper understanding of what was at stake was simply absent. The regime evidently did not understand the tradition that they were putting on the block.

However tempting it might be to turn immediately to the issues raised by the recent US administration, the enormity of the potential loss cannot be understood if the focus is on these defendants alone. The crisis is not truly about them. The rule of law cannot be understood in terms of the US Constitution alone, or international law, or war crimes. The problem is deeper than codes or laws. The rule of law is, as it turns out, about more than law.

So let us begin at the beginning. We have been working on this for some twenty-five hundred years. We would do well to understand what we are made of, and what we are not.

Epimenides was a sixth-century-BC sage who crossed the Aegean Sea to Attica in order to advise the ancient Athenians about how to get along in the world. He was probably right when he said that Cretans lie, and he might well have said the same about strangers in general. Aegean culture was slowly evolving from the chaos today labeled "the Greek Dark Ages," wherein piracy, plunder, and patriarchal murder were givens.

At about this same time, the Greek poet Homer gave to the Western world the story of the warrior hero Odysseus on his journey home from the Trojan War. Odysseus was a wily fox who outsmarted the Trojans with the great hollow horse, then deceived the one-eyed Cyclops (location unknown), the goddess of enchantment Circe on her island, the hospitable Phaiakians on their island, and then the suitors of his wife, Penelope. In general, Odysseus was a capable liar. Homer called him "crafty," and craftiness, for Homer, was a most honorable quality. The trick was to know *when* to lie. When Odysseus was with his son, he did not lie at all. When he was with his wife, Penelope, he only lied sometimes. She was, however, a female, and thus weaker, and was from different family stock, and therefore a stranger, and lying to the weak or to strangers was usually acceptable. A whole bundle of values were tied up in that one story. But these were not just Homer's values. Epimenides saw the same thing: in an ancient society at the birth of Western civilization, don't trust anybody you don't know very well.[1]

When the Greeks went to war against Troy (about 1220 BC),[2] Agamemnon was the king, leader of all other kings, and Odysseus was a minor ruler of a small island who followed Agamemnon. Agamemnon's power was the final arbiter of right and wrong. Even the great warrior Achilles was a vassal of Agamemnon, because fewer villages followed him and he commanded fewer warriors. The content of Agamemnon's character was largely irrelevant to his position of power. Agamemnon had at an earlier time murdered the first husband of his wife, Clytemnestra, then killed her nursing child by her former husband, and finally sacrificed his own daughter Iphigenia to get a fair wind to sail off to Troy.[3] Whatever Iphigenia might stand for—the sacred feminine, the rights of inheritance, the quality of reproduction, or even just beauty—all that was and would continue to be sacrificed, both literally and symbolically, to the power of the supreme patriarch and the requirements of war.

In Agamemnon's world as Homer described it, the highest social value was clan or family and the assurance of continuation of the patriarchy, the family line through sons. Maintenance of the clan required serious attention to hierarchy, by any means. Secrecy, brute force, cheating, and cruelty might sometimes be necessary. Might makes right, and power, so long as it is successful, contains its own moral justification. Put another way, if someone is more powerful, he must be right. Thereafter, in the train of the king, those who are *not* the most powerful must use other devices. According to Homer, therefore, Odysseus survives because of his craftiness. These became values by which patriarchy would be maintained for most of history until 1776.

Through the study of Homer by Greek and Roman schoolchildren for a thousand years, deception became a blueprint for heroes and eventually for Western civilization.[4] In external relations, or those matters between clans, raw power became the first moral value; but when such power was not available, clever deception was the next choice. It was at the heart of the patriarchal mind. Lying was accepted by Athena and Zeus and was thus acceptable at the highest levels on Mount Olympus in the transcendent, eternal natural order. What might be called the Odysseus Principle—lying to strangers when necessary—was at the foundation of ancient patriarchy and, as we shall see, of modern feudalism. The dramatic, contrary story of how honesty emerges to have its own economic importance is the remarkable story of the struggle for the rule of law against the traditions of kings.

2

THE SHORT LIFE OF AN HONEST MAN IN ROME

Roman Virtue and Roman Liberty expired together.

—Cato

Some two hundred years after the death of Julius Caesar, Marcus Aurelius came to power in ancient Rome. He was a sort of ideal, a philosopher king. His leadership was benign and forthright and his care of the great empire conscientious and thoughtful. When Marcus died, his son Commodus succeeded him. No father and son could have been more different. Commodus was not interested in philosophy but rather styled himself a great gladiator. He sought out swordsmen and archers as teachers and held games in the Colosseum during which he himself took the field, using his extraordinary athletic ability to shoot at the lions, elephants, zebras, giraffes, and other creatures imported for his sport. Commodus fought and killed people too. He chose for himself the habit and weapons of the Secutor, armed with a helmet, sword, and buckler, and he would take the field against a naked antagonist who might be armed only with a net and trident. The poor prisoner and Commodus then engaged in mortal combat before the roaring multitudes in the Colosseum. And the emperor never lost, of course. According to Edward Gibbon in *The Decline and Fall of the Roman Empire*, Commodus donned the clothing of Secutor 735 times. That would mean that he personally murdered at least 735 men.[1]

All the limits of stoic philosophy that had been his father's dignity were Commodus's disdain. He proudly called himself the Roman Hercules, prostituting his person and dignity to violence and blood. His model of cruelty spread among the administrators of the empire, and destruction hung over the heads of any who might challenge his authority or whim. This despicable man was at last poisoned in his bed by his mistress, for even she was afraid that he would soon turn on her. His death is an early and telling example of how tyranny turns even apparently loving associates to treachery.

When the word of Commodus's murder raced through the streets of Rome that night, there was at first disbelief and then huge relief. Laetus, commander of the Praetorian Guard, bodyguards who were supposed to protect the person of the emperor, quickly settled upon an ancient senator named Pertinax to replace the murdered man. In his years, Pertinax had risen from the ranks to the first honors of the state. He was known for firmness and patience, prudence and integrity—the exact opposite of Commodus.

Laetus had been one of the conspirators with the dead emperor's mistress, and he now took the old senator to be introduced to the Praetorians. Laetus said to them, This is our new man. They quietly acquiesced, but there was no enthusiasm among them, for Pertinax was not their kind of man. He had more respect for the laws of Rome than they thought necessary.

Pertinax immediately instituted widespread reforms, opening commerce, reducing taxes, replenishing the public treasury, rehabilitating the finances of a regime that Commodus had left in desperate poverty. He remitted all the oppressive taxes invented by Commodus, canceled unjust claims on the treasury, declaring that he "was better satisfied to administer a poor republic with innocence, than to acquire riches by the ways of tyranny and dishonor."[2] At the same time, he turned title to his own private fortune over to his wife and son, to avoid any pretence that his role should bring gain to himself. He also refused to anoint his own son with the title of Caesar, which would have dubbed him successor; rather, he required time for both him and his son to prove themselves. He proceeded steadily to prosecute a band of assassins who had been a part of Commodus's reign, then gave over their process to the orderly forms of justice rather than seek to have them summarily executed. In all this Pertinax yielded nothing to popular prejudice and resentment but kept most high the interests of the whole of Rome and its people. He was the sort of man through whom the rule of law might emerge.

All these virtues in one man were, however, gall to the Praetorians. They had been on the receiving end of the booty of empire for a very long time, through a great many emperors. They were accustomed to controlling military power in the city of Rome at the heart of the state. Over the years new emperors, upon entry to the office, had been wont to pay the Praetorians or to promise them large fees, "donatives," that would vary according to the demands of the bidder and his resources. The Praetorians were thus so powerful that they had to be paid off to allow any new man to come to the head of the empire. Virtue in the person of Pertinax was not in their interest. Virtue was not a substitute for a donative. Virtue, worse, threatened donatives in the future. Virtue, therefore, was good cause for killing Pertinax.

The Praetorians rose in rebellion and, on only the eighty-sixth day of Pertinax's reign, stormed the palace and confronted him. After seeing that he would not run but would only appeal to their sense of justice, they killed him, separated his head from his body, and carried it on a pike through the streets. Those Praetorians still at the palace rushed out to the ramparts and proclaimed loudly that they would make the next emperor that man who would be the highest bidder at public auction. Before the night was over, they sold the empire to one Didius Julianus, a wealthy senator. The senator spent his fortune at the foot of the ramparts and bought the royal purple. Money and money alone purchased the right to lead the world's greatest military power. The great republic of Rome, the state ostensibly bound by law and tradition, or by the restraints of the Roman senate, which had previously been the source of the emperor's nomination, was now for sale. The law had been sold. Justice had been sold. Personal rule akin to that of Agamemnon had been restored.

The Praetorians had by this time, AD 193, evolved into a small, elite class more apt to claim privilege than to do any work. Over long periods they never used their weapons except to install or remove emperors. Praetorians had become parasites on the laurel branch, sucking up to themselves much more than they gave. Thus, Pertinax's crime had been his attempt to subordinate them and the rest of Rome to the law. It may be that during the earlier times of the Roman Republic, the law had held some sway over emperors and consuls, Praetorians and generals. After the murder of Pertinax, the law was more likely to be a prostitute to power.

In the millennium after the fall of the Roman Empire, Europe fractured into a thousand fiefdoms and bishoprics. Kings and popes, dukes and bishops replaced any single emperor. Exceptions to the rule of kings, such as in the republics of Venice or Florence, were rare, but even these produced leaders who manipulated and controlled the law to their personal benefit. For the most part, including within the so-called republics, Europe's territories were ruled by self-proclaimed royals, and not one of these kings, great or small, was forced to bow to, serve, or treat equally the urban poor or peasants or women or slaves or Jews. The law provided to all of these—who must have been the great majority of the population—no protection against royal power, no door to opportunity or protection against the torrents of misfortune.

3

THE MISERABLE LIFE OF A FEUDAL KING

Wherefore we will and firmly order…
that the men in our kingdom have and hold
all the aforesaid liberties, rights, and concessions,
well and peaceably, freely and quietly, fully and wholly,
for themselves and their heirs, of us and our heirs,
in all respects and in all places forever, as is aforesaid.

—Magna Carta, par. 63, 1215

As patriarchy grew into feudalism, the law became servant to kings. In Rome, after Pertinax, the established codes did not rule the emperor or his successors but were among many tools by which the rich and powerful sought to maintain hierarchy and inequality, separation and privilege. For at least a millennium, well into modern times, the law served the principle that might makes right, and that principle is bedrock for feudalism. "What the Emperor has determined has the force of a statute" was the principle encoded by the emperor Justinian in the sixth century.[1] The will of the emperor *is* law.

Following the ancient Roman tradition encoded by Justinian, King John I of medieval England was among those who wielded nearly absolute power: he enforced his own choices for High Church offices, though he was not the head of the church. He meddled with the property rights and inheritance of his barons and liege lords, though he was not a judge. He made war wherever he chose, unilaterally, though he was not by any means the only one to pay for war's exorbitant costs.

In AD 1204, King John insisted upon sailing with an army to attack France, but he was not a good general and his knights were badly defeated. The loss emptied the royal treasury, so the king issued a decree to raise taxes, which he had already done on more than one occasion. Hurt by his defeats, his prestige was declining and his barons and subjects becoming increasingly restless. During the next ten years they tolerated him, but with growing resistance. Dissenters such as Robin Hood were also now taking rebellion to the forests.

Then, in 1214, the king again sailed for France and lost yet another battle. This time he lost all of England's possessions in France. It was a crushing blow, a stunning loss of prestige, dignity, and English treasure. England was now ruled by a despotic and defeated king who saddled his subjects with oppressive taxation for an ill-conceived war. He exacted properties and feudal privileges arbitrarily, sometimes without consideration for widows or the weak and often with no respect for the great landowners. "Send me your son," he ordered William Marshal, Earl of Pembroke, taking the child hostage to ensure the loyalty of Marshal and his wife.

Finally, a remarkable gaggle of bishops, earls, barons, constables, and other persons of high estate rebelled. Without doctrine or religion to justify their cause, they nevertheless resisted their king. A showdown was forced in the meadow at Runnymede, in the open, outside the ramparts of Windsor Castle. On a warm summer's day, in one afternoon, the principle of absolute royal power collapsed. The scene was described by Winston Churchill:

> On a Monday morning in June, between Staines and Windsor, the barons and Churchmen began to collect on the great meadow at Runnymede. An uneasy hush fell on them…Many had failed to…[attend] and the bold few who had come knew that the King would never forgive this humiliation. He would

hunt them down when he could, and the laymen at least were staking their lives in the cause they served. They had arranged a little throne for the King and a tent. The handful of resolute men had drawn up, it seems, a short document on parchment. Their retainers and the groups and squadrons of horsemen in sullen steel kept at some distance and well in the background. For was not armed rebellion against the Crown the supreme feudal crime? Then events followed rapidly. A small cavalcade appeared from the direction of Windsor. Gradually men made out the faces of the King, the Papal Legate, the Archbishop of Canterbury, and several bishops. They dismounted without ceremony. Someone, probably the Archbishop, stated briefly the terms that were suggested. The King declared at once that he agreed. He said the details should be arranged immediately in his chancery…They were sealed in a quiet, short scene, which has become one of the most famous in our history, on June 15, 1215.[2]

King John had been forced to sign a document, a contract forever after to be known as the Great Contract, the Great Charter, or the Magna Carta. *Contract* is the best word because it states an ongoing obligation, an enforceable commitment—more than just a declaration or statement of purpose or a weak king's weak intention. In feudal terms, the foundation of friendships and alliances as well as loyalties and conspiracies had been critically undermined. Violence, pillage, blood, and mayhem had been the alternative to this contract, and these had been rejected in favor of a nonviolent contract.

The document named all the high potentates and lords to whom kings would thenceforth be forever bound, including the archbishop of Canterbury, Stephen Langton, the preeminent religious authority in all of England and a leading philosopher of his time. With him were the bishops of Lincoln, Worcester, and Coventry; the pope's own personal representative; the aforementioned William Marshal, Earl of Pembroke; the Earl of Arundel;

and other holders of broad lands and marvelous castles. Of all these nobles, William Marshal was perhaps most noteworthy. He had served three kings in his long life and was known from his early days as "the greatest knight" for his incomparable prowess in tournaments. In trial by combat, none had ever proved his superior. By now, as an older man, no longer just a knight, he had become the most powerful of all the peerage and the most influential.

Since the days before Richard the Lionheart, Marshal had ever been loyal to his king and he remained so now. When the assemblage gathered at Runnymede that day, Marshal therefore stood with King John. Marshal's counsel had always been more conciliatory than belligerent, and now he both stabilized King John and awakened him to the necessities of compromise. He brought the king to the table, and in so doing saved England from civil war. Marshal's reason trumped King John's unbounded arrogance. After years of building crisis, the king reluctantly, angrily, spitting nails, bent to the counsel of his greatest knight.

And in this, the greatest knight became known to history as a conciliator. Because he was most powerful of all and because he had been closest to the king, had Marshal taken the more usual courtier's course and urged John I to resist the upstart nobles at Runnymede, had he flattered the king and reinforced that man's unbounded self-pity, it is likely that the Magna Carta would never have been signed. Rather than that of a historic contract that initiates the rule of law in England, the date June 15, 1215, would have just recorded another bloody battle.

In the evolution of the rule of law, the appearance of a man or woman of character in the right place and at the right time has often been critical. This was one of those times, and Marshal was one of those people. It is hard to imagine a turning point or even an accident in history that might have had greater ripples through time than did the signing of the Magna Carta. Marshal was certainly no democrat, much less a rebel. But he did an honorable thing. He aided a tyrant in climbing down off his high horse and in so doing in turning a corner that had not been turned elsewhere in Europe.

The introductory paragraph of the Magna Carta names all the great lords and then begins a long list of promises from the sovereign king to his liege subjects. *Liege* means that they are loyal to him and *sovereign* that he should have supreme authority. The document that follows, however, turns those concepts—and the absolute authority recommended by the widely prevailing Justinian Code—upside down. The Magna Carta makes the loyalty of the people dependent upon the king's correct use of his royal power. The bargain would now be *two-sided*. Rule well and we will follow, say the nobility, but rule badly and we have the right to resist in every way at our disposal. No English king, nor French, nor Spanish, nor Italian had ever before been forced to write down such a bargain to the disadvantage of supreme feudal authority.

Here the history of civil liberty begins. It may even be the beginning of what we today call civil society. It is certainly the beginning, in English history, of the rights of assembly and open debate concerning matters of public interest. Not since the republic of ancient Rome had any society, even in the rest of Europe, been governed by the principles to be spelled out in the Great Charter. Not since the Caesars *ended* the Roman Republic had the governed exercised effective power over their governor. Here also is the foundation of the principle that the authority of the ruler comes not from his power, wealth, or family line, nor from his connection to God, his character, or even his sublime personal dignity. Rather, the authority of the ruler in this case, now in England, will arise from his contract with the ruled. A *contract*, unlike the blessing of God, is enforceable and can be rescinded. If one side does not perform his part of the bargain, the whole contract can be rejected by the other side, which is to say, in effect, that if a king does not honor *his* duties to his people, *they* may rebel. Now, in 1215, arose the principle of the law above personal rule, a principle that still is not in actual practice in Russia, China, Nigeria, Azerbaijan, Kazakhstan, Venezuela, in countries the world around—take your pick.

In the first paragraph of the Magna Carta, King John grants "to all freemen of our kingdom, for us and our heirs for ever, all the underwritten liberties, to be had and held by them and their heirs, of us and our heirs for ever." Then begins a recitation of sixty-three paragraphs, details stating what these liberties are that are to be held forever. He grants the noble lords their right to inherit lands without excessive taxation. He grants rights to minor heirs and to widows. He agrees—fully conscious of the emblazoned knights assembled in battle armor in the green fields around him—that before the levy of royal taxes he will summon an assembly of those to be taxed:

> And for obtaining the common counsel of the kingdom [before] the assessing of a…[tax]…we will…cause to be summoned generally, through our sheriffs and bailiffs, and others who [will be subject to the tax a meeting] for a fixed date…after the expiry of at least forty days, and at a fixed place…and in all letters of such summons *we will specify the reason of the summons*.[3]

This paragraph is doubly significant because it is not just about creating an assembly or the beginning of a parliament, or even because it ties taxes to the assembly. Here is the foundation of the great American constitutional principles of notice and due process. Not only will those who must bear the tax be summoned to a common counsel, but the summons shall inform them of the *reasons* for the assembly, thus to give notice *in advance* and time to prepare to all who might be adversely affected. The king promises to give them a full forty days' notice, at a fixed time and place, and they will come to a meeting, to counsel and reason with him concerning such taxation. This principle of fair notice and due process is today spread throughout the width and breadth of US law and has its roots right here, in this promise of King John eight hundred years ago.

The Magna Carta goes further: courts of law shall thereafter not wander about trailing after the king, but rather be convened in a fixed place where suitors who need relief are themselves located. Courts will be accessible by general rule—not only by the grace of a self-interested or sometimes craven king. Here, for the first time, as a practical matter, justice becomes a concept *independent* of the royal will. No principle may be more at the heart of the division between today's democratic and autocratic worlds.

King John further promised that cases concerning land should be convened only in those counties where the land is actually situated. It is a simple provision that adds to the reliability of the evidence, but it is important because once again it establishes that it shall be evidence, and not the king's will, that shall be determinative in England's courts.

Finally, the Magna Carta promises that no one shall be imprisoned or lose his land or be exiled or in any way destroyed "except by the lawful judgment of his peers or by the law of the land."[4] It also goes on to give more detail to the new brand of justice, with the king vowing that "to no one will we sell, to no one will we refuse or delay, right or justice"[5] and that he would "appoint as justices, constables, sheriffs, or bailiffs only such as know the law of the realm and mean to observe it well."[6]

These newly described liberties were to be enforced by a council of twenty-five barons, and they in turn were to be given allegiance similar to that of the king. Power was to be shared, and shared permanently. The twenty-five nobles were to be replaced when they died.

> Wherefore we will and firmly order...that the men in our kingdom have and hold all the aforesaid liberties, rights, and concessions, well and peaceably, freely and quietly, fully and wholly, for themselves and their heirs, of us and our heirs, in all respects and in all places forever, as is aforesaid.[7]

Within this remarkable first list of limitations of royal power were the foundations of today's requirement for fair notice, equal access to courts, trial by peers, political judgments after consultation, taxation only after discussion, and above all, that the law shall be above the whims of even the sovereign king. Had there been no Magna Carta, there likely would not have been a US Constitution. Our true American story, therefore, begins at least as far back as 1215.

Three months after he signed the document, King John renounced the Magna Carta and also persuaded Pope Innocent III to renounce its "shameful" provisions, including the council of twenty-five nobles and the doctrine of majority rule. The pope had for some time intended a Vatican-English alliance against the French, but he had had absolutely no intention of creating an independent secular power of haughty nobles. Even though Stephen Langton, the archbishop of Canterbury, was theoretically the pope's representative in England, the archbishop had turned out to be more English than Catholic. So the pope denounced the whole thing.

With this support, King John went back to war. He died fighting the next year. His nine-year-old son, Henry III, took the throne. He was weak simply because of his age, and under the considerable influence of his regent, William Marshal, he reaffirmed the charter in 1217 to reassure England's nobles that its promises would be maintained.[8] In this reaffirmation, Marshal, no doubt more than any other person, was responsible for the Magna Carta's preservation.

Henry reaffirmed the charter once more when he reached his majority, in 1225. These reaffirmations were apparently necessary to keep the throne in balance with the authority of the nobility, to hold England together, to halt the civil turmoil. Two generations later, in 1297, King Edward I was in similar trouble; he too needed the cooperation of his nobles and subjects in the villages and shires, and he too grudgingly renewed the royal commitment. Thus, after nearly a century of resistance and uncertainty, did a limit on unbridled royal power become an assumption of English law.

The councils of nobility to which John I had acquiesced, or to which later monarchs paid careful attention, arose at first simply as a substitute for civil war. Fair process or trial by jury or the right of assembly arose when tensions were highest and the social fabric was at risk of unraveling. There was an urgent need for an alternative, for discourse, for a nonviolent process when major conflict was on the verge of erupting. The English Parliament, or the US Congress, therefore, did not arise out of a *theory* of democracy so much as a desperate need—experienced by John I, his son, and his grandson—for an alternative to pitched battle. It is perhaps telling that this turning toward a collaborative process was midwifed into existence by the most prominent warrior of his times, the renowned "greatest knight," William Marshal, who apparently already in 1215 foresaw the limits of combat when faced with inexorable forces for political change.

$$\mathcal{L}$$

THE HALF-LIFE OF FEUDALISM AND THE BIRTH OF LAW

When the vassals must go to join the host,
the bourgeois rest in their beds;
when the vassals go to be massacred in battle,
the bourgeois picnic by the river.

—*Renart le Contrefait*, fourteenth-century satire[1]

Kings in France, Italy, Spain, and even (for the most part) in England continued to rule by fiat, without control from anyone, least of all from their subjects. In these European civilizations, royal knights were the equivalent of Odysseus and his pirates. Nobles in Europe were programmed to get rich by plundering cities of neighboring princes, bringing home carpets and jewels and horses and gold. They were essentially doing the same thing that Odysseus had done as a pirate on the Aegean twenty-five hundred years before. The road to wealth had not changed very much in that whole time.

Now increasingly successful merchants in medieval Europe could not help but notice that all those nobles and knights had to win their riches at the risk of their very lives. So this merchant class had gradually, for some generations, begun acquiring wealth in ways that did not involve killing or, perhaps more important, did not create risk of being killed themselves. The merchants of Paris, in particular, had discovered banking and finance. This was a much easier way to get rich and was certainly safer than joining in the king's lists, going off flailing about with lances and swords— nobody died making loans, weaving cloth, or selling wool. In the great scheme of things, and to the despair of the monarchs, the warrior ethic was simply dissolving from underneath their feudal feet. Commerce was, unknown to all, subversive. It undermined the acceptability of both violence and lying.

Merchants had discovered an alternate way to gain entry into the upper ranks of wealth and therefore into the government. War was becoming obsolete for those smart enough to choose another way. They were gradually becoming unwilling to either serve in or finance endless wars. The finances of the new urban class were increasingly secure without a king, and as this class emerged, it proved to have interests entirely different from those of either the king or the landed aristocracy. As, from the fifteenth century on, commerce expanded all over Europe and even into areas at the far end of the Mediterranean touched by the Crusades, more and more strangers speaking different languages, holding different views of God, of different skin color and customs were coming into direct contact with one another.

Cities became crowded with people with whom no one had previously had intimate personal knowledge. These would be urban people who had never herded one another's cows or helped put up hay, had neither dug ditches together nor traded a turnip for a radish. The bonds forged by repeated contact that characterizes village life—and are the basis of clan—were simply absent in these growing cities. Nevertheless, trade absolutely depended upon commerce with such strangers, and success required that deals made between such strangers be reliable: that goods be delivered when promised, that payment be in the amounts promised, that there be some process for handling disputes. Simply killing or conquering one's commercial adversary was now counterproductive because one might someday want that trading partner again. The feudal principle of violence and power as the arbiter of disputes was, to say the least, clumsy in the marketplace. Nor did secrecy and hierarchy foster trade so much as an open declaration of prices and the reliability of sales. Craftiness, the principle lauded by Homer and valued through the ages, was now often counterproductive. Diversity tended to open new markets even more than homogeneity. Commercial deals now fell under the shadow of the long future, and the short-term solutions of the sword were useless for planning inventory or as a bond for shipping, or for sophisticated conflict resolution such as, say, partial rescission of contract. If to chop off a man's head might be complete rescission, that would be quite useless to make a transaction go forward. Power alone did not make this new commerce work. Raw power was not the explanation for the success of capitalism.

So if, as society in the Middle Ages unraveled, power was not to be the single source of moral authority, then what would be? The natural place to look might have been toward the Church of Rome. The Catholic religion dominated all of Europe, and the Church certainly had great power. But by the fourteenth and fifteenth centuries, even the Church was losing its hold over commerce, its ability to regulate or prohibit interest rates, or to connect the law of contract to the law of God. In addition, the Church was evidently and at best morally ambiguous itself, governed primarily by patriarchal and feudal principles that were increasingly strained by commerce and contact with the far worlds of Africa and China.

The Church demanded absolute loyalty, enforced secrecy and rigid hierarchy, feared diversity, scorned equality, and benefited from lying and deceit whenever useful. Thoroughly engaged in the struggle for territory and political power in Italy and France, manipulating vassal states in Germany, attempting to control monarchies in Spain and England, the Church was itself an embodiment of Machiavellian principles. These were not principles that could provide security in an increasingly commercial world. Commerce, to the contrary, bred increasing numbers of consumers and widely dispersed wealth and opportunity for innovation that stemmed from originality and creativity regardless of social class. People who found new ways to succeed in the markets were less interested in the laws of God than in the laws of exchange. They were doing all right on their own. Commerce worked demonstrably better when it observed fairness and process, as might two men playing chess, rather than the principle that might makes right. Commercial values were therefore the opposite of royal values, or values of the Church, which were anchored around the central purpose of securing and maintaining hierarchies of military or political power.

It was by this time becoming apparent that none of the hallmarks of the Church or of ancient Greek, Roman, and even medieval feudal loyalties were sufficient to promote and spread emerging capitalism. A tectonic shift was under way as merchants, traders, artisans, and a growing professional class of lawyers and accountants, bankers and lenders sought to bring reliability to business. A network of personal or clan loyalties, however carefully woven between the Medicis and the popes of Rome and linked back to the Venetians, or to the dukes of Milan, was too attenuated, too clumsy to keep up with the opportunities of expanding commerce. Things were moving too fast; not every deal could be cemented with a ducal banquet. The Medicis rose to prominence as bankers, but not even the Medicis could control the whole of a thousand transactions taking place from the bazaars of Constantinople to the bookstores along the Seine. Silks from China brought in by the Venetians and paid for with Spanish gold might leak into Paris or fall under the control of the Holy Roman Emperor, and all the spiderwebs of Medici control could not hold these in check or in one set of accounts. Further, reliability depended upon simple market values rather than violence, and an increasingly wealthy and influential commercial class needed another standard, something more discerning, more articulate, more nuanced than the sword. They needed new rules to allocate failures and guide risk. They needed the rule of law.[2]

In England, therefore, the common law became the mediator of these values, or, when there was no feudal tie, the mediator between strangers. By 1540, contract law had become highly developed. There were remedies for breach and restitution, for damages, and for specific performance, all remarkably nuanced and all to the aid of reliability in commercial affairs. None of this new law had anything to do with knights of the tournament or trial by combat. Agreements were being forged between tradesmen and multiple buyers and sellers every day, and these could not be welded together by feudal or family allegiances. All this created a commercial dependability not just at the end of a lance, but without lances at all, by order of court. As Shakespeare saw it, Shylock the Jew would do business with Antonio the gentile merchant of Venice, and Antonio's bond would be enforceable to the strictest letter of the agreement.

Trades of cloths and seeds, pots and shoes, knives and ploughs—the whole world of bargain and exchange—are by nature consensual and most efficiently accomplished in an environment that is free from fear or violent disruption. Trade therefore has the power to bring about a sea change, a transition to new tactics concerning how to prosper or how to survive, and it is bottomed upon assumptions quite different from those that underlay the world of Odysseus, or, for that matter, of the kings and princes of medieval Europe.

It is assumed, for example, that commerce functions best when it is dependable, when sellers produce the goods that they have promised to produce and buyers hand over the money that they have promised to hand over. It is assumed that the goods will be produced without the need for renegotiation or reinforcement at the end of a sword, or that one's word or bond will be reliable because such reliability is of mutual benefit. It is assumed, most significantly, that the cow that is represented as pregnant is in fact pregnant and that honesty (building a business reputation) enhances commerce, is not counterproductive at all, but is actually an overall benefit to all parties and produces wealth rather than diminishes it. These assumptions were the exact opposite of the Odysseus Principle.

Ever since Homer's hero was able to lie his way home to Penelope, honesty between strangers had been considered a rarity. It is still, today, considered naive in much of the world.[3] But in Western Europe's emerging commercial world at the end of the Middle Ages, the experience increasingly must have been that lying and bribery do not ultimately enhance commerce at all, that deals must be planned, and that reliable partners are more apt over the long term to fit into plans than are unreliable ones. Reliable partners naturally seek out other reliable partners, while cheating partners tend to find willing victims harder and harder to locate. Clusters of reliable partners tend to grow while clusters of unreliable partners gradually shrink. A cheating seller typically wins the prize of that first sale, it is true. But when the purchaser gets home and discovers that the cow is not pregnant, he is less likely to return to that cheater for the next deal, and the cheater's range of possible transactions begins to contract. The cheater's circle of business partners therefore inevitably shrinks over time while reliable partners are all the while seeking each other out and building larger and larger circles of cooperation. Truth-telling therefore would ultimately become not just a moral or a religious principle but commercially useful and important to the propertied classes and their courts. Words like *fraud* and *covenant* and *contract* would be given nuanced meanings as judges tried to make commerce ever more reliable. Reliability meant profitability. For that practical reason alone it would be enforced in courts, supported as a matter of law. It would be assumed in this new world of trade that transactions speed up when a deal is performed as originally described and is not forever the subject of one more cup of coffee or evening of vodka or promise of one more daughter in marriage. Planning and financing are most efficient if deals are objectified, and they ought not be, cannot be, always personal. That, by itself, stands feudalism on its head.

Feudalism leads to ambiguous deals, constantly renegotiated by an unhappy king, subjected to changing family alliances and changing winds of war. Ambiguity or uncertainty is feudalism's natural environment. Don't try to force a promise from the king. In fact, it is impossible to force a promise from the king. And therefore it is impossible to enforce promises from anyone else, either, because if the king changes his mind the whole power structure—including the courts—will shift, and when the power structure shifts, all deals are off. In such a system, one's only protection is personal connection to the king (or the president in those countries that are still feudal), or at least to the hierarchy that leads to the king.[4]

Rapid, complex commercial interchange is most effective when it does not depend upon personalities and ambiguities at all. Don't trouble the seller with the buyer's clan name or ethnic origin, just name the price, name the goods, name the date of delivery, seal the bargain, and everyone will move on. That is commerce in the emerging world of the Renaissance as it unfolded into the fifteenth and sixteenth centuries, and that world was moving too fast for enforcement by the territorial invasion of some king's knights. Commerce had become too particular, too dependent upon complex facts. Only an emerging law could handle this complexity, and only a nonviolent court process could be sufficiently nuanced to handle what had become by then too complex to settle with a sword.[5]

Legal principles of fairness, mistake, and rescission were all therefore occasioned by the need for reliability in commerce, for some general, or objective, principles that would govern whether or not the king or lord of the manor was involved. These principles would begin to apply outside the feudal hierarchy and between people who might have had no family, clan, or historic ties of any kind. All this accompanied the growth of cities; increasing commerce up and down the Rhine, the Seine, and the Thames; sea trade along the coasts back and forth between the Netherlands, Spain, and Italy; and Venetian trade eastward throughout the Aegean to Constantinople and Jerusalem. The more trade, the more need for principles of fairness when the ship did *not* come in. A body of law grew and was intended to apply to all those who were not the king.

Here, in emerging capitalism, is also the emergence of a new morality gradually incorporated into law. It remained, however, to be determined whether such morality or law could ever apply beyond commerce, whether it could ever be applied to limit the powers of kings and dukes, archbishops and magnificent bankers. And for that to happen, someone had to nibble away at the core of the ideology that power is the source of righteousness or morality. Someone had to undermine the plant at the root, to question the myths of kings. That someone turned out to be neither lawyer nor professor, neither philosopher nor ascetic, but a simple playwright.

5

POETS AS MIDWIVES

For you have but mistook me all this while:
I live with bread like you, feel want,
Taste grief, need friends: subjected thus,
How can you say to me, I am a king?

—William Shakespeare, *Richard II*

In the centuries following the Magna Carta, Europe experienced the ravages of war like waves of tides washing back and forth over France and Italy, splashing into England and Spain, with feudal knights as bottom-feeders scouring plunder out of Normandy, Aquitaine, Languedoc, Florence, and Venice, even threatening Rome.

In the fourteenth century, King Edward III of England fought to seize a part of France. In response, King Jean II marched his lords and knights, archers and pikers off to do battle with King Edward's son, the Black Prince of England, outside the city of Poitiers. The English had for some time been ransacking central France and were loaded with plunder. King Jean suddenly attacked, attempting to steal all that plunder back. To everyone's great shock, although he outnumbered the English, he was defeated and captured. Dozens of the French king's nobles, hundreds of his knights, and thousands of his foot soldiers were killed. The king himself was then taken to England and held for ransom. The Battle of Poitiers was a disaster for France.

The year was 1356. King Jean's son, the dauphin Charles, rushed back to Paris to raise ransom for his father, demanding of a growing commercial class in France that they contribute money to pay for his father's release. To his surprise, he met stolid resistance. As we have seen, an emerging merchant class had gradually grown independent of feudal hierarchy. These merchants were now unwilling either to serve in Jean's endless wars or to finance his ransom. For all they cared, he could rot in England.

In February 1357, meeting as the Estates General and led by a powerful merchant—a draper named Etienne Marcel—the bourgeoisie took control of Paris. They formulated a Grand Ordinance of sixty-one articles, a sort of Magna Carta of France, stating that the monarchy could levy no tax without approval of the Estates, that, in addition, they had the right to periodically assemble, and that a Grand Council was to be elected to advise the Crown. At first the dauphin had no choice but to agree and even to sign the Grand Ordinance. But then the prince retreated to the countryside and rallied landsmen, nobles, and knights across the land.

Gradually, through the course of 1357 and 1358, chaos spread across France while some nobles came to the aid of, and then deserted, the cause of the bourgeoisie. Peasants in the countryside, joining the fray, rose in armed rebellion, and slaughter followed upon slaughter as the idea of some limitation to the power of the monarch was now openly contested by force of arms. Finally, in the face of such utter chaos, the dauphin regathered the landed and aristocratic warlords from outside Paris, and, with all their knights, they hammered the Estates General back into the ground. The Grand Ordinance was denounced and largely forgotten.[1] This is the course of events that might also have nullified the Magna Carta in England, more than a century before, had it not been for the influence of William Marshal, the Earl of Pembroke. But without a man of Marshal's unusual stature and vision, France instead descended into chaos and war, and the nonviolent, potentially more democratic solution that the Estates General had proposed was abandoned. It was not to rise again until the Revolution of 1789, more than four hundred years later.

Twenty years after the uprising in France, Edward III's English subjects also grew restless, and in 1376 they too rose to contest the huge taxes of the king. This time they were especially upset at monies levied to pay for the king's outlandishly expensive mistress, whom they said was, among other things, a witch. More substantively, Lords and Commons combined to protest the venality of the king's ministers and to insist, again relying on the principle of the Magna Carta, that Parliament must consent to taxes. The House of Commons, now called the "Good Parliament," went so far as to elect for the first time a real Speaker. From this day forward, Parliament would not only meet to raise revenues for the Crown, but, appointing its own leader, would offer its opinions and even counsel to the king. In this case, however, in 1376, they had offered more than counsel; they forced the king to cut off the monies to his mistress. They then went further and indicted the most corrupt of the king's ministers, and when challenged to know by what authority they did so, they asserted that *the House of Commons*, as a body, would bring the charge. It was the first ever impeachment of a minister of the Crown, a daring assertion, and the strongest assertion yet that Parliament had power independent of the king.

The king's mistress was sorely displeased, of course, as were other great nobles such as John of Gaunt, the Duke of Lancaster, but for a time the Good Parliament seemed able and determined to give voice to the new commercial and middle classes of Britain. Commerce cannot function without reliability or dependability of contract and is therefore ultimately dependent upon the rule of law. Parliament had increasingly been filled with commercial men, squires, and landholders, and these persons naturally gave voice to the need for fair courts and objective principles by which to arbitrate disputes, not just between the monarch and his subjects, but also between buyers and sellers all over the land.

But then King Edward's son, the Black Prince, the very hero who had twenty years earlier captured King Jean of France, fell ill. A sudden outpouring of national pride swelled to defend the memory of the prince and the glories of monarchy. Unfortunately for the parliamentarians, the prince then died. He left behind his enfeebled father, old Edward III, and a young son, Richard II. It might have been a time for Parliament to secure its position, but the wily Duke of Lancaster rallied the nobles of England to the memory of the dead prince. The lords were bought off, the Good Parliament dismissed, its impeachments overridden, previous ministers reinstated, the wicked mistress returned, and the rule of law buried once more in the cold soil of personal rule.

Having reestablished his base, the Duke of Lancaster decided to go to war to win himself a kingship in Spain. His taxations of the English did not at first raise enough money, so he levied a second time. This caused a popular explosion, and a man by the name of Wat Tyler organized a mass of peasants armed with rusty swords, scythes, and axes. They seized Canterbury, liberated political prisoners, and protested against a sort of peasant slavery called villenage. Villeins were bound to service, tied to the land, and effectively had no rights or privileges in the law. Wat Tyler's "mad multitude" marched from Kent to Essex, opened prisons, sacked manors, and burned records, killing judges, bishops, and tax collectors along the way. A peasant spokesman swore to kill "all lawyers and servants of the King they could find."[2] As Barbara Tuchman puts it in her marvelous recounting in *A Distant Mirror*, the men of the land, peasants and villeins, were especially after men of the law because the law "was the villeins' prison."[3]

Eventually, Tyler and his rebellious rabble laid siege to London. King Richard II was fourteen; he was forced to negotiate. The rebels razed the Tower of London and murdered Simon of Sudbury, the archbishop of Canterbury. Tyler and his followers also burned the Duke of Lancaster's palace; destroyed the Temple, where all the legal records were kept; and then confronted the young king. Tyler demanded that all inequalities of rank and status be abolished, for all men to be equal below the king, that the Church be disendowed and its estates divided among commoners. (Four hundred years later, even Thomas Paine would not ask for more.) The king, perhaps rather clever himself, promised everything "consistent with the regality of his crown."[4] Unfortunately for the democratic principle, in this proviso King Richard II opened up an exception to the rule of law that would justify the royal prerogative and bloodshed for centuries to follow.

A day later, at an arranged meeting, Tyler, perhaps in the heat of passion and flush of success, picked a quarrel with one of the king's squires, drew a dagger, and was instantly struck down himself. His head was stuck upon a post and paraded before the multitudes, and with the king promising to meet all their demands, Tyler's peasant armies lost courage as quickly as they had gained it. Lacking organization other than the feudal principle of personal loyalty to Wat Tyler, lacking even the building in which to meet or means by which to remain assembled, they dispersed and all was lost. The Peasants' Revolt crumbled absolutely. Richard II thereafter reneged on his promises to end villenage, rebels were hanged, charters that had been issued from the landowners' parliament were canceled. Noble reaction set in to support the absolute rule of the king even more strongly than before, and Richard II would himself become the symbol of the tyrant. On the continent, England, France, the Italian city-states, and Spain warred on.

A half century later, in 1431, a young peasant maid in the French village of Arc heard heavenly voices urging her to assist her king. Saints Michael, Catherine, and Margaret instructed her to restore the rightful authority of the French Crown, to help King Charles VII regain territory that was still held by the English. She obediently saddled up, rode off to the king's court, and persuaded a pusillanimous collection of wasted courtiers to give her armor and a better horse, whereupon she rode off, with banners flying, to the front lines. At first "the Maid," famously known to history as Jeanne d'Arc, was so courageous in battle, so inspiring to the king and his soldiers that she led them to victory after victory and the English were driven back. But unfortunately for the wild woman on horseback, they were never entirely defeated.

One fateful day Jeanne was captured in battle, trussed and shamed, and imprisoned to await trial for religious apostasy. At once the French king and his parade of bishops abandoned her, more allegiant to principles of feudalism and hierarchy, status and privilege than to a woman's honor or dignity or even the glory of France. The solidarity of aristocracy—nobles more bound to each other than to their own subjects—was more binding than any affection for an illiterate, troublesome maiden who should have been at home tending ducks. Without any provision of due process, without any jury, without any proof of legal violation, without a single witness on her behalf or a lawyer or advocate of any kind to assist her, the bishops pronounced her a witch. They burned her alive for heresy, idolatry, blasphemy, superstition, sacrilege, and sorcery. With the connivance of the English who had captured her, the trial was presided over by French bishops.

The Magna Carta did not apply in Rouen, or, of course, in a Church trial that was presumptively a trial under the laws of God. Here, in Jeanne's final days, there was no law to restrain the whims of either kings or bishops. The long, slow evolution of the rule of law had made no dent whatsoever, had in no way weakened, was completely irrelevant to the absolute power of the Church. When the powers of Church and king were combined, no farmer's child could claim aid of the law. When the Church of Rome, the king of France, and the king of England were combined, a girl could be burned alive without the protection or support of a single voice on her behalf. She was lower class, she was a woman, and she was a free thinker, more religious than anyone had ever seen and therefore more apt to think new. To do so was dangerous to property, dangerous to hierarchy, dangerous to religious orders, dangerous to the mystique of kings whose personal will—in 1431—was still more the law than the law was law.

Outside the castle walls of medieval Europe, courts met, cases were decided, sheriffs challenged criminals, and contracts were enforced, but inside the castle and in all matters affecting the castle, the law was still a stranger. This royal isolation was the norm throughout the Middle Ages. In the sixth century, the Justinian Code had declared the will of the emperor the law of the land for no other reason than because it was his will. In spite of the Magna Carta, the Justinian principle would still prevail right down into the sixteenth century. A king had signed the Magna Carta, but because there was no one to enforce his promises, it would remain largely unattended for three centuries.

Nothing changed to upset this coalition of the wealthy and privileged and their "absolute right" to govern with personal will until a hundred years after Jeanne d'Arc, when Henry VIII sat upon the throne of England. Henry wanted a son more than he wanted or needed the aid of the Roman Catholic Church. He ruled with an iron hand and, removed as he was on his island from the armies of Rome, could act with more independence than monarchs in France or Italy. Ironically, it was Henry's act of supreme self-will, his flaunting of his own peevish and selfish intentions and his defiance of any authority above his own that ultimately brought down the whole structure of personal rule in England. Henry single-handedly threw out the Catholic Church so that he could marry the wives he wanted in order to get the sons he must have to secure his patrimony. In so doing, he planted the seeds of division that required his successors to weave and dodge among the nobles and commons for two centuries until ultimately Church and Crown were irrevocably split and the rule of law painfully sprouted through the cracks.

Henry died—after six wives—with only one son, who was to become Edward VI. Like his father, young Edward favored the new Anglican church, the Church of England, which had been established to ratify his father's divorces. Now, in the 1540s, Anglicans allied with the Crown and Roman Catholics went into full retreat throughout England. Henry had looted and seized monasteries and appropriated the enormous wealth of the pope to his own ends. His son continued the Anglican alliance, but then died while still a teenager. Unfortunately for the Anglicans, Henry's first daughter, Mary, then became queen. Mary was the daughter of Henry's first wife, a Spanish Catholic, and she immediately set about reinstating the one true catholic and apostolic faith. By royal decree, England was turned upside down—again. Protestants were burned in the village squares and the furious, self-righteous queen became known as "Bloody Mary." Anglicans who resisted were rounded up and sent to the Tower or simply hung, drawn, and quartered for heresy and sedition. No law of the land restrained this queen in her ferocious attempt to bring God back to her people. At this point in English history, any queen who claimed to know God could trump the common law.

But then after only five years Mary, too, died and was succeeded by yet another of Henry's children, this time the girl Elizabeth, who had been raised in an Anglican household. In 1558, Elizabeth, age twenty-five, came to the throne of a divided and unhappy country riven by conflict over religion and in terror of the unbridled power of willful monarchs. Elizabeth had herself been locked for a time in the Tower—by her sister Mary— and knew the trembling fear of those who might be killed at any moment. She began to consult with, remonstrate with, or disagree with, but nevertheless to engage Parliament. She did not subject her will to theirs—England was not yet to that point—but she did know that Parliament could help to hold her kingdom together, and she acted in ways calculated to keep their loyalty.

Queen Elizabeth was no saint. She was no advocate for women or for the rule of law. At one time she cut off the hand of a printer who objected to her prospective marriage to the Duke d'Anjou of France. At another, she allowed to be executed a certain poor Mr. Penry, who had been caught with papers in his pockets that merely said that the queen had sufficient royal prerogative to "establish" the laws. Penry had avoided the usual terms of *making, enacting, decreeing,* and *ordaining* the laws, which—said the Lord Keeper—imply "a most absolute authority." Not having sufficiently fawned over the royal prerogative, Penry was condemned.[5]

Indeed, Elizabeth liked to be fawned over, to be addressed as the Thrice Blessed, Thrice Divine Queen. She had no small share of royal pride, peevishness, and temper. But Elizabeth, as history knows, was clever enough to weave her way between Catholics and Anglicans and to establish peace within the territory of England. She was not the equivalent of, say, her Russian contemporary Ivan the Terrible. She had no sons of her own, but unlike Ivan, if she had had a son, she would not likely have killed him herself. Still, the differences were subtle. One of the reasons that Elizabeth never married was her fear of the contest that might emerge between herself and any husband or son. She avoided those conflicts by simply refusing to breed.

Elizabeth was highly educated. She could read Latin and Greek, spoke French and Spanish, was comfortable with poetry and the language of scholars. She did not give full rein to the law, was perhaps even ignorant of the Magna Carta, but she did give wide rein to poets, and this too is part of the unexpected story of the evolution of the rule of law.

Just before Marlowe and Shakespeare, the most heralded poet in Queen Elizabeth's court was a young courtier named Philip Sidney. His sister Mary was also a poet, and the two were devoted to one another. Although Philip could publish, Mary could not. Women were allowed to *translate* from French and Italian into English, which Mary did, brilliantly, and she read Greek and Latin, but she was not allowed to appear in plays or publish anything original because everyone agreed that women were inferior. In 1586 Philip was sent off to one of Elizabeth's wars and was killed in Holland. Mary was devastated. She fell into two years of prolonged grieving and silence. But in the early 1590s she emerged from the shadows, intending to finish Philip's work. Disguising her words as those of her brother, she found a way to publish her own ideas. She concluded a translation of the Psalms of David and delivered the translation direct to the insulated, isolated Thrice Divine Queen. She also translated French plays into English and chose those that carried a political

rather than purely personal message. In her translation of
Robert Garnier's *Antonious,* a pre-Shakespeare tale of Antony
and Cleopatra, she uses Roman soldiers to condemn those who
make wars. She is writing into the teeth of royal arrogance,
penning perhaps the first antiwar lines in English history, and
Mary Sidney aimed them right at the war-making sovereign who
had sent her brother to his death:

> Shall euer civile bate
> Gnaw and deuour our state?
> Shall neuer we this blade,
> Our bloud hath bloudie made
> Lay downe?...
> But as from age to age,
> So passe from rage to rage?[6]

Sidney was a woman of grace and intelligence and one of
the first to use language to advance not just the cause of peace,
but to lever open the doors of tyranny. Eventually she gathered
around herself such a flock of literary lights of her age, such a
band of worshipful followers, that her home at Wilton House,
away from London, became a magnet. Her husband, the Earl of
Pembroke, was the patron of Pembroke's Men, a theater company,
and among others, she attracted to the acting troupe a young
player by the name of William Shakespeare. It was Shakespeare
(or Sidney; there is a decent argument that it was she) who eventually wrote a great caution to kings in the play *Richard II.*[7] This was
the same Richard II, of course, who had betrayed his promises to
the peasants during the Wat Tyler rebellion and who was thereafter deposed and murdered. The poet proclaims a warning for
the world to see in language more dramatic than any ever before
hurled at the throne:

For God's sake, let us sit upon the ground
And tell sad stories of the death of kings;
How some have been deposed; some slain in war,
Some haunted by the ghosts they have deposed;
Some poison'd by their wives: some sleeping kill'd;
All murder'd: for within the hollow crown
That rounds the mortal temples of a king
Keeps Death his court and there the antic sits,
Scoffing his state and grinning at his pomp,
Allowing him a breath, a little scene,
To monarchize, be fear'd and kill with looks.

This mocking of royal arrogance would be sedition were it not in a stage play. The poet then goes even further, telling the monarch, the royal being supposedly anointed by God, that kings are mortal, that they are going to die:

Infusing him with self and vain conceit,
As if this flesh which walls about our life,
Were brass impregnable, and humour'd thus
Comes at the last and with a little pin
Bores through his castle wall, and farewell king!

Then, at last, Shakespeare (or Sidney) uncovers the truth of kings in words no person, then or now, can misunderstand. It is presented as if said by a king himself, disguising the fact that a playwright is actually bringing into question the myth of royal power.

Cover your heads and mock not flesh and blood
With solemn reverence: throw away respect,
Tradition, form and ceremonious duty,
For you have but mistook me all this while:
I live with bread like you, feel want,
Taste grief, need friends: subjected thus,
How can you say to me, I am a king?

The poet is speaking of royal frailty in words that, had they been uttered in Parliament, would most likely have been considered seditious. But here, semidisguised, a truth is out in the open to be heard for the first time by the English public: the truth that kings are, at the very base of it all, no different from any other mortal.

The Shakespeare histories do not, as a whole, glorify princes. Not only is Richard II made humble, the hunchback Richard III is demeaned, Henry VI is cuckolded, Hamlet is a mama's boy, and Coriolanus (though not precisely a prince) is done in by arrogance, Julius Caesar done in by the inevitable conspiracy, Macbeth done in by an evil wife. "All murdered," muses Richard II, forecasting his own demise.

After Sidney and Shakespeare, kings were never the same, never cloaked in quite the same mystique. The seventeenth century would become one of turmoil and tumult, transition and the triumph, finally, of the principle of the law above the king. But the moving force this time had not been a law in Parliament, a revolt of the middle class, a philosophic tract, a migration of peasants, nor any of the standard events we usually recognize. The spread of commerce and trade had indeed spawned both a new diversity and a new morality that would stir feudal culture and challenge privilege. But it would remain for the poets of the sixteenth and early seventeenth centuries to attack the majesty of princes, to erode the patriarchal myth from which feudalism ultimately derived its power. When the playwright put into the mouth of Richard II the self-effacing words "I eat bread like you," English culture was being prepared for revolution.

6

THE CRADLE CENTURY

Magna Carta is such a fellow that he will have no saving.

—Sir Edward Coke in Parliament, 1628[1]

During the three centuries after the Magna Carta, English kings forgot, ignored, discredited, and simply refused to enforce the idea of a parliament assembled to advise and approve royal taxes. During this whole time, only Queen Elizabeth had worked with Parliament as an ally, skillfully blending royal ends with theirs, but it would be hard to dredge up the name of one sovereign in these three hundred years who bent to the law as King John had been forced to do in 1215.

The barons at Runnymede had demanded due process in the courts and that no free man should be jailed without being lawfully charged. Courts, they said, should be separated physically from the king and not held under any royal thumb, or, more appropriately, any royal hammer. Instead of adhering to these principles, however, the law had been so subjected to the will of monarchs that by the time of Tyler's Rebellion, lawyers were considered evil agents of the Crown employed to enforce the personal power of the landed, propertied, and already wealthy.

Personal rule and the rule of law are a contradiction, utter opposites. But so melded had they become that the law in 1381 was far from the rallying cry of the poor; it was the scourge of the poor. Nor had the law any relevance in the proceedings of the Church, and while Jeanne d'Arc was the best known, she would be but a symbolic victim of the unbridled, untrammeled, arrogant powers of bishops and priests who operated as if they alone understood the laws of God. These were the conditions of tyranny, not only in England, but all over Europe, and so it was to remain until the seventeenth century.

After Queen Elizabeth's death in 1603, the Stuarts came to the English throne. They asserted divine guidance and the authority to tax, make war, imprison, and torture; an authority that ought not, could not, be limited by Parliament. The Stuarts sought to fight back against any idea that kings ate bread, tasted grief or needed friends. They had roots more deep in Europe than in England, were more attuned to absolute power than the English, and would resurrect, if they could, the old Justinian rule.

The first Stuart to follow Elizabeth was James I. He ruled erratically but more or less harmlessly. It was his son, however, Charles I, who bridled at the mere idea that his power should be limited by a parliament of burghers, lawyers, landowners, and merchants. Who had anointed them? Charles therefore sought to ignore Parliament and govern by decree, just as if he were instructed by God, or at least by the ancient Justinian Code.

At this time, as it happened, a lawyer by the name of Sir Edward Coke turned his talents to uncover, or to rediscover, the great promises of King John of 1215. At first, King Charles paid little mind. But this time not only the great nobles who sat in the House of Lords but also the burghers, knights, sheriffs, and landowners who now sat in the House of Commons rose to support Coke.[2] The old man proclaimed loudly, "Magna Carta…will have no saving!" He meant to say that no part of it could be saved out or carved away, not even by the sovereign.

Charles did not agree. No prince in Europe would have agreed. Many in England's House of Lords did not agree. The bishops of the Anglican church—themselves now wedded to royal power—did not agree. Here—the assertion four hundred years later of the principles of the Magna Carta against a willful king, against his lords and the high bishops of the church—was a third, head-on confrontation with royal power. Wat Tyler's rebellion had been the second, but Tyler's success was too personal, too dependent upon one man and not sufficiently grounded in the existing powers to hold up against the wealthy Duke of Lancaster, and Tyler's Rebellion dissolved into the sand just as had the rebellion of the French Estates General only a few years earlier. Now, in 1628, came a most unusual advocate, a lawyer willing to stand up to the king not just for personal reasons but for the security of the realm. Some said that Coke and his supporters were disturbers of the peace, radicals, even traitors, and should be hanged. But some did not, and this became one of the pivotal moments in the history of the rule of law.

The first great conflict came over Charles's insistence that he had the right to imprison people upon his own authority for as long as he chose and that this right stemmed from the royal prerogative from God. Arising from that insistence, the second great conflict was over his claim that he might, like Roman emperors of old, make law by his own will, without Parliament. The struggle between Charles and Parliament turned out to be critical, as now the crocus of liberty emerged from a frigid winter of royal power.

In 1626 Sir Nicolas Hyde, lord chief justice for Charles, issued instructions to commissioners who were to collect "loans" to finance Charles's wars. The loans were to be extracted from unwilling knights, merchants, and artisans. These loans, since they were not voluntary, looked to the people who paid them exactly like a tax. But it was a tax that had not been approved by Parliament and therefore was illegal under the Magna Carta. Money was therefore being raised by order of the royal chamber, unilaterally, without consent of the people's representatives. Opposition was widespread. Hyde therefore instructed certain royal commissioners to go among the dissenters and to find out who told them not to loan to the king. Who was a part of their conspiracy to resist the Crown? Who was with them in this opposition to the legitimate orders of an anointed monarch? The commissioners were instructed to keep watch and make a written record.[3] They should certify to the king's privy council the "names, qualities and dwelling places of all such refractory persons, with all speed, and especially if they shall discover any combination or confederacy against these proceedings."[4] Catharine Macaulay, the great radical historian of the eighteenth century, later reported that as a result of such investigations by the Crown, "prisons all over the kingdom were full of illustrious sufferers." Their imprisonment, of course, knew no bounds in time and might last forever.

Charles had imprisoned not just the unwashed but also merchants and knights, men of distinction. These now called upon the law of habeas corpus dating back to Edward III, Edward I, and to King John and the Great Charter. According to all these statutes, no man in England might be imprisoned except "according to law," which meant that some legal cause must be shown. A "legal cause" is not simply the disfavor of the king or his lord chief justice, said the king's opponents; a legal cause is rooted in the common law as it has been enforced for generations.

Oh, no, answered Lord Chief Justice Hyde in response to these pleas, this is imprisonment *"per speciale mandatum domini Regis,"* by royal prerogative, and no cause need at all be mentioned. Royal prerogative trumps the law, is beyond law, and is therefore the supreme law.[5]

But, no, indeed, cried out those lawyers for the imprisoned merchants and knights, does not the Magna Carta state that it shall be the law of the land that freemen ought not be imprisoned but by due process of law?

Now many English lawyers, enjoying perhaps their finest hour in the history of that green island, rose to the case and stood up to oppose these imprisonments by the unilateral decision of the king or his minions. A certain Mr. Calthorp remembered a case from Edward III, in the fourteenth century, that no man should be taken before his sovereign "until it be by indictment or presentment of his good and lawful neighbours where such deeds are done, in due manner, or by process, made by writ original at the common law...And if any thing be done against [a man's freedom] it shall be redressed and holden for nought."[6] A man brought to jail *without cause*, even by the king, exclaimed Calthorp, must be set free! Calthorp then recited a total of six other ancient statutes that would keep a king from summarily imprisoning his enemies. In going this far and in such detail, Calthorp was probably putting his own life on the line. If ever he lost the general agreement and support of his fellows in the Commons, or if he too far alienated the Lords, the king would certainly try to maneuver him toward Star Chamber, a royal court where the king could himself be the judge or could appoint his own judges, and where the end result was often mutilation or hanging. The personal stakes were very high.

The king's response was confident. He enlisted his chaplain, Roger Manwaring, who might one day, as everyone knew, aspire to become a bishop, and would, of course, be appointed by the king. Manwaring should, instructed the king, say something to the crowds, some word from God. Whereupon the preacher, who did indeed wish to become a bishop, enlisted divine authority to the cause of the Crown: "The king is not bound to observe the laws of the realm concerning the subjects' right and liberties...his royal will and command in imposing loans and taxes without common consent in parliament doth oblige the subjects' conscience, upon pain of eternal damnation." Obey the king, he proclaimed, or *God* will melt you down. "Those who refused to pay [loans to the king] offended against the law of God...and became guilty of impiety, disloyalty and rebellion." Parliament, warned Manwaring (his eye upon that bishopric), "was a mongrel, overcome by sloth and faction, and instead of doing its duty to God would rather produce sundry impediments to the just designs of princes."[7]

The battle was on. Sir Francis Seymour rose in the Commons to reply to Vicar Manwaring. Seymour accused Manwaring of simply selling God's grace: "When preachers forsake their own calling, and turn [into] ignorant statesmen, we see how willing they are to exchange a good conscience for a bishopric."[8] You are not a preacher, chided Seymour, but merely an office seeker. To which the king himself now rejoined with mounting fury that if Parliament did not give to him what he demanded, he would "*use other means* which God has put into my hands in order to save that which the follies of some particular men [like Calthorp and Seymour] may otherwise put in danger."[9]

With these words, the stakes were raised again. The king would accept no bounds; he would do whatever it took to get what he wanted. "Take not this for a threatening," he purred, "for I scorn to threaten any but my equals."[10] He would, rather, if he chose, "use other means." However, the king's threats turned out to be a bluff. Lacking any clear alternative means beyond those he had already used, he sent his lord keeper to warn Parliament of "necessity *and the sword*." "Remember his majesty's admonition," said the lord keeper. "I say, remember it."[11]

It was in the face of these threats to use the sword in times of "necessity"—a necessity that the king alone might declare—that the courage of these seventeenth-century lawyers was especially remarkable. Sir Frances Seymour—again raising his head above the crowd in the Commons—asked how the king could unilaterally make laws, lest England was to become like ancient "autocratical Persia"? And "How can we express our affections [to the king] while we retain our fears, or speak of giving till we know whether we have anything to give? For if his majesty may be persuaded to take what he will, what need we to give?"[12]

Now the fires of dissent began to spread ever more widely through the House of Commons. A firebrand, Sir Robert Philips, rose in passionate accord with Seymour: "Oh improvident ancestors! O unwise forefathers! To be so curious in providing for the quiet possession of our laws and the liberties of parliament and to neglect our persons and bodies, and to let them [the merchants and knights] lie in prison and that *durante bene pacito*, remedieless. If this be the law, why talk of liberties!"[13]

King Charles was no dullard. His demands were, he said, modest: "I only require 30 ships to guard the channel, 20 more to guard the Elbe, 20,000 horse and foot and all their provisions and victuals, ordnance for forts and arrears for merchant ships that have aided me in the past. I have heard your pleas and paid attention, mine is certainly a limited request, humble even, far less than I originally asked and the glory of England depends upon your support to me."[14]

The king's sycophant attorney general weighed in for the Crown. A king has more important things to do, he said, than to worry about habeas corpus. A king must consider wars, money, pardons.

Many of those who sat in the House of Lords agreed with the king. They were defenders of the rights of the powerful. They claimed that civilization, stability, and justice all depend upon a strong core of authority. Not incidentally, it was a healthy *center* that guaranteed their own continued dominance in English affairs. Not only the lords, therefore, but also the bishops of the Anglican church, the established Church of England, now joined with the Crown. The bishops were successors in power and prestige to the now-outlawed Catholic Church, and they too were in strong support of the king's prerogative. It did not pass unnoticed that the powers of a king to proclaim right and wrong were similar to those powers of the church and that to question the king's authority might lead to questioning of the bishops' authority as well. Lawyers Calthorp, Seymour, and Philips were pushing against a rock wall of aristocratic privilege, an entrenched establishment fully armed with doctrine and tradition, wealth and lands, and the ability to wage war. The claim of the lords and bishops was of course never outright for themselves, for privilege. Their claim was that the *peace of England* depended upon the established order against which a few pettifogging, pernicious, and rebellious lawyers so ruefully struggled.

Many in the House of Lords therefore argued that without a royal prerogative, all society would crumble. On the other side, however, were a growing number of those who now, for a second time in English history, seemed gradually to be repersuading themselves of the idea of the law above the king. Men in the Commons would live or die for this principle, as the king himself would eventually discover.

Before his sovereign's unhappy end, Charles's first secretary made the case for temperance and belief. The issue was still those false imprisonments, the king's right to throw into jail whomever refused his commands or questioned his authority to raise money by fiat. The first secretary argued that habeas corpus did not apply to a king in time of war.[15] As reported by Catharine Macaulay, here was the first secretary's plea:

> Do not think that by cases of law and debate we can make that [royal prerogative] to be no law, which, in experience, we every day find necessary. Make what law you will...if I will discharge my duty...and the oath I have taken to his majesty, I must commit [a prisoner], and neither express the cause to the gaoler nor to the judges, nor to any counselor in England, but to the king himself.[16]

The first secretary's plea was in vain. Parliament was by now emboldened by years of a gradually increasing sense of its own authority. Elizabeth had consulted them. The poets had demystified the royal person. Shakespeare had humanized not only Richard II, but also Richard III, Henry VI, Coriolanus, Caesar, and even Henry IV. Hamlet was a prince, ill done, but of ill temper as well. Princes who argued their direct connection to God now had a more difficult case than even one hundred years before, in the time of Henry VIII.

Charles would not yield. His authority came from God. He dismissed Parliament and for a time attempted to rule England without those most unfortunate, irreverent tormentors, men to whom he would not speak directly because they were beneath his station. Ultimately, Coke, Calthorp, Seymour, and Philips held their ground. After a prolonged confrontation, in 1628 they rallied the House of Commons to pass the famous Petition of Right. It is the second most dramatic moment in the history of English and American constitutional law.

> III. And whereas also by the statute called The Great Charter of the Liberties of England [the Magna Carta], it is declared and enacted, that no freeman may be taken or imprisoned or be disseized [dispossessed] of his freehold or liberties, or his free customs, or be outlawed or exiled, or in any manner destroyed, but by the lawful judgment of his peers, or by the law of the land.

> IV. And...[under]...King Edward III, it was declared...that no man...should be put out of his land or tenements, nor taken, nor imprisoned, nor disinherited nor put to death without being brought to answer by due process of law.

> V. Nevertheless...divers of your subjects have of late been imprisoned without any cause showed; and when for their deliverance they were brought before your justices by your Majesty's writs of habeas corpus, there to undergo and receive as the court should order, and their keepers commanded to certify the causes of their detainer, no cause was certified, but that they were detained by your Majesty's special command, signified by the lords of your Privy Council, and yet were returned back to several prisons, without being charged with anything to which they might make answer according to the law.

The king's subjects were being thrown into prison, and when brought to court under the common law, their jailers were supposed to say *why* they were being held, for what legal cause. But "no cause was certified, but that they were detained by your Majesty's special command" and then they were returned to prison. The courts were holding that, the law aside, it is enough that His Majesty wills it.

The situation could not have been more tyrannical had Emperor Justinian himself sat upon the English throne.

This, said Parliament in 1628, is not mete, Your Grace, not good for the comfort and safety of your people, and contrary to four hundred years of our law, ever since the Great Charter. They drafted the famous Petition of Right, proclaiming that habeas corpus may not be denied, that a person may not be kept indefinitely in jail without demonstration of legal cause, even if it is the king who puts him there.

Defense of the petition produced one of the famous moments in the history of civil liberties. The House of Commons had sent the draft to Lords, which then met, with the king presiding. All waited for His Majesty's assent. Instead, he spoke obtusely, neither accepting nor rejecting, offering a "compromise" that would save out the royal prerogative. There was fury when the Commons went back to its own chambers, and it was Sir Edward Coke, the venerable old man of the law, whose words were remembered:

> In my opinion sovereign power is no parliamentary word. It weakens Magna Charta, and all the statutes; for they are absolute, without any saving of sovereign power: And should we now add...[this claimed royal prerogative to our law], it will weaken the foundation of law, and then the building must fall. Take we heed what we yield unto: Magna Charta is such a fellow that he will have no sovereign.[17]

"Sovereign power is no parliamentary word." It is the statutes that are absolute, the law that is absolute, not the will of any man, and the law will have no sovereign. Coke risked his life to say those things, and he got away with it.

King Charles was mightily offended. He forthwith dismissed Parliament and sought to govern in outright defiance, solely upon royal prerogative, not just in taxes, but in all things. For some years, he sought to rule independent of the law. The issue of the prerogative remained central throughout the whole of the

1630s all the way up to 1640. For a full ten years, English lawyers like Coke and Calthorp, Seymour and Philips staked their lives and fortunes on the precious idea that *no* prerogative, not even one given by God, was absolute. Charles might be sovereign among his lords and sovereign above his subjects, but he was—they argued—not sovereign above the law. He was not sovereign above habeas corpus. He was not sovereign above the right of Parliament to approve taxes. He was not sovereign above the rights of fair trial.

The king may have privately thought these ideas treasonous. But the lawyers had some basis for their claims and could trace them back, as we have seen, through four hundred years of legal history. They had something to go on that was stronger than simple opposition to Charles himself.

In the end, the king again ran out of money. The Petition of Right had effectively narrowed his options. He could not enforce "loans" as he had done before. Reluctantly, he called Parliament back into session. Once more he had to deal with those he considered to be recalcitrant, obstinate, self-interested, decidedly lower-class lawyers, merchants, and farmers. In spite of their humbling by years out of London and out of power, the surviving friends of Coke and Seymour still would not concede the unlimited royal prerogative. Their resistance was so strong, in fact, that it would frame English and American history for centuries to come.

7

A REBEL EVEN A KING WOULD SAVE

Truly Jenny, (and I know that you may easily
be persuaded to it), he was a gallant man,
an honest man, an able man, and take all,
I know not to any man living second.

—Arthur Goodwin, after burying John Hampden, June 25, 1643[1]

The memory of this deceased colonel is such
that in no age to come but it will more and more
be had in honor and esteem; a man so religious,
and of that prudence, judgment, temper, valour,
and integrity, that he hath left few like behind him.

—*The Kingdom's Weekly Intelligence*, a week after Hampden's death[2]

During the period immediately following Sir Edward Coke's
confrontation with King Charles I in 1628, Parliament and king
settled into a long, pitched battle. Charles was neither incompe-
tent nor a dolt, and he ruled for seven years, keeping Parliament
at bay the whole time. His rule was not especially egregious or
tyrannical, but it was absolute. For a time, the Magna Carta, due
process, and the rights of assembly lay as concepts foundering
in the memories of old lawyers. Still, the unbridled prerogative
could not last forever.

Coke was old and soon passed from the scene, at which time
the mantle of moral authority slowly passed to another lawyer,
John Hampden, an ally of Seymour and Calthorp, a landsman

from Buckinghamshire, not far from London. Hampden was a devout Puritan whose chief attribute was neither oratory nor wealth nor military prowess nor scholarship, though he was accomplished in all of these. Another parliamentarian, John Eliot, was the flaming orator who most often confronted the king, and William Pym was the leader in Parliament who made the set oratories to denounce illegal taxes and royal indifference to the ancient constitution. But according to the reports of those who were in Parliament at that time, it was John Hampden who was regarded by most as the great man, the leader of stature whose calm voice and reasoned opinion led Parliament in the direction of independence from the royal prerogative.

As the years progressed, Charles showed no less appetite for war and ships. He therefore sought to impose a new property tax for the direct support of his navy. A great many in Parliament, including Hampden, were alarmed that ship-money could be used both to protect English shipping against Barbary Pirates and, more likely, by the English king *against his own Parliament*. Hampden publicly declared that he would not pay. The case went to court, where it was certain that he would lose, since the judges were appointed by and served as the loyal supporters of the Crown.

Futile as Hampden's effort was in court, however, it was perceived by the nation as taking a stand on behalf of Parliament against yet another onerous royal tax. The king won the battle in his courts but was losing the popularity contest among his subjects. Finally, violating all protocol and tradition, Charles marched into the House of Commons seeking grandly to arrest Hampden and four other ringleaders. Someone tipped the rebels off, and they escaped out the back door just before the king arrived. The word spread. Hampden was becoming a hero.

Perhaps he appealed to the people because, as a man of character, his motives seemed larger than property or family. It was he who prayed to God that he do the right thing by his country and his conscience. It was Hampden whose advice and counsel were sought in committee after committee of Parliament during the stormy years leading up to the civil war, and it was his combination of character, learning, balance, and calm that led Lords and Commons alike to ask his opinion.

Most assuredly, not all men of those times were of high moral character, but John Hampden serves as an exemplar for a certain high-mindedness that characterized the leadership of that century from which the principles of republican government eventually arose. This was the century that anchored habeas corpus in the minds of freedom-seeking men, and this was the century that gave rise gradually to the principle that power derives from the governed, not from the governor. Hampden was one of those few who, after Coke, was the next midwife to constitutional government as we now know it.

People said of John Hampden that he did what he said he would do, that when he said no, he meant no, and when he said yes, he meant yes. When he rose in Parliament to say he did not favor something, he did not favor that thing, and when he rose to say that he did favor something, he could be counted upon to stand for that, and those who sided with him could depend upon the fact that no bribe or honor from the king would ever sway him from his principle. Most significantly, when he rose to say to the king that he would not pay His Majesty's illegal ship-money, it was because he genuinely thought the tax illegal and not just because he was protecting his own twenty shillings.[3]

But when at last His Majesty Charles I drew his forces off to the north of London, refusing Parliament's demand that he remain close to them physically and their request that they—not he—be in control of the militia, when, that is, at last the conflict had grown to the point where a clash of arms was inevitable, Hampden went home to Buckinghamshire to raise a troop of his own. He would contest tyranny, if need be, by arms. The debater and mediator was no longer young, now in his late forties, when he climbed aboard his horse to take up the sword. He had become the emotional and spiritual leader of the disparate forces gathering to defend Parliament, and in the course of the first year of conflict he became the communicator between Parliament and the field command. He fostered a kind of special affection among the men who followed him, and as war broke out in 1642, it was he who became an inspiration for Parliament's raw, newly created army. It was he who pulled them from the fields and farms and drilled them into combat readiness with their muskets and pikes.

In 1643, when the war was not a year old, riding into the midst of fierce action Hampden was shot directly in the back and gravely wounded. He rode manfully from the field to a local tavern either to recover or to die. As he lingered there, word of his fall quickly spread to King Charles's encampment in nearby Oxford. Charles at once sent word that he, the king, would, if requested, send his own physicians across the lines to Hampden's care. Hampden unfortunately declined the royal offer, and within the week he was dead. Thereafter, negotiations between the king and Parliament worsened, and war unfolded mercilessly for years.

In the end, Hampden's death was a tragedy not only for the republican cause but also for Charles Stuart. When the war was lost, in 1648, the king was captured by parliamentary forces and brought before a jury of sixty commissioners in Westminster Hall. There was no moderate hand remaining who might mediate a settlement; no one played the role that William Marshal had played in 1215 or that Hampden might have played had he still been alive. Thus, in January 1649, when John Cooke went on reading the charge in the great trial in Westminster Hall, the die was already cast. The king was declared a tyrant and guilty of treason, and before the month of January was over he was brought onto an open balcony at Whitehall Palace and beheaded.

From these twin tragedies we can take this: the life of John Hampden—a man of commitment to the public good, a reliable man whose word was his bond, whose goal was not alone to secure the Hampden family or the king's dynastic powers, whose primary method was reconciliation rather than the sword—stands out as a symbol of something larger than himself. He was an embodiment of seventeenth-century civic virtues beyond law, outside capitalism or parliaments or codes or grand political ambitions, an example of something often overlooked but that somehow lies at the heart of the "civil" in civilization. Hampden is a reminder that some intangible adhesive is required for the rule of law, something beyond law and capitalism. Call it character.

It may in the end be true that, more than capitalism, more than the law, some quality called civic virtue, some attendance to the larger welfare, some decency and compassion, some regard for the ways to resolve conflict that are *not* violent is the hallmark of a functioning democracy. Commerce may be the stomach of a civil society and law its muscle, but its heart is character. John Hampden was the heart of the English revolution. We will see, when we come to it later, that without values similar to Hampden's, the American Revolution, with all its attendant codes and laws, would have been meaningless.

UNPARALLELED COURAGE, FRAUD, AND REVOLUTION

We live in an age that makes truth pass for treason.

—Sir Algernon Sidney, from the scaffold, 1683

Charles I died for the principle of an unbridled royal prerogative, put to death by a parliament determined to curb kingly power. His death did not, however, finally solve the matter of royal taxes or habeas corpus or tampering with the courts. He was followed by a decade of reforms during which the English attempted to establish a sort of republic, though they eventually established a leadership model similar to a monarchy by appointing (rather than anointing) Lord Protector Oliver Cromwell. But the new government also settled the collar of Puritanism like a yoke around the stout English neck. The well-fed new urban class now began to chafe and choke.

After a decade of rules concerning when to go to church and what to do there, how to pray and how not to pray, a decade of military control in which Parliament played little role, the burghers of England had had a bellyful. Cromwell died in 1658; his son Richard briefly attempted to rule, but the English had had their fill and threw him out. So it was that in 1660, the Stuarts were welcomed back to London with cheering and acclaim. The tide had again turned, and once again the whole idea of laws to restrain kings fell upon the consciences of a few good men.[1]

Charles II was brought back from exile in France, where he had fled in 1649. One of the new king's first initiatives was to search out and brutally hang, draw, and quarter John Cooke, the commoner who had prosecuted his father. Without Cooke's courage to read on from the charge when Charles I commanded him to pick up the broken tip of the royal cane, the story of the law might never have been writ large. Cooke was a hero whose name is seldom if ever mentioned, but it should be remembered. He died an awful death.

The restored Stuart monarchy at first avoided any serious confrontation with Parliament. Charles drank, swaggered, bedded the lovely Nell Gwyn (and at least twelve others), and for several years did not force the issue of rights for Catholics. Charles was not openly Catholic,[2] but his brother James—the Duke of York and probable next in line of royal succession—was. The question of whether a Catholic might soon be allowed to come to the throne of England created great bitterness and hostility on the streets of London. Since Henry VIII, the monarch had also been "protector of the faith" of the Church of England. How could a Catholic be protector of the Anglican faith?

Now to the story of democracy comes Sir Algernon Sidney, descendant of a long line of independent Sidneys. Years earlier young Sidney had opposed Charles I, had been present when the most forthright statements of people's power had been uttered in the House of Commons, and had been infected with the virus of popular sovereignty. After Charles's death, however, Sidney had had little taste for the Puritan oppressions of Lord Protector Cromwell. He had therefore retired from politics and even from England for many years. But when, after the Restoration, Charles II regained power, Sidney also returned to London.

Sidney's writings show a severe distaste for royal power, pettiness, and arrogance.[3] He was among those who objected to the king's prerogatives, and before very long he may have actually joined a conspiracy to forcefully oust the king. He was, as it happened, also socially prominent, which was dangerous because it meant that he was closely watched by the Crown. At first, no one could catch him in an actual act of treason. But as time passed and public anger against the Catholic leanings of the monarchy increased, a small group plotted the death of Charles II. They planned to gather a band of armed men to surround the king on a public road and to kill him then and there. The king would be on his way to a festival in Newmarket, with the royal route leading past Rye House, a private home owned by one of the plotters—hence the name known to history: the Rye House Plot. Here on the fateful day the conspirators would gather, and perhaps they even did. But alas, at the last moment a fire in Newmarket forced the king to change his plans and not go to the town. He did not pass by Rye House at all. Unfortunately for the conspiracy, the plotters were soon thereafter discovered and done away with. No actual evidence linked Sidney directly to the conspiracy, but historians believe he may have been one of the conspirators. Still, if the law is king, and the king not above the law, the matter would have to be proven by real evidence, according to common law rules developed over centuries. This was a capital offense, and in such matters, where lives were on the line, most Englishmen expected that such rules should be followed.

Sidney was charged with treason. The common law required that in capital cases there be at least *two* incriminating witnesses. The Crown could find only one: Lord Howard, who was widely believed to have purchased his own freedom by agreeing to testify. Howard had a scurrilous reputation and might have been an unreliable, or even unpersuasive witness for that reason alone. But the Crown had found no one else who could claim to know Sidney personally and to have talked to him. The defendant therefore argued that under the law requiring two witnesses in capital cases, he should be immediately freed.[4]

The only other evidence against Sidney, other than the uncertain Lord Howard, was a manuscript. This had been taken from a book upon which Sidney had been working for many years. The papers had been found in the defendant's closet. In Elizabeth's time, poetry and theater had been the only recourse of dissidents.

Now Sidney was at work on a philosophical writing that held out-right that kings rule by the consent of the people, subject to the control of Parliament, and are accountable to the people for acts of misgovernment. In extreme cases of tyranny and oppression, he wrote, resistance would be justifiable. In that one fateful thought, that resistance would be justifiable, the Crown saw treason. If that was not enough, Sidney also had written that monarchy was typically accompanied by "slavery, misery, infamy, destruction and desolation."[5] In the event, he would be tried as much for his loathing as for his actions.

The case for the Crown was based upon these closet papers from Sidney's life's work. His tract on government showed, said the solicitor general, a purpose to kill this king. General philosophy could be fairly interpreted to mean a specific intention to murder Charles Stuart.

Did the criminal law, responded Sidney, not require evidence of involvement in this specific plot to kill this specific king? His book had not even been published; how then an incitement to rebellion? No one had read it! And if no one had read it, how could there be a conspiracy that requires at least two people? And how could an unread document be a concrete act in furtherance of a specific crime? How could it be an act to commit murder of anyone, anywhere, at any time?

To which the solicitor general replied for the Crown that the papers that had been found in Sidney's possession manifested an imagination to kill the king. Such writing (or imagination) was itself an overt act in the conspiracy; the writing was, he said, a substitute for the second witness required by law. [6]

To defenders of the royal prerogative, the idea that the people's power translated to *Parliament* and not to the king at all was outright sedition. The court of King's Bench, under the jurisdiction of the infamous Lord Chief Justice George Jeffreys, quickly found Sidney guilty and sentenced the writer and philosopher to death.

Less than a month later, standing in his final moments upon the scaffold, brave Sidney handed to the sheriff a paper. He had written what he wanted the world to remember and no doubt feared that were he to speak it out in that desperate travail, he might forget something. In this writing (which quickly spread through radical circles all over England), he urged his countrymen to respect the rule of law even above their innate respect for authority and grandeur. Like Edward Coke before him, he cried out, "These laws [of ancient England] are to be *observed* and the oaths taken by rulers are to be *kept*" (emphasis added). The law is not an empty thing; the law is not a hollow shell; the law is the heart and backbone of a nation.

Sidney argued that England should respect freedom of thought and speech of any man. This was the essence of the matter, of course. Freedom of speech was not yet guaranteed to anyone in England. It was not a man's right to disparage the authority of a king. It was not his right to say that a king was morally wrong or personally corrupt. It was not his right to say that moral authority arose from some source other than the sword, or that the law was for some purpose other than to preserve power. It was not his right to say that intelligence mattered in a leader, or that competence mattered in a minister, or that truth-telling was of more power than incense or the wafer at Communion. "If nevertheless the writer were mistaken," he wrote, "he might have been refuted by law, reason and Scripture. No man for such matters was ever otherwise punished than by being made to see his error...but... we live in an age that makes truth pass for treason." Flinging law and truth into the faces of kings, in 1683 Sidney went to his death.

Within a century, Sidney's words would provide a candle in the darkness of England's royal past, but it would take that long. The darkness of tyranny had some time left yet. When Charles had returned to England in 1660, his Catholic brother, James, the Duke of York, had come with him. It was over the issue of James's probable succession to the throne that serious controversy now exploded. James was avowedly Catholic, and his second wife was Catholic. But most of England was not Catholic. While Charles was still alive, therefore, the House of Commons attempted to pass a law to exclude James from any right to become king. With this direct confrontation, the issue of religious toleration broke into the open.[7] Anger ran high and threatened even the innocent mistresses of the king. One story has it that on a certain day an angry crowd surrounded Nell Gwyn's carriage, as she rode through the streets of London. They fell upon the carriage, threatening to attack Gwyn and tear her apart. The mob apparently thought she was the king's Catholic lover, Louise de Keroualle. Gwyn saved herself—so the story goes—by crying out through the window, "No! No! I am the king's *Protestant* whore!"

Habeas corpus now enjoyed one of its greatest successes, and the story about how it came about is a wild tale. In 1679 there was enormous pressure on Charles to exclude his brother from the succession. Charles refused to relent, but to soften his opponents in the Commons he allowed them to consider a bill to establish habeas corpus in its full detail, including provisions for time limits to hold a prisoner in jail, prohibitions against double jeopardy, and a time certain for criminal trials.[8] As the story is told, the Commons supported the bill but the Lords opposed, and the bill went back and forth between the two houses. At last the issue was whether to hold a conference. Failing that, the bill would die. By tradition, the means of voting in the Lords was that those who supported the conference had to pass out of the chamber and be counted as they passed back in. Two "tellers," or counters, were required: the one to be sure that the other did not cheat. The supporter of the conference in this case was the first teller. He noted to his delight that his counterpart was rather in his cups. When a particularly fat lord came through the door to be counted, the teller, in jest, counted "Ten!" His opponent teller, having nodded off, missed the joke, and the first teller proceeded to count forward from that number. Habeas corpus passed that day by a margin fifty-seven to fifty-five, with ten of those in favor having been in the form of one fat lord. The Act of 1679 remains in effect in England to this day, though with amendments, and is a pillar, still, of English constitutional law.[9]

In 1685 Charles II died and the Catholic Duke of York assumed the throne against the concerted opposition and accumulated legal knowledge of two generations of English lawyers. The execution of Sidney had left many disgusted and outraged. They now determined to persist against the royal prerogative, and, now that the new king was more egregious than the last, they considered the issue to be one of national survival. To be Catholic, they thought, was not to be English at all.

In 1688, five years after Algernon Sidney's death, the Test Act of 1672 still prohibited Catholics from serving in official positions in English government. The act had been the result of a century of intermeddling in English politics by Roman popes and Spanish kings. The new king, however, would, if possible, overturn this hostility and reunite England with the rest of mostly Catholic Europe. King James II openly intended to reverse a century of English Protestantism. He was publicly supported in this objective by the very powerful French king, whose armies dominated Europe. Shortly after ascending to the throne, therefore, James ordered his Anglican clergy to announce from all the pulpits in the land his decision to appoint Catholics to certain positions then held by Anglicans. He would override the Test Act and reassert Catholicism in England; he called the override a Declaration of Indulgence. That declaration at once became an announcement of religious war between the king and his Protestant subjects. James said that the royal prerogative allowed him to render an act of Parliament a nullity. Now, again, the issue would be whether the king could *make* the law or be *subject to* the law. Kings John, Richard II, and Charles I had all fought the same fight. Until Charles I, they had all won. Now, James II wanted to go backward to a time before his father, to rule like Elizabeth or Henry VIII or Edward III. The very principle of feudal authority now hung in the balance.

In a state of shock, seven of the highest-ranking Anglican bishops immediately gathered in London. They huddled together in the palace of the archbishop of Canterbury for some days, fearful for their lives if they rebelled but even more fearful for the future of their church and their country. Finally, they agreed that they would not—could not—obey the king's order. They could not order their clergy to announce from every pulpit the news that the Anglican church was in effect to be destroyed. For these bishops, however, to engage in outright resistance to their sovereign was certain danger. Everyone knew that Sidney had lost his head for suggesting a limit to the power of the sovereign. Further, the Church of England had long been the king's ally. The bishops reluctantly decided to act respectfully, without raising any public standard of rebellion or popular protest. They would privately petition the king—with full deference, but with the intention to reasonably dissuade him from his intended course. They would try to hold him to the Test Act, which prohibited such appointments. They would warn of the civil discord that would follow if the king insisted upon setting Catholics in charge of Anglicans.

These seven bishops requested an audience directly with His Royal Majesty. They did not announce their outright resistance and hostility from their pulpits all across the land, where they might have raised the realm to outright rebellion. Instead, they thought it best and more moderate to bring to the king a one-page paper written by the archbishop of Canterbury. He was the nation's highest prelate; they would all seven sign. They would plead with King James that he not insist upon this royal power to do away with an act of Parliament. He should not insist that he could dispense with law on his own. No king should have an unbridled power to say when and where and how he would enforce the laws.

In due course the seven bishops were admitted to the king's chambers. They entered in an attitude of obeisance, kneeling in front of their sovereign. The king, who had not seen the petition, met them with smiles, thinking that they had come to plead for pardon. He expected apologies for recalcitrance, religious insensibility, irreligious arrogance. Instead, from their position kneeling on the floor, the archbishop's petition was handed to him.

The king read the paper, then folded it, and his face grew dark. These rebels were not asking forgiveness; they were asking a royal retraction, a royal humiliation, a forfeiture of rights afforded to a king by God.

"This is a standard of rebellion!" cried James, holding aloft the petition. "I *will* be obeyed. My declaration shall be published [in all the churches]. You are trumpeters of sedition!...God has given me the dispensing power and I will maintain it."[10]

James immediately convened a special council and gave it authority to indict the bishops. In a matter of days, the council ordered the seven to be rounded up and imprisoned. The brightest red cassocks in London were then collected on barges and rowed down the River Thames to the Tower of London. But by now—and to the king's great disadvantage—the modest petition of the bishops had found its way to local printers. They in turn had made thousands of copies, and these soon spread throughout all the public houses of London. The people of London responded in great numbers. As the barges loaded with the arrested and indicted bishops floated down the Thames toward the Tower, half the citizenry of the capital city seemed now to swarm to the shores to cheer them on.

The bishops were to be tried, having already been imprisoned, in a common law court. Lawyers would have to choose sides. Any prominent lawyer at this time would have had a very difficult decision. He could come to the defense of the laws of Parliament or the defense of royal power. He could stand with Sir Edward Coke and attempt to enforce the Magna Carta or he could look out for his personal career, which could only truly be assured by the continued and constant approval of the Crown. He could decide for the memory of Algernon Sidney, holding that power came from the people, or he could seek favor at the palace, as most lawyers had done down through time.

One of the greatest lawyers in England, William Williams, a former Speaker in Parliament and therefore a man of the people, was approached by the king—seduced, some would say, by the promise of riches and station—and agreed to represent the Crown against the bishops. After a long career representing the Commons, Williams went over to the king.

But six other lawyers, including a young legal scholar named John Somers, searched their souls and saw in the bishops' case the fundamental principle that must underlie the rule of law: they saw that if the king could throw bishops in jail for merely petitioning their prince to uphold the law, there was no point in having law, no point in even having courts, and no safety for the beliefs or the person of any man. If the king's Declaration of Indulgence was allowed to overrule Parliament's law, then what law was safe?

The four unhappy judges who sat on King's Bench for that trial were in a decidedly difficult position. They were caught between a furious monarch and a furious public. They most surely did not want be at that place at that time and would have gladly retired to a quiet life in the country. Half of London seemed to be gathered in the streets outside Westminster Hall. This was the same hall in which Charles I had been tried by John Cooke and found guilty of treason forty years before. Now that king's son was staking his life on reclaiming the prerogative, including the royal right to dispense with laws he did not like. Those outside Westminster Hall were clearly opposing their king. This was a head-on collision between a monarch asserting feudal authority and his people expanding their own claims to the law.

The king waited in his palace. He fully expected his court to do his bidding. He had reason to be confident. He had appointed the judges, one of whom was Catholic (in violation of the very law that was being tested). Tradition was all in the king's favor. Without question, personal rule was the norm in all the world, and James had gone no further in personal rule than any monarch was apt to go in any civilized realm. The king's resolution was fixed. "I will go on," he said. "I have been too indulgent, indulgence ruined my father."[11]

Young John Somers stood against this traditional feudal principle. He argued a standard that would, in the event, shape history and one day lay the groundwork for the American Republic. The import of his case was so great that it was perhaps even unknown to him. He argued against the principle of personal rule, the most widespread principle in history. He argued that the law mattered in the abstract, as a general principle, that the statutes of Edward III mattered, that before these the Magna Carta mattered, and that all these statutes contained a promise to prosecute no man except under the law. He demonstrated through chapter and verse that he had excavated from the oldest and mustiest buried law reports that if to petition the king was sedition, then England had no secure foundation, and that a country without a secure legal foundation would come to chaos, forever without rule or safety. This was the soil from which only tyranny could ever spring.

Fearing the crowds outside on the streets as much as they feared the king's rage, the four judges turned the case over to the jury without a clear legal instruction that would force a finding for the king. One judge even instructed the jury that the king had no dispensing power and that if such a power were to exist, it would destroy Parliament. The jury was then locked in a room, deprived of food, and ordered to decide. With the king's guards outside the door and with friends of the bishops in turn guarding the king's guards, those inside deliberated all night. At seven in the morning, the last of the royalists gave in and assented to acquittal. "Not guilty," read the jury foreman as a roar of approval erupted from the galleries and then flowed like a wave through all of London. That night bonfires burned in the countryside and seven candles, for the seven bishops, appeared in windows throughout the city. Subjects of the unhappy king flowed into the streets of London, dancing at his humiliation.[12]

James at first sulked, and as he did, the initiative passed from his hands. Lawyers were once again leaders in Parliament, and they now rallied one more time. They demanded that Parliament should be respected, that taxes should be levied by that house and not directly by the king, that royal favors should not be granted willy-nilly to royal favorites, that laws once in place were to be honored by the Crown and not "dispensed" with, or "suspended." All these abuses had been combined with James's insufferable royal arrogance, incompetence, and an unwillingness to truck with those who—though of lesser rank—might have saved him. James would not stoop to rally churchmen or bishops or the naturally supportive leaders in the House of Lords. In these days, as respect for the English Crown gradually unraveled, Parliament once again began to challenge the royal prerogative.

The overarching issue was the same as it is today: What is the extent of executive power? Does it indeed come from God or from the nature of the office, untrammeled? Does its exalted source mean that it overrides the established law? Does the fact that the king is sovereign mean that he can dispense with the law as it applies to his friends and suspend some laws altogether because he simply does not like these laws? Can he dispense and suspend at will? Is that the true meaning of the royal (or the executive) prerogative? In 1688 the issue was framed thus: Can the need for stability and tradition, the need of every subject for social order and safety, carry with it the allowance that those who are the most elite of all, those who are kings and bishops, lords and barons, rule unhindered, in spite of four hundred years of English law? Does the criminal law apply only to some imagined criminal class but not to the class of kings? May those whom the king fears be put in jail, while those whom he does not fear be turned free?

In the end, those who asked these questions at this turning point in the seventeenth century decided—staked their lives— *against* a royal prerogative of such unlimited extent. In so doing they came down contrary to the prevailing opinions of those who governed throughout the world.[13] After only three years of James's tyranny, they threw him out, forced him to abdicate, to leave the country. They then invited two new monarchs who were more pliable, more willing to give due regard to Parliament and to the rule of law, or, that is, who would not again persecute men like

Algernon Sidney, to take the throne. Before William and Mary could assume power, they were forced by Parliament to agree to principles that would thereafter be known as the English Bill of Rights of 1689:

> That the pretended power of *suspending* the laws or the execution of laws by regal authority without consent of Parliament is illegal;
>
> That the pretended power of *dispensing* with laws or the execution of laws by regal authority, as it hath been assumed and exercised of late, is illegal;
>
> That levying money for or to the use of the Crown by pretence of prerogative, without grant of Parliament, for the longer time, or in other manner than the same is or shall be granted, is illegal;
>
> That excessive bail ought not to be required, nor excessive fines imposed, nor cruel and unusual punishments inflicted.[14]

To be king would no longer include the power to suspend or to dispense with existing law. This bill of rights expressly stated that it applied to the "dominions" of which the American colonies were the principal example. The colonists, and therefore we today who have inherited this legal tradition, are beneficiaries of this language:

> That all and every the particulars aforesaid shall be firmly and strictly holden and observed as they are expressed in the said declaration, and all officers and ministers whosoever shall serve their Majesties and their successors according to the same in all time to come.

This was a second royal promise that the principle of law above the king was to prevail "in all time to come." In 1215 King John had promised:

> Wherefore we will...that the men in our kingdom have and
> hold all the aforesaid liberties, rights, and concessions, well
> and peaceably, freely and quietly, fully and wholly, for them-
> selves and their heirs, of us and our heirs, in all respects and
> in all places forever.[15]

So it was that through one improbable triumph at a time—
victories sometimes centuries apart—a legal foundation was
emerging from the arrogance, wars, and oppressive feudalism of
the Middle Ages. In 1215 the Magna Carta had been singular in all
of Europe to establish the principle of the law above the king. That
principle came inextricably bound to the right of assembly, and
that, in turn, to the right of those assembled to approve taxation
and that the courts should be free of royal control. It was the contrast of these principles to the rest of government throughout the
world and even in Europe that made the Magna Carta so stunning.

Then, in 1628, the Petition of Right proclaimed that a king
could no longer punish his enemies—or enforce his taxes—by
putting men in prison under his order alone. Habeas corpus, the
right to have an objective legal justification demonstrated to a
court of law, would be defended, even though a king might have
to be killed to enforce the point. To the Magna Carta, then, add
the Petition of Right of 1628.

Finally, in 1689, the English Bill of Rights marked the third
and most important of these foundational triumphs. James's
forced departure ensured for all time the end of rule by royal
decree and the suspension of statute by the royal will. The law
would no longer be suspended, dispensed with, or abrogated
simply because the chief enforcer did not like it.

These three great moments in legal history had not occurred
elsewhere. In France, King Louis XIV ruled with absolute power.
Of him it could fairly be said, "L'Etat, c'est moi." There was no
parliament in his equation. In Spain, Germany, and Italy, the
rights of man were still only the subject of philosophical tracts.
In Switzerland and Holland, republican governments had taken

root but lay in deep shadow beneath the sway of the powerful surrounding monarchies. The next giant leap for the rights of men (and, eventually, women) would have to occur somewhere out from under that shadow. But as time passed it became clear that not only monarchies were a problem; by 1776, it was becoming increasingly clear that parliaments, too, could become corrupt.

9

THE BIRTH OF A REPUBLIC

All just power is now derived from
and conferred by the people.

—Solicitor General John Cooke, in *King Charles,*
His Case, January 1649[1]

We hold these truths to be self-evident, that all men
are created equal, that they are endowed by their Creator
with certain unalienable Rights, that among these are Life,
Liberty and the pursuit of Happiness.—
That to secure these rights,
Governments are instituted among Men,
deriving their just powers from the consent of the governed.

—Declaration of Independence, July 4, 1776

The so-called Glorious Revolution of 1689 in England had established decisively, for the third time, that the king may not unilaterally determine the law. Law may only be created by Parliament and king combined. But what if Parliament too was corrupted by wealth and greed? What if landowners and rich merchants, the knights and squires of that body were also to become self-interested or to hold themselves out as a propertied class above the law?

This issue was not addressed by any nation until it burst upon the scene in advance of the American Revolution. The ultimate source of law, argued the people of the new American continent, is neither king nor Parliament, but the people—all the people. "We the people" became for the colonists not only a slogan but a profound political foundation. That foundation, however, was not foundation anywhere else. Across the sea in Europe, it was revolution.

By the mid-eighteenth century, it had become clear in the Americas that the Glorious Revolution of 1689 had not in any way secured the fortunes of those small farmers or artisans or shopkeepers who underlay the established classes. Upper-class leaders like Sir Algernon Sidney, a knight and colonel in the army, had been persecuted by Charles II, distinguished bishops were imprisoned by James II, and before them the persecuted had been sheriffs, burghers, and lawyers who had been imprisoned without the remedy of habeas corpus by Charles I. *Poor* people were most likely *not* petitioning for habeas corpus and were not in jail at all unless it was debtor's prison. One imagines that habeas corpus was not being enforced by Sir Edward Coke to the benefit of these poor debtors so much as for those wealthier men from whom Charles was extorting large sums of money for his warships. The Petition of Right works to this effect: "Don't force us (rich people) to pay for your warships."[2]

The fundamental change wrought by the American Revolution of 1776 was to inject into respectable political debate the idea that equality of opportunity, economic security, and reasonable prospects for education for the masses might produce more stability than do hierarchies of kings and dukes and squires and sheriffs. Habeas corpus and rights of assembly and fair process should extend to them as well, because if they did not, there would still be no stability, and if no stability, no security of property.

That Thomas Jefferson should write in 1776 that it was "self-evident" that "all men are created equal" was a stunning assertion. The idea was not, of course, self-evident to most of the world. Nor was it original to the Americans. Jefferson and George Washington and prominent women like Abigail Adams and Mercy Otis Warren had each in turn been in correspondence, before 1776, with English radicals, including especially the historian Catharine Macaulay. Macaulay had argued vigorously, after Algernon Sidney, that the authority of government derived originally from the people, from *all* the people, not from some mystical connection between God and kings, not from some authority residing in the rights of property, or the rights of the richest and luckiest. Macaulay saw property rights and titles for kings and dukes and lords all as trappings to ensure the stability of those who wish to maintain themselves in power and who will do anything necessary to subordinate, suppress, and destroy the liberties of those who might wish to raise themselves up. Liberty must be for all, she wrote, because there is a "natural love of freedom which lies latent in the breast of every rational being."[3] As a female historian challenging the conservative history of David Hume (who was worried about the "extreme liberty" in the Habeas Corpus Act of 1679), she was striking into a territory rarely if ever pioneered by her sex. But, she said, as she launched into her eight-volume *History of England*, playing a "proper" female role could not "keep [her] mute in the cause of liberty and virtue while the doctrine of [political] slavery finds so many interested writers to defend it by fraud and sophistry."[4]

During the years when the American colonists were restive under King George's arbitrary taxation, arrests, and billeting of British soldiers in private houses, Macaulay wrote to encourage their independence. You are not the rebels, she said, it is the *conservatives* "who are rebels in the worst sense; rebels to the laws of their country, the law of nature, the law of reason and the law of God." The American colonists must not forget that

> there are in every society a number of men to whom tyranny
> is in some measure profitable; men devoid of every virtue and
> qualification requisite to rise in a free state. The emoluments
> and favours they gain from supporting tyranny are the only
> means by which they can obtain distinctions.[5]

The first volume of Macaulay's history was published in 1763. In the course of the next years she was read by prominent Americans including Benjamin Rush, John and Abigail Adams, James Madison, Thomas Jefferson, and Mercy Otis Warren. Already in 1770, John Adams wrote in his diary:

> I have read with much Admiration, Mrs. Macaulay's History of England & c.. It is formed upon the Plan, which I have ever wished to see adopted by Historians. It is calculated to strip off the Gilding and false Lustre from worthless Princes and Nobles, and to bestow the Reward of Virtue, Praise upon the generous and worthy only.[6]

Macaulay was, however, tame compared to Thomas Paine. When colonial tensions were at their highest, it was Paine who hammered home the point about the endless and inevitable abuses of kings. Perhaps unlike any other writer of his time, he was himself of the working class, an emigrant, rough around the edges, not well connected or established in his new country. In the fall of 1775, further, after blood had been shed at Lexington and Concord, the colonies were profoundly divided on their future. Dr. Benjamin Rush of Philadelphia, himself a writer and thinker but of the upper classes and afraid for his own reputation, opined that Paine had little to lose and therefore urged him to write openly as the doctor himself could not.[7]

Paine agreed:

> The independence of America would have added but little to her own happiness, and been of no benefit to the world if her government had been formed on the *corrupt models of the old world*. It was the opportunity for *beginning the world anew...* of bringing forward a *new system* of government in which the rights of *all* men should be preserved that gave *value* to independence.[8]

In his pamphlet published in January 1776, *Common Sense*, Paine went full bore for independence, once and for all. He wrote not only for the silent wealthy like Rush, but also to mechanics and laborers, and wrote with the heart of a revolutionary offended by extreme wealth. Of what use were all their fineries and estates to the lot of the rest? "I was struck," he wrote later, "with the order and decorum with which everything was conducted [in America]; and impressed with the idea that a little more than what society naturally performed was all the government that was necessary, and that monarchy and aristocracy were frauds and impositions upon mankind." These were strong words, indeed. "Frauds and impositions" were worse than parasitic or unnecessary; fraud can be criminal. Of the storied and widely admired English monarchy he wrote: "A French bastard [William the Conqueror, in 1066] landing with an armed banditti and establishing himself king of England against the consent of the natives, is in plain terms a very paltry rascally original."[9] He even quoted scripture for his purpose: "And all the people said unto Samuel, Pray for thy servants unto the Lord thy God that we die not, for WE HAVE ADDED UNTO OUR SINS THIS EVIL, TO ASK FOR A KING."[10]

If the Bible was the word of God, warned Paine, then beware. How could a king, *scorned* by the Bible, rule *by divine right*?

> In England a king hath little more to do than to make war and give away places, which in plain terms, is to impoverish the nation and set it together by the ears. A pretty business indeed for a man to be allowed eight hundred thousand sterling a year for, and [to be] worshipped into the bargain! Of more worth is one honest man to society, and in the sight of God, than all the crowned ruffians that ever lived.[11]

Paine's *Common Sense* rallied an uncertain colonial nation to fight for independence. In a few months it is said to have sold over 150,000 copies. Whereas before its publication the colonies were divided concerning the question whether to merely fight for a repeal of the Stamp Act or for a halt to billeting of troops in people's homes, after *Common Sense* the idea of independence broke into the open. And this was more than just squirming free from Britain; it was about a new order in which law would be king.

> Let a day be solemnly set apart for proclaiming the charter [the Constitution]; let it be brought forth placed on the divine law, the word of God; let a crown be placed thereon, by which the world may know, that so far as we approve of monarchy, that in America THE LAW IS KING. For as in absolute governments the King is law, so in free countries the law *ought* to be King; and there ought to be no other. But lest any ill use should afterwards arise, let the crown at the conclusion of the ceremony be demolished, and scattered among the people whose right it is.[12]

In 1775, as fighting broke out in Lexington, Massachusetts, Virginians began to organize a new college to be named after those two English patriots of the seventeenth century, John Hampden and Algernon Sidney. Sidney had written that power ultimately derives from the people; in June 1776 Jefferson penned the famous words that all just powers derive from consent of the governed and, in so doing, gave the ultimate victory to the martyred radical.[13]

Sidney's *Discourses Concerning Government* had been on James Madison's required reading list when he was a student at Princeton,[14] and in 1775 Madison took a seat on the first board of trustees of the newly-founded Hampden-Sidney College.[15] Patrick Henry was a trustee there too. Indeed, the tapestry of liberty was woven by many friends. In a famous case in 1770, the defense lawyer John Adams wove together Sidney and the idea of the rule of law to defend the hated British soldiers who had participated in the Boston Massacre. In one of the more stirring closings in American jurisprudence, Adams told the jury that the law trumps even patriotic passion or fury:

The law, in all vicissitudes of government, fluctuations of the passions, or flights of enthusiasm, will preserve a steady unde-viating course; it will not bend to the uncertain wishes, imagi-nations, and wanton tempers of men. To use the words of a great and worthy man, a patriot, and an hero, and enlightened friend of mankind, and a martyr to liberty;...ALGERNON SIDNEY,...'The law (says he), no passion can disturb. Tis void of Desire and Fear, Lust and Anger.'[16]

Any lawyer would die for a summation like that. The jury was impressed and acquitted the British soldiers.

The Constitution of 1789 would eventually include a protec-tion for habeas corpus that may not be suspended except in time of invasion or rebellion, would prohibit billeting of troops in pri-vate homes, and would balance the powers of the chief executive and Congress, retain the power to tax in Congress, provide for election of the president rather than for a hereditary king, and establish a Supreme Court independent of either Congress or the president. But neither Madison nor those who had met at the Constitutional Convention in the summer of 1787 were unani-mous for democracy. Madison was himself one of the richest landowners in Virginia. His proposal for the Constitution would insulate the presidency from the people through the device of the Electoral College, would take away the rule of the majority by providing for two senators from even the smallest states with the least population, would allow for judges to serve for life, would make no provision for women to vote, and would refuse to take a stand against slavery.[17]

Yet, having said all that, it is undeniable that a turning in world history was under way. By 1791 a profound change was emerging from the feudal fog: the first ten amendments to the US Constitution do not only protect property, hierarchy, and the dominion of princes, or for that matter, the dominion of Congress or the newly created presidency. These amendments for the most part protect people, and where they protect property it is the property of all, including the smallest shopkeeper, not just the farms of the landed gentry. The amendments protect even those people who may dissent from the existing property distributions, or precisely those people who dissent from their government. The opening of rights to all was therefore more from the impulse of Paine than of the plantation owners or bankers. The new American Bill of Rights would include freedom of speech, freedom of assembly, and the right to petition for redress of grievances (remembering the seven bishops). It would include freedom from unreasonable search and seizure (recalling Mr. Penry's pocket and Algernon Sidney's closet), and a prohibition against cruel and unusual punishment (remembering punishments without number that had occurred in the Tower of London). All these had nothing to do with the ancient role of government to protect hierarchy or clan or the dominant role of force. Rather, the opposite was true: these were rights that would be needed to guard the common man and woman against the power of those very persons who had ever before been the ones to dictate the terms of their lives.

One would have to look hard to find any equivalent event earlier in the history of the Western world. Yes, there had been revolts of underclasses against the aristocrats of Athens in the sixth century BC, and, yes, the Roman Republic had sought to protect the masses through the office of Tribune, but here was a complete written constitution that in its first set of pre-agreed amendments added the rights of commoners, with or without property, with or without social position, with or without powers of their own. The Constitution in its original part, it is true, granted to senators the rights of privilege, allowed the continued ownership of slaves, and allowed state legislatures the leeway to grant property owners the rights to vote and to deny women the right to vote. All that occurred in Articles I, II, and III, and all of that represented a balancing of traditional patriarchal interests. It was the American Bill of Rights, however, the first ten amendments to the US Constitution, that signaled the world was changing, new values were emerging, and these were not about property and power alone.

One may appropriately add the American Revolution and the resulting Constitution of the United States as a fourth glorious benchmark in the story of the decline of personal rule, or, that is, of the dissolution of feudalism. The reservations for privilege in the Constitution make it clear, it is true, that there are two streams in American political culture, and even today only one of these is Jeffersonian or derives from Paine and Macaulay and Sidney and Cooke. Only one side of our culture agrees that all men are created equal, or that equality of opportunity is the basis of social stability. The other substantial political current throughout our last two hundred years has been fed by the desire to rehabilitate the central power of plutocrats and kings, even if they are now called presidents and CEOs. It is the rising tide of this executive power within the last forty years that has brought democracy to a crossroads again, to an equivalent moment to those of 1215, 1628, 1689, and 1776.

REBIRTH
OF THE FEUDAL MIND
IN THE UNITED STATES

10

TO SUSPEND THE LAW, AGAIN

Before he enter on the Execution of his Office,
he shall take the following Oath or Affirmation:
I do solemnly swear (or affirm) that I will faithfully
execute the Office of President of the United States,
and will to the best of my ability, preserve, protect
and defend the Constitution of the United States.

—Article II, Section 1, US Constitution

The executive branch shall construe
such provisions in a manner consistent with
the constitutional authority of the President.

—President George W. Bush's signing statement for HR 4986,
the National Defense Authorization Act for Fiscal Year 2008,
January 28, 2008

The new federal Constitution of 1789 was stunning in its brevity. With all its amendments, it still fills less than a score of pages.[1] Nevertheless, despite its conciseness, the drafters of the federal constitution spelled out the wording of the oath of office for the president. They included the exact language. He should take a solemn oath to "*faithfully execute*" the office and "preserve, protect and defend the Constitution." Two hundred years later it might seem surprising that they should have been so particular. But their particularity is not surprising when one remembers those people whose stories we have here encountered. Nothing had been more egregious, no argument had been more prolonged, no issue was more at the heart of the rise of the rule of law than that the king should *not* have the power to make his own laws or to decide when and where he should administer the laws made by Parliament. Kings, the founders well knew, did not much like to abide by the law, and the framers were worried that presidents might be tempted to act like kings. They knew the cost, measured in centuries and lives, of this temptation. They knew full well all of the history, from Emperor Pertinax up through John Somers, of the sacrifice and bloodshed to reach this point of definition, and they knew how fragile it all was.

When the framers began writing in Philadelphia in the summer of 1787, therefore, "faithfully execute" was no platitude. To "faithfully execute" was a mandate to abide by a principle to *distribute* rather than to concentrate these powers. The chief executive would have no royal prerogative to act on his own (with the exception of the power to pardon). The president's office would consist of executing those laws enacted under the consensual processes of Congress. There would be no executive power drawn from God or from natural law or law of the church, and most especially none based merely upon a president's personal preference. Not here, not in this country. Law would come from the compromises fashioned in the assembly drawn from the people. The oath of office would be an explicit and solemn remedy for the severe grievances against which the colonists' ancestors had been struggling for more than five hundred years.

It had been treason for Charles I to refuse to abide by the will of Parliament and to repeatedly attempt to enforce his personal rule against the rights of his subjects. The English civil war had therefore been more than a clash of personalities or a dispute of parties or even a dispute over the financing of wars. Rather, it had been the clash of great principles concerning executive powers, and when Charles spoke of the royal prerogative, he sought to retain whole and entire the personal rule of feudalism. When Parliament spoke of the rule of law, it meant to assert the exact opposite.

A century and a half later, the framers of the US Constitution would have known this background, chapter and verse. They had read Catharine Macaulay, who had spelled it out in eight volumes. They would have also known from the Bill of Rights of 1689 "that the pretended power of dispensing with laws or the execution of laws, by regal authority, as it hath been assumed and exercised of late, is illegal." They had also read David Hume, the Scottish philosopher who contended that men were governed by crass self-interest and that the masses could only be controlled if they were scattered or dispersed into small units so that they could not unite. The primary drafter of the US Constitution, James Madison, studied Hume's writing at Princeton and in 1787 turned the philosopher's pessimism into institutions constructed to balance the multiple passions of every rank and class.[2] John Adams, writing from London in 1787, included in his book *A Defence of the Constitutions of Government of the United States of America* a chapter devoted to Machiavelli and another to Algernon Sidney.[3] Adams had had an important impact on political thinking before the Revolution when, in 1775, he published his *Thoughts on Government*, and he was entirely convinced that neither reason nor the rule of law could ensure a civil society. Only a strong system of checks and balances could contain man's ambitions.[4]

In today's world the words *balance of powers* may have become a cliché, but when one recalls the powerful antipathy of Thomas Paine to kings, the experiences of excessive power out of which men like Paine and Patrick Henry had shaped their repugnance to the institution of monarchy, and when we recall the conviction that "in America THE LAW IS KING," the phrase is not a cliché. Restraint on the power of the commander in chief was not a slogan. For two centuries, for so-called national security purposes, kings had thrown dissenters into jail, raised taxes, or enforced only those laws of which they personally approved. The colonists knew that after the Magna Carta, creeping feudalism had again invaded the English psyche, taken over its loyalties, and bankrupted its treasury. When we today speak of the balance of powers, we speak of the primary protection sought by these framers to avoid forever the return to feudalism and with that the return to tyranny. In the minds of Paine and Henry and Adams and Madison at the birth of this republic, tyranny was the certain outcome of the *im*balance of powers. The loss of such balance would be something far more significant than mere discontent or dissatisfaction or an aberration in a democratic ideal. *Oppression* would be the result. This concern was therefore far more than a mere concern for congressional inconvenience or executive incompetence. Tyranny would be the outcome, and that would in turn lead to social unrest, instability, and, in a vicious cycle, instability would justify a return of royal oppression.

Historically in England and in modern times in the United States, the wedge issue, the excuse for such imbalance, has been prosecution of war. It is the camel's nose under the tent. It is the opening for even larger imbalance, and it is the extent of that larger imbalance that made the administration of George W. Bush singularly abusive.

Not since World War II has Congress been called upon to exercise its constitutional function of declaring war. Harry Truman took the country into Korea without such a declaration. Lyndon Johnson took us into Vietnam without such a declaration. Congress was not altogether happy with these unilateral actions and became especially upset after it became public knowledge that Johnson had fabricated evidence as an excuse to widen the war in Vietnam.[5] In their fury about these revelations of presidential deceit, Congress passed the War Powers Act, requiring that any president report to Congress after any use of military force abroad, and such report must include the circumstances necessitating the introduction of those forces. The president must state the constitutional and legislative support for such action, and the estimated scope and duration of the hostilities or involvement.[6]

But presidential war-making continued. President Carter sent helicopter gunships to Iran without a declaration of war. Ronald Reagan invaded Grenada and armed contras in Nicaragua without a declaration. Unusual in this tradition, George H. W. Bush sought the approval of Congress before the first Gulf War, although, consistent with his predecessors, he maintained that he was not required to do so by the War Powers Act. Bill Clinton sent troops to Bosnia without a declaration, and George W. Bush invaded Afghanistan and Iraq without a declaration of war. President Barack Obama has continued to unilaterally strike at Taliban targets in Afghanistan and Pakistan without a declaration. Most often these military excursions have been tacitly supported—after the fact—by Congress, through the passage of financing legislation. The will of the framers that war be only the result of discourse and debate—before the fact—has not in these instances been observed.

At the time of the American Revolution, even the idea of a standing army had been repugnant to the framers and to the early administrations of Washington, Adams, and Jefferson. By 1973 a standing army was not only routine in America, its use appeared to be totally at the discretion of the philosophy, the politics, even the mental health of the one person who might be sitting as president. Congress therefore also included in the 1973 War Powers Act the requirement that US forces be withdrawn from hostilities within sixty days after their introduction unless expressly authorized to stay longer by Congress. Vietnam had been an excruciating experience for American families and American politics. The Nixon administration had not made the war more popular, and although the president vetoed the War Powers Act of 1973, the House and Senate both repassed the act by two-thirds majorities, overriding the veto. That the veto was overridden, a rarity in US politics, showed the extent of congressional conviction that something needed to be done to control the unilateral engagement of military force by the chief executive.

At the time, President Nixon and his staff aide Dick Cheney vigorously objected. They viewed any limitation on presidential power as a serious mistake, and it is from these origins that Dick Cheney has since been on a widely reported crusade to restore what he considers to be the rightful powers of the office of the president of the United States.

The battle over presidential power therefore has fifty-year roots and has developed not only in response to specific wars but also ideologically. The debate has spawned the theory of the unitary executive. Cheney was assisted in the formulation and expression of that concept by his philosophical allies, his neoconservative, or neocon, colleagues, all of whom stood upon the principle that presidents since Lyndon Johnson have been unconstitutionally undermined and weakened by Congress. Here in the neocon movement was the reemergent conservative undercurrent in American politics that was apparent in the debates at the Constitutional Convention in 1787. Privilege, as we have noted, had been protected in the idea of the Electoral College, in provision for longer terms for senators (who were to be American patricians); and it was reflected in the protection of the so-called property rights of slave owners. In modern times the privilege of power was at the heart of the idea of the unitary executive. Alexander Hamilton was a champion of such power in the early years of the Republic; Dick Cheney was its champion in the Bush administration.

The concept of the unitary executive is that the president controls the executive apparatus, all the agencies, all the departments, the environmental efforts, the civil rights efforts, the education efforts, and so forth, and that his duty derives from the constitutional provision that he is to "take care" that the laws under which these agencies work are faithfully executed. To "take care" is in effect an unlimited power and difficult to distinguish from powers Charles I claimed for the royal prerogative. According to Cheney, the chief executive is the *sole executor* and therefore must add his interpretation of the law to those of Congress and the courts. This is stunning. Not only were the courts to interpret the laws, but so was the president. And if courts were asked to refer to legislative intent—a search that historically has required them to investigate congressional debates—under the doctrine of unitary executive, they were now also to refer to the president's signing statements. He would add his intention to that of Congress as if he were a coequal legislator. Bush and Cheney argued that the president's personal conviction was as relevant as that of Congress, and in the form of signing statements the chief executive would arrogate to his office not only the powers of Article II of the Constitution but also those of Article I. If this were a good faith attempt to interpret the Constitution, it would be entirely honorable. If this were, however, an attempt to reshape the document to give a president the powers of a king, it would roll back seven hundred years in the evolution of the rule of law.

There *is* a point at which the unitary principle makes sense. How can a president, it may be argued, enforce a law that he fundamentally believes to be unconstitutional or immoral? He cannot. He must, say the neocons, be able to draw the line and not violate his deepest legal convictions. He would not be "taking care" to faithfully execute the laws if he believed that one of these laws was truly unconstitutional. The problem comes, therefore—and this is where the unitary argument runs into trouble—in the case of those laws with which a president merely disagrees and searches for a pretext to frame an objection. If he refuses to enforce a law concerning affirmative action simply because his party platform has opposed the policy, or if he refuses to enforce an environmental regulation because he thinks it onerous for his campaign contributors, or if he refuses to spend money on stem cell research because he believes that God has instructed him otherwise, does "taking care" allow him to quietly and effectively override Congress?

This is different than if a president has been advised that the courts would disallow such legislation because of its unconstitutionality. That is another case. But where his resistance is rooted merely in the fact that Congress has reached a different legislative compromise than the president would himself have reached, has passed a law the president would himself not have passed, he is merely substituting his personal legislative judgment for that of Congress. He has done what James II did when he "suspended" the application of the law in instances of his own choosing, contrary to legislative intent. He has effectively usurped the powers of the legislature, or, that is, upset the delicate balance at the heart of the US constitutional system.

In the event, George W. Bush did not see fit to restrict his signing statements or his refusals to enforce laws to those that he was advised would be declared unconstitutional. Far more broadly, he refused to enforce laws that he argued *ought* to be unconstitutional according to his own view (if not the court's view). In that regard, he went further than any president before him. During his terms in office, President George W. Bush issued 125 signing statements expressing his intention to abide by congressional law only insofar as he personally approved such law. According to a 2005 study funded by the American Bar Association,

> from the inception of the Republic until 2000, Presidents produced signing statements containing fewer than 600 challenges to the bills they signed. According to the most recent update, in his one-and-a-half terms so far, President George W. Bush (Bush II) has produced [challenges to] more than 800 [provisions].[7]

Other reports now make the number of challenged provisions in Bush signing statements at above a thousand. In the words of Charlie Savage of the *Boston Globe*:

> I went back and read all these signing statements…that had been put into the Federal Register since the beginning of the Bush administration. What it turned out to be was a road map, essentially, to the implication of the unfettered presidency that Dick Cheney's legal team was trying to create, because when you march down the hundreds of different laws that Bush had declared himself and the executive branch free to disobey, you saw that it's not just a torture ban here or a question of surveillance there, but in hundreds of matters, now over a thousand, large and small, anywhere the Congress had tried to say the

executive branch had to do something, couldn't do something else, had to go about doing something in a certain way…the implication [of the statement] was that Congress could not regulate the government.

It was none of Congress' business what the government did, how it went about it, what the limits of its conduct were. All these matters were solely for the president to decide. So Congress could make laws for the rest of us, but not for the government. The government existed to do what the president wanted it to do at any given moment.[8]

Parliament in the 1600s and the people of the United States during the Bush terms were both confronted with a legitimate question: how much power must the executive have in order to be able to effectively govern? That is a fair consideration on the one hand. On the other hand, how much power must reside in Parliament, or Congress, the people's body, the body that most reflects the compromises and trade-offs necessary to respond to all parts of the country, all traditions, and all social concerns?

Proponents of the unitary executive answered by saying that congressional compromise—or the accumulated judgment of the people's representatives—cannot override the president's personal judgment, because he alone is the one official elected by the whole people. This argument is oft repeated. By their vote, the people may be said to have authorized plenary powers. The president may have such powers because he is commander in chief under Article II of the Constitution and they voted for him in a time of war.

These arguments are flawed. The people may have voted for a president because of Iraq, or terror, or immigration, or religious affiliation, but it is unlikely that they did so because of a desire, for example, to override scientific research at the EPA, or the torture statutes, or the habeas corpus clause of Article I of the Constitution, or, more unlikely, all of these. The people manifestly, for example, did not vote for President Bush specifically hoping that he would override the Coastal Zone Management Act of 1972, a law that he subsequently unilaterally amended by executive order. In spite of a provision in the act prohibiting certain sonar usage because of its potential impact on coastal sea life, and in spite of court orders enforcing the statute, the president issued his own order in January 2008 suspending the statute and authorizing the navy to do precisely what the statute and the courts had ordered not be done. Congress and the courts, in accordance with their constitutionally assigned powers, had therefore both created that act and supervised its enforcement. In summarily ordering the suspension of the act, the president asserted that he might dispense not only with the law, but with those parts of the Constitution that empower courts and Congress.[9]

Bush's argument was that when exercising his Article II powers to "take care" to enforce the laws, he might ignore or abrogate those very laws. He might care for the Coastal Zone Management Act by nullifying it. He might wipe out the act in whole or in part; it would be up to him. In February 2008, a federal district judge issued a thirty-six-page opinion *reasserting* the principle that in the Coastal Zone case, the law is above the president. But on that same date, without hesitation or pause, the Bush White House announced its intention to continue its claimed special dispensation.[10]

Ultimately, it has to be said in Bush's defense that when this case was appealed to the United States Supreme Court, that court upheld the president's decision to override the Coastal Zone Management Act on grounds of national security, granting that right to the commander in chief.[11] The president was ultimately vindicated, legally. But the gravity of the constitutional matter resides in the action of the president to override the then-existing law in advance of, and regardless of, court opinions to the contrary and that he did so, as he put it, to "take care" of such laws.

The justification for the unitary executive is that a wartime commander may ignore Articles I and III. He may ignore the greater part of the Constitution establishing courts and Congress as if only Article II were operative. This he may do even when it is he, the president, who has declared the war without Congress. He may eviscerate the old Constitution; hang it and draw and quarter it. He may do all this because he is the single official elected nationally, by all the people.

Sir Edward Coke, Sir Algernon Sidney, and Thomas Paine were among those who said that such conduct—even when under royal authority, claimed to come from God himself—would never be tolerated again. When Charles I did these things, he was indicted by John Cooke as a tyrant; when James II did them, it was sufficient cause to throw him out, exile him, banish him forever. When George W. Bush did them, no one did anything. Bush assumed this unilateral power notwithstanding that in Article I, Section 8 of the Constitution, it is the people's body, not the president, that is given the regulatory power over the government, and it is Congress, not the president, that is *explicitly* authorized to regulate our military forces. The language is straightforward: "Congress shall have the power…To make Rules for the Government and Regulation of the land and naval Forces."

The framers seem to have contemplated the very question that arose under George W. Bush and explicitly decided that question in favor of Congress. Nor was that constitutional provision likely to have been casual or arbitrary. Immediately preceding the English civil war, in 1642, Parliament had sought to create and control the militia and demanded that the king relinquish such control. In a desperate attempt to avoid the collapse of the country into all-out war, messages were hurriedly exchanged between the two camps. If the king would yield on this point, war might still be avoided. In this critical moment, knowing full well the consequence, Charles proclaimed, "[I] would no more part with [control of the militia] than [my] crown."[12] Shortly thereafter, the war began.

In 1787 this history was broadly known, having been the subject of histories by both Catharine Macaulay and David Hume, both of whom were familiar to Madison and his colleagues. It is unlikely therefore that the drafters of the American Constitution only casually or accidentally adopted the position of that earlier Parliament, the pivotal question that might have avoided England's civil war. They chose to state that Congress, not the president, shall regulate the army. And yet, this is another provision that Bush wholly ignored.

In 2008 President Bush authorized construction of permanent military bases in Iraq. These bases, as originally sited, were located coincidentally with substantial Iraqi oil reserves, and, except for bases within Baghdad, were largely missing from areas such as Al Anbar province that did not contain oil reserves. Permanent bases at the chosen locations would have guaranteed permanent control by the United States of major sources of Iraqi national income and, very likely, control of the resources themselves. Many observers suspected that these military bases, in these locations, were the original and most important justification for the Iraqi invasion of 2003.[13] Congress, however, in opposition to this permanent presence, and responding to elections of 2006, which had sent a message that withdrawal from Iraq should be a top national priority, passed the 2008 Defense Authorization Act with a prohibition against permanent construction of such military bases. But in signing the act on January 28, 2008, the president flatly asserted his power to override Congress, attaching the following text:

> Provisions of the Act...purport to impose requirements that could inhibit the President's ability to carry out his constitutional obligations to take care that the laws be faithfully executed, to protect national security, to supervise the executive branch, and to execute his authority as Commander in Chief. The executive branch shall construe such provisions in a manner consistent with the constitutional authority of the President.[14]

In other words, the president shall treat any restraints imposed by Congress as null and void and shall operate according to his own policies and judgments regardless of any law passed by Congress that make such action illegal.

The president in effect asserted in this statement that his election in 2004 overrode the elections of 2006 and that he had the constitutional power to ignore the expressed will of the people in later elections. He asserted, further, that his was the only power that could apply to foreign affairs and that his was the only power to regulate the land and naval forces.

Nowhere in the Constitution does it say that a president may abrogate the statutes of Congress and the decisions of the courts. It could not be fairly argued that in the election of 2004 the voters of the United States had intended to give the president power to preempt the role of Congress and federal courts. It could not be fairly argued that a president could do so whenever in his sole judgment he had an intention or conviction different from that of either of those constitutionally created bodies. Thomas Paine would have screamed bloody murder.

A president may only have such plenary power if he suspends the law. But he is not merely suspending a statute. He is suspending Article I, Section 8 of the US Constitution, the clause that gives Congress power to regulate government and our land and naval forces. He must therefore suspend not only the law—whether it relates to torture or sea coasts or corporate reporting or anything else—he must suspend the delicate political balance drawn from the lessons of the Magna Carta of 1215, the Petition of Right of 1628, the Glorious Revolution of 1689, and the American Revolution of 1776. Between 2001 and 2009, the United States experienced a president willing to do just that. He was willing to mimic the arrogant incompetence of James II and to assume the bloodstained mantle of Charles I, and in effect to reintroduce to us the royal code of Justinian. Everything the leader does is legal because he does it.

When the law is violated at the highest levels, and when the courts do nothing and Congress does nothing, this is taken by the world not as an omission but as permission. If nonenforcement is taken as a permission by one president, it must be permission to all presidents. If a permission to all presidents, it is permission to any successor to George W. Bush. If it is a general permission to any successor, the Constitution has been rewritten and revised without any convention or agreement of the people, without any vote, without any knowledge that the social compact has been dismantled. And when the leader can violate the law and no one knows thereof, he acts like a king.

In June 2009 President Barack Obama proved the point. He signed a bill providing funding for the International Monetary Fund and included a signing statement saying he would not enforce labor and environmental standards in the making of IMF loans. Such restrictions would "interfere with my constitutional authority to conduct foreign relations by directing the Executive to take certain positions in negotiations or discussions with international organizations and foreign governments, or by requiring consultation with the Congress prior to such negotiations or discussions." The House of Representatives immediately responded, amending a subsequent foreign operations bill to restrict funding for such operations unless the president did indeed abide by the labor and environmental restrictions in the earlier IMF bill.[15] The rebuff was bipartisan and passed by an overwhelming margin of 429–2. Still, Obama's willingness to follow the Bush example makes clear that the issue of the signing statement is not permanently resolved.

History gives us few examples of executives willing to retrench. Like the descendants of the Caesars, they are elected or appointed or chosen to take action; movement is their mandate, the lumbering bureaucracy their curse. Congress is provincial; the people are impatient; something must be done, and in today's America only those eighteenth-century precedents stand in their way. The temptation to use power must seem not so much the temptation to immorality, or to illegality, or the intention to do something against the Constitution so much as the simple desire to break a governmental paralysis that seems itself immoral. That imagined paralysis then, at its deepest levels, is the conundrum at the heart of democracy's trauma today.

Is the paralysis necessarily a bad thing? James Madison saw this coming and thought it good. Better that government not act at all, he wrote in *Federalist #10*, than that it coalesce its powers in the hands of a few. His intention was not unity, but countervailing interests. Gridlock, he thought, is better than tyranny.[16] But things move faster today than they did in the eighteenth century. Faced with global warming and even networks of international terror, gridlock may no longer be a guarantor of freedom. In general, Republicans in Congress during the first nine months of the Obama administration have chosen gridlock, although they do not cite Madison. President Obama on the other hand has chosen action, however he can get it, although he does not think he is James II. Liberals who railed against George W. Bush's abuses of executive power now are apt to wish that Obama had more power. Conservatives who never saw a Bush war they did not like now tend to find Obama's wars far too expensive. Can our eighteenth-century Constitution contain and direct these contradictions?

The modern demand is for leadership and, in a simple denial, for the restraint of leadership at the same time. The ancient Athenians once willingly gave over authority to a powerful orator named Psistratus and in the act straight out named him a tyrant. The Romans once willingly gave over powers to Augustus Caesar and named him a god. Is this, then, the way of republics? That they gradually give way to that greatest of all temptations that the Greeks—faced with the same problem 2,600 years ago—called tyranny? Or can a modern republic, breaking from the temptation, call itself back to enforce the widespread dispersal of power and with that the preservation of freedom?

11

SPECIAL COURTS, AGAIN

There needed but this one court [Star Chamber]
in any government to put an end to all regular,
legal, and exact plans of liberty.

—David Hume, *History of England*

In lands in which the king is king—and the law is not king—
those citizens on the outside of the mainstream, the fringe, the
unlikely, the unpopular, or even the too successful, are targets
for persecution. We are a herd species, and most of us hunker
down in the crowd to avoid notice, to stay safely away from the
lions. For some reason, however—genetics, perhaps, or egotism
or integrity even—some of us hang out on the margins, and in
traditional feudal societies these are the ones who are easiest to
pick off. For kings and autocrats, courts are the easy means to
keep the crowd together. Political dissidents and troublemak-
ers are eliminated through the careful orchestration of legal
prosecutions.

Where feudal principles are residual in the culture, sometimes the autocrat himself plays judge or sometimes he appoints
the judges or sometimes simply creates courts for a particular
purpose, to do his bidding. When the society is knit together and
the public peace is maintained by a web of personal allegiances,
personal policies, and personal aggrandizement outside the law,

then judges do not become judges except by their willingness to become servants of elites or insiders. Criminal accusations are then used to eliminate outsiders. Those who are not friends are enemies. In Moscow, in December 2008, the Putin government moved against the billionaire mining oligarch Dimitri Rybolovlev, suggesting that his firm had violated laws yet to be named, presaging a government takeover of his company. The accusations originated from Prime Minister Putin's right-hand man and former KGB associate, Igor Sechin. This is the same treatment that in 2003 was accorded another billionaire oligarch, the owner of Yukos Oil, Mikhail Khodorkovsky, who was prosecuted and sent to a labor camp on tax charges. Khodorkovsky, once a fabulously wealthy man, remains incarcerated today, and no one in Russia believes that his real crime was failure to pay taxes. It had much more to do with his willingness to spend money to support Putin's political opposition.

Bribery, cheating, the use of government to serve one's personal interests are feudalism's visible markers still today. But to label personal rule as simply moral depravity is to underestimate its deeper root. Payoffs to officials, the use of courts to eliminate competition, and permits obtained more through personal contacts than through objective legal standards are the surface evidence of a profoundly significant, and widely prevalent, understanding of how the world works. The underlying conviction is that the natural organizing principle of society is personal relationship. One is powerful or successful depending quite simply and primarily upon one's contacts and connections. Family and classmates, cousins and vodka companions are the key to permits, opportunities, university admissions, official posts, payoffs, and extralegal exchanges. In all such transactions the law can be a tool against competition but is seen as no restraint against enforcing one's personal advantage. According to this point of view, it is naive *not* to pay bribes when necessary and, if one is an official, equally naive not to expect reward for concessions given. Power is then achieved by weaving together a network of personal allegiances whose decisions can ultimately be enforced, if necessary, through the courts. These courts, in turn, are not expected to operate in obedience to any objective standard of law or evidence so much as in obedience to the requirements of personal loyalty or fealty.

In modern times the feudal mind is shielded behind democratic names, but it is nevertheless feudalism. It is rule according to which rights belong to the most powerful and are given moral authority precisely because of such power. It is rule that is based upon violence and intimidation. It is clan based, or friends based, and rejects diversity or equality as a standard of value or predictor of social stability. It rejects truth-telling as a social adhesive and substitutes fear for trust. Living in a Western culture, one has the impression that feudal governments were left behind after the Middle Ages and that modern civilization has moved beyond. That would be a wrong impression. The feudal principle of personal rule is still today—under other names and to a greater or lesser degree—dominant in governments all over the planet. It is the feudalism practiced by Medvedev and Putin in Russia, by the heads of the party in China and the imams of Iran, and by the autocrats of Central Asia and the Caucasus. It is the feudalism of the patrôns of Mexico and of tribal chiefs in Afghanistan and Iraq.

Seldom do establishment lawyers in countries where personal rule is the norm defend those accused of crimes against the state, or of slandering the leader, or of speaking badly of the leader's policies. Were one do to so, he would likely himself be persecuted.[1] During more than seventy years of the Soviet tyranny, lawyers were facilitators of cruelty and torture. They existed in great numbers, but they did not apply the can opener of human rights to Soviet tyranny. To the contrary, they were tyranny's civilized face, its servile enforcers sent to accomplish an end that had nothing to do with the rule of law.[2] One might look therefore with some awe and a sense of wonder at the accidents of history that produced an alternative, nonfeudal mentality.

The story began, as we have seen, when the barons demanded of King John in 1215 that he separate the courts from the royal train, that they be allowed to convene in counties where the aggrieved parties resided or where the relevant property was located.[3] The desired effect was to establish a distance between royal power and justice, even to make a shield of the law against royal abuse. The nobility certainly had no idea at the time what new paradigm they were introducing. Considering, however, the extent to which all of society—probably from Ireland to China and everywhere in between—was dominated by the absolute centrality of government based upon personal relationships, the idea that law had standing outside the reach of the sovereign was wickedly subversive. But the revolution did not come quickly.

More than 150 years after the Magna Carta—and in spite of its provisions—peasants were still not able to plead in court against the lords who held them in perpetual bondage. They were treated as agricultural slaves and could not access the law at all when the issue was any one of them against any one of their lords. In 1381 came Tyler's Rebellion, a mass of peasants who came toward London burning and pillaging and chanting, "Kill all the lawyers and servants of the king." They burned every lawyer's house they could find, and when they got into town they seized and summarily executed Sir John Cavendish, the chief justice of England. Such was the reputation of the law and courts in 1381. As we have seen, the peasants lost this battle, and in the four-teenth century the idea that law ought to be servant to the people, that courts should be governed by due process, sank like a wave back into the sand.[4]

Another two hundred years passed and in 1601, Robert Devereux, Earl of Essex, tiring of the life of courtier, restless at the limited rewards that Queen Elizabeth would afford him, deprived, further, of his wine patents and desperate for income, mounted a rebellion against the queen in the city of London. He was the distant descendant of royal blood[5] and rallied a number of other discontented earls and counts. They assembled a troop of two hundred and marched toward the palace wherein the queen awaited, apparently not terribly frightened. Essex was immediately taken, imprisoned, and brought to trial in front of an assembly of lords the queen herself had chosen.[6] The remarkable thing about the case is not that Essex was convicted and executed—he was most certainly guilty of treason—but that even by 1601 the queen would pick the court to which he must answer. When matters were most dangerous, the sovereign assumed the power to name her justices and to decide the sentence. Wat Tyler's complaint had been that his peasant class was terrorized by the law; Essex's complaint should have been that the monarch who had been offended could determine herself who should rule upon his guilt. She would assay the injury to the Crown by appointing not some independent authority to rule on the evidence, but men of her own choosing, bound to her service.[7] From the standpoint of the rule of law, this is monstrous.

As the centuries unfolded, various means had been developed through which kings or the great crimson-robed bishops could evade the common law or circumvent those courts where commoners or dissenters might have had some minimal protection. In 1351 a unique—and now infamous—court had been created to do the king's bidding in matters he thought too serious to leave to the ordinary courts. These would be matters involving people the king especially did not like: people on the margins, people whom he deemed dangerous, or people whose words or language might embarrass the Crown. The new court consisted of the king's privy councilors and judges, all of whom served at his pleasure. Or, when the king himself was present, he could be the sole judge.

These special proceedings were held in a narrow back room in ancient Westminster Palace. They took place under a white ceiling upon which were painted blue stars, and the place was therefore called Star Chamber. The room was not very big. It was not accessible to the public. Here were conducted trials of treason, riot, or sedition. Star Chamber was a perfect example of personal rule. Far from *insulating* the public from abuses by the Crown as it might be hoped that the law would do, to the contrary, Star Chamber now became an instrument of orchestrated persecutions.[8] Mary, Queen of Scots was tried in absentia in Star Chamber and thereafter beheaded. The English historian and philosopher David Hume later wrote:

> There needed but this one court in any government to put an end to all regular, legal, and exact plans of liberty; for who durst set himself in opposition to the crown and ministry, or aspire to the character of being a patron of freedom, while exposed to so arbitrary a jurisdiction? I much question whether any of the absolute monarchies in Europe contain, at present, so illegal and despotic a tribunal.[9]

David Hume—writing in the eighteenth century, years after Star Chamber was abolished—was not a flaming radical. In fact, he often supported the rule of kings. But he was a mighty critic of Star Chamber. The framers of the American Constitution, including Adams and Jefferson, both of whom had read Hume, would certainly have known of that chamber and of the famous case of Mary, Queen of Scots, and quite probably of others, like that of William Prynne.

In 1632 Prynne, a Puritan, published pamphlets attacking immorality on the public stage in London. Prynne's work was widely interpreted as an attack against the morals of Charles I's queen, Henrietta Maria. It appears that the queen had danced— to the mind of Prynne—lewdly and lasciviously in many private stage performances. "Pagan dancing," wrote Prynne, "[was] to Christ's dishonor, religion's scandal, chastity's shipwreck, sin's advantage, and the eternal ruin of many precious souls."[10]

King Charles did not suffer lightly Prynne's effrontery, no matter how indirect, and neither did the Anglican church. Anglicans did not much want morals to be dictated by Puritans. The archbishop of course could speak directly to God, who in general was on the side of kings, no matter what their morals. The Prynne intrusion into his territory therefore mightily offended William Laud, who was at the time King Charles's archbishop of Canterbury. Laud dragged Prynne into Star Chamber. The man was definitely from the outermost Protestant fringe. The assembled bishops and judges had no trouble finding him guilty of seditious libel. In this court Prynne had no protection in rules of evidence or common law standards that usually govern trials for sedition. Star Chamber simply took an unpopular person, a dissenter, away from the law and subjected him to the whim of the sovereign. Laud's judges ordered that the defendant be fined five thousand pounds (a princely sum), and that in addition his ears be partially cut off. Further, he was to be imprisoned in the Tower of London without book, pen, or paper.

Prynne survived. After some years, he was eventually released from the Tower. Having apparently learned no humility or respect for kings, he immediately again took up his writing. He once more condemned rampant immorality in the kingdom. Now, in 1637, Archbishop Laud was forced to bring the poor man to trial a second time, the result of which was like the first. This time the rest of Prynne's ears were cut off. For good measure, "SL," for "seditious libel," was branded upon each of his cheeks. Star Chamber was not at all good for a man's health.

Sir Algernon Sidney was tried a generation later, in 1683. King Charles II ordered him brought before the court of King's Bench, where the Lord Chief Justice George Jeffreys presided, on a charge of high treason. Jeffreys was only thirty-two years old but already known as a terror to all who came before him. In other trials he was recorded to have interrupted witnesses attempting to defend themselves. One report has him attacking a defendant who had tried to undermine the credibility of state's witnesses by showing that one was a papist and another a prostitute. "Thou impudent rebel," exclaimed Judge Jeffreys, "to reflect on the King's evidence! I see thee, villain, I see thee already with the halter round thy neck."

When Sidney was brought before him, Jeffreys quickly suspended rules of evidence and allowed two men who had never met the defendant to testify regarding Sidney's state of mind. This they knew based on general conditions of conspiracy abroad in the land. Jeffreys then also allowed Sidney to be convicted by the testimony of only one witness with direct knowledge of the defendant himself, although the common law required two. That old rule was waived. Sidney lost his head.

These well-known cases serve to stand for some of the thousands of nameless victims of personal rule persecuted when kings and courts were not separated. The victims included Mary, Queen of Scots, the Earl of Essex, William Prynne, Algernon Sidney, and unknown numbers of those no longer identifiable.

After James II was deposed and William and Mary came to the throne in 1689, they were forced to agree not to create any more such special courts as had been done under James II. The English Bill of Rights contained this additional clause:

> That the commission for erecting the late Court of Comm-
> issioners for Ecclesiastical causes, and all other commissions
> and courts of like nature are illegal and pernicious.

James Madison and the framers of the US Constitution knew of Star Chamber. They knew too that law and religion had often been mixed and of the prosecution of dissident religious belief as treasonous or seditious. To equate heresy with treason or sedition had been common, especially during the reign of Queen Elizabeth. They therefore drafted Article III of the Constitution, creating courts separate from the president and separate from Congress. They sought to guarantee what the nobility at Runnymede had at first attempted. They sought to separate the executive from the interpretation of law.

Now, in the modern era, comes the so-called war on terror. After being chastised by the Supreme Court in June 2006 for imprisonments that had evaded the Constitution,[11] the Bush administration proposed, and a compliant Congress quickly passed, a new law, the Military Commissions Act of 2006.[12] While none claimed the purpose, and few were probably aware of this reality, the act substantially re-created special courts in the manner and for the purposes such courts had played as servants of English kings. The act authorized indefinite imprisonment without evidence of probable cause, and for imagined crimes. Detainees in the war on terror would be treated as if they were subjects of James II, or Charles I, or even King John in 1215. In sum, the act claimed to establish the right of an American president to conduct trials, suppress evidence, deny habeas corpus, and try prisoners that he alone—or those acting on his behalf—might identify as enemies.

The Military Commissions Act (MCA) was signed into law by President George W. Bush on October 17, 2006, only days before the midterm elections in which Republicans suffered loss of control of both houses of Congress. Enacted in haste, as if disturbed by a premonition that such political losses might soon occur, the MCA provided ultimate and plenary power to the president in his courts. Certain persons might be labeled "alien unlawful enemy combatants," and such persons should be explicitly denied the right to speedy trial or the right to constitutional protections against compulsory self-incrimination, meaning that evidence produced by torture might be used to convict. The MCA further, and egregiously, denied to such defendants the right for their cases to be considered under existing law, holdings, interpretations or other precedents, even of other military commissions. Finally, flying in the face of the international community, the act denied the right to protection of the Geneva Conventions. In 1683 Chief Justice Jeffreys had denied Algernon Sidney the protection of traditional common law and rules of evidence; hundreds of years later, President Bush's military commissions would provide no better protection for enemy combatants.

A person falls into this abyss of lawlessness as a result of having been designated an "alien unlawful enemy combatant." That designation, in turn, is to be made by a special tribunal appointed by the president. The decision of the special tribunal shall be final. Once having been so designated, a person may rot in jail for life. The designation, whether founded upon hearsay, rumor, the pointing of a soldier's finger during a midnight raid, the accusation of a jealous neighbor, the nod of a rival tribal leader, or the confusion of a terrified widow, shall be dispositive.

That any such tribunal should have been appointed by presidential order, to hold and prosecute enemies the president himself—or the lowest private on the battlefield—selects, to advance a war he himself declares and that he prosecutes in violation of both international treaties and domestic law, is of course entirely contrary to the legal tradition upon which the Republic was founded. It was reminiscent of those extraordinary tribunals appointed by Queen Elizabeth to try and execute the Earl of Essex and of Charles I's Star Chamber, which ordered chopping off the ears of William Prynne. The penalty that may be ordered by a military commission under this 2006 act is no less medieval. It too includes the penalty of death.

These changes in American practice, authored by President Bush and supported by Congress, give credence to the accusation that rather than dissolving personal rule, we are now once again, after two hundred years, moving in that direction ourselves. Rather than feudal societies, as in Russia, becoming more like us, we are becoming more like them. Not all courts serve the will of the president, for sure. Not even a small minority of courts do that. But that would also have been true at the time of the Magna Carta and it is true in Russia today. The major business of courts was handled far from the influence of King John or Vladimir Putin or, when he was in office, from George W. Bush. What *is* similar in all three situations is that when a matter of grave national concern or concern to the executive has arisen, as when Penry threatened the prestige of Queen Elizabeth, or Khodorkovsky threatened the prestige of Putin, or "enemy combatants" threaten the success of the "war on terror," then the executive seeks to take over and create courts that he can control. In our system, this is an erosion of Article III of the Constitution. In the case of Putin, it is simply business as usual. The more we do it, the more our practice becomes like theirs and the greater the inching back toward feudalism.

12

WAR PRIVILEGES, AGAIN

> Where law ends, tyranny begins.
>
> —William Pitt, Earl of Chatham

> The writ of habeas corpus is itself an indispensable
> mechanism for monitoring the separation of powers.
> The test for determining the scope of this provision
> must not be subject to manipulation by those
> whose power it is designed to restrain.
>
> —Justice Anthony Kennedy, *Boumediene et al. v. Bush*

After 9/11, the ensuing wars once again raised the issue of the king—or a president—above the law. Again, it would come to the surface under the banner of habeas corpus. In spite of the fact that there was no invasion or rebellion in progress, the Bush administration swept up and imprisoned hundreds of persons living within the United States. Suspected of being terrorist sympathizers, they were locked up and accorded the protections of neither prisoners of war nor criminals. The roundups appear to have been based solely upon national origin, skin color, or religion and particularly targeted Arabs and Muslims.[1] On its face, such a roundup violated equal protection and due process guarantees of the Constitution,[2] and persons held in violation of such provisions would ordinarily have a right to raise that defense in a habeas petition. But that was not to be.

Many of those imprisoned in 2001 were held incommunicado indefinitely, for months at a time, without bail, without right to counsel or to communicate with their families.[3] Their number was apparently more than one thousand.[4] They were taken from the streets of New York and Chicago and Los Angeles and Santa Fe. In the general climate of the time—with the battle cry of the president for a "war on terror" and the willingness of the national media to exploit war's sensation—the plight of these detainees was largely neglected by the general public. These persons, perhaps living on the margins of American society, had nothing of the high social standing of the friends of Edward Coke in 1628, and for them, in 2001, the ancient writ of habeas corpus was of no practical relevance. The writ had become a casualty of war hysteria.

Thus stood the situation at the beginning of 2003. In spite of an extended history and its prominent position in the Constitution, through the course of the next six years the Bush administration would make a concerted effort to limit the application of the writ in order to expand the powers of the president. They thus attempted to tip the balance in favor of the chief executive and away from the Article III courts, an effort consistent with the effort we have already seen to shift power away from the Article I Congress.

It was not long, however, before the courts reacted.

A fellow by the name of Yaser Hamdi was picked up by the tribal chiefs of the Northern Alliance in Afghanistan and turned over to the US military in the fall of 2001. He was subsequently labeled by the Bush administration as an "enemy combatant" and brought to a navy brig in this country. (Someone had discovered that Hamdi had been born in Louisiana and, thus, was an American citizen.) Hamdi's father then filed a habeas petition saying that Hamdi had gone to Afghanistan only two months before 9/11, could not have been trained to be a combatant in that short time, and had in reality been in that country to do relief work. The father said that the boy had a right to see the evidence against him. What proof had they that his boy was an enemy combatant? Was it enough that the notoriously corrupt tribal chiefs of the Northern Alliance said so? Did not habeas guarantee some showing of the evidence to the defendant himself?

Yes, said the Supreme Court, he does have that right.[5] There is a due process right to know the evidence according to which one is being tried, and habeas allows Hamdi to pursue that right. After three years and after at first being washed under the tide of war hysteria, in 2004 the famous old writ reemerged.

Another prisoner rounded up in Afghanistan after the invasion of that country in 2001 was Osama bin Laden's driver, Hamdan. Unlike Hamdi, he was not an American. He was sent to Guantanamo, was also labeled an enemy combatant, and was held for some years without trial. Finally, the government proposed to try him for conspiracy, he allegedly having been present with bin Laden when plans were made to train terrorists. The trial was planned to be before a specially created military commission. By act of Congress, defendants in these commissions would not be allowed to either see or hear the evidence against them. Here, again, the Supreme Court came to the defendant's rescue and more importantly, perhaps, the rescue of habeas corpus.[6] A defendant, said the Court, even a foreigner picked up abroad, has a right to be present in the courtroom, a right to hear and see the evidence. Congress, said the Court in *Hamdan v. Rumsfeld*, had not been explicit in saying that such right *did not* exist, therefore it still did. The justices had discovered a loophole in the statute.

It was now late in 2006. A Republican-controlled Congress moved quickly to close the statutory loophole, to explicitly create a military court in which there would be no right of habeas corpus for enemy combatants. Shortly before the autumn congressional elections, the Military Commissions Act was enacted.[7] Congress, in effect, overruled *Hamdan*. The new law explicitly stated that once the determination was made that someone was an enemy combatant, he would have no further right to the ancient writ. For the moment, the Bush search for broad presidential powers had been affirmed by Congress. Under the leadership of the executive branch, the Article I Congress said that the role of the Article III courts may be curtailed. There the matter lay until October 2007.

Now came the case of Lakhdar Boumediene, an alleged terrorist picked up in Bosnia and sent to Guantánamo. Could habeas corpus be applied to him, a foreigner, picked up overseas and held in a jail in Cuba? Congress had answered no. The matter came to the Supreme Court for one more review.

The pressure upon the Court was enormous. Four justices, Roberts, Scalia, Alito, and Thomas, wrote scathing dissents, sounding much the same as those who had defended Charles I before he was beheaded or James II before he was exiled. In 1643 a royalist by the name of Dudley Digges had written that "God is not a God of sedition, of mutinye, and confusion, but of unity, order, and of peace."[8] In June 2008 Justice Scalia, dissenting in *Boumediene et al. v. Bush*, wrote, "The game of bait-and-switch that today's opinion plays upon the Nation's Commander in Chief will…almost certainly cause more Americans to be killed." To insist on habeas corpus in the war on terror would therefore be "devastating." Chief Justice Roberts wrote that habeas corpus may be replaced by lesser legislative protections and that the greater protection provided by the old writ would be "fruitless" and "misguided."[9] These were personal attacks in the spirit of Alexander Hamilton lambasting Jeffersonians.

Justice Anthony Kennedy responded for the majority. He at first described in great detail the long evolution of habeas corpus from the time of King John through more than eight hundred years. We have to consult the law and learn from its teachings, he wrote, and one of these teachings is that liberty and security are reconciled *within* the framework of the law, not outside the law.[10]

Kennedy acknowledged the fears of the four justices in the minority and that the old habeas history may seem far removed from the nation's present, urgent concerns. But, he said:

Security subsists, too, in fidelity to freedom's first principles. Chief among these are freedom from arbitrary and unlawful restraint and the personal liberty that is secured by adherence to the separation of powers. It is from these principles that the judicial authority to consider petitions for habeas corpus relief derives.[11]

In accord with those principles, neither the president nor Congress may deprive a prisoner in Guantánamo of the right to know why he is there and under what law. Like Sir Edward Coke in 1628, in the face of a furious storm, Kennedy wrote that habeas corpus will have no sovereign.

Abstaining from questions involving formal sovereignty and territorial governance is one thing. To hold the political branches have the power to switch the Constitution on or off at will is quite another. [This Court will not accept] a regime in which Congress and the President, not this Court, say "what the law is."[12]

Habeas is above all, wrote Kennedy, about the balance of powers. It has been important all these centuries to bind the powers of the commander who thinks he is omniscient, to restrain the ruler who thinks he knows more than the legislators, to limit the very idea of limitless powers that seems to come naturally to the minds of those who think they are acting according to God's will.

And so, as of the summer of 2008, habeas corpus, the great writ, had been at first ignored and then restored by act of the Supreme Court of the United States, and for a time and in this limited way the Court had enacted a significant restraint on expanding presidential power. But the war on terror[13] was now being used not only to attempt to limit habeas corpus. There were other ways executive power was expanding and effectively nullifying important rights contained in the Constitution. The massive roundups in the United States that occurred in the wake of 9/11 also flew in the face of the plain meaning of amendments to the US Constitution.

> The right of the people to be secure in their persons, houses, papers, and effects, against unreasonable searches and seizures, shall not be violated.[14]

The Fourth Amendment says "people"; it is not limited to "citizens." These detainees, whether citizens or not, were obviously not secure in their homes. They were rounded up and transported to jails without warrants or probable cause but because of the color of their skin, their religion, or their national origin. They were also denied other constitutional protections, this time from the Sixth Amendment:

> In all criminal prosecutions, the accused shall enjoy the right to a speedy and public trial, by an impartial jury of the State and district wherein the crime shall have been committed, which district shall have been previously ascertained by law, and to be informed of the nature and cause of the accusation; to be confronted with the witnesses against him; to have compulsory process for obtaining witnesses in his favor, and to have the Assistance of Counsel for his defence.

In may be argued that the midnight roundups were not "criminal prosecutions," since Muslims were only being caught up and interrogated, held as "persons of interest," or were being deported because of suspected immigration violations. From the standpoint of the victim, however, the result was the same. It was indefinite detention, and that is the same result as from a criminal trial. If the result is the same, the distinction between what is and what is not a criminal prosecution may have meaning for advocates of presidential power but no meaning for the victim or the victim's families, and was no protection to preserve the victim's place in society or the health of his or her business. A punishment without criminal prosecution that is just as harsh as punishment with criminal prosecution should not escape the Constitution only because it is even less the result of due process.

Nor did the Bush administration erosion of human freedoms end there. The Eighth Amendment provides that "excessive bail shall not be required, nor excessive fines imposed, nor cruel and unusual punishments inflicted."[15]

In modern times, the detail of what constitutes cruel and unusual punishment has been codified in the Geneva Conventions, proclaiming that no physical or mental torture, nor any other form of coercion, may be inflicted on prisoners of war to secure from them information of any kind whatever,[16] and that definition has in turn become subject to US enforcement through the Uniform Code of Military Justice, the US Criminal Code, and several acts of Congress.[17] But the codes and Geneva Conventions did not keep the Bush administration from waterboarding.

Waterboarding—intentionally creating terror that one is being drowned—was defended by the Bush administration justice department, the president's personal counsel, and by the president himself. "Because the danger remains, we need to ensure our intelligence officials have all the tools they need to stop the terrorists," Bush said in a press statement on March 8, 2008. The White House claimed that waterboarding, although admittedly used, was not cruel and unusual punishment and was only "simulated drowning." Simulation no doubt accurately reflects the intention of the investigators because a dead prisoner can give no more information. For that reason alone they did not intend to kill him. But the experience of the victim is not simulated. The victim experiences the beginning stages of actual, real drowning. He actually goes through the first, or perhaps even advanced, stages of asphyxiation, which may or may not be interrupted in a timely way by his captors.[18] According to an Associated Press report based upon government data, by March 16, 2005, at least 108 people had died in American custody in Iraq and Afghanistan, many of them violently.[19] How many of these deaths may have resulted from waterboarding that was not terminated soon enough is unknown. But it is plausible or perhaps even likely that not all the drownings were "simulated." Nor do we know how many took place abroad and how many under US jurisdiction at Guantánamo.

The US military once issued a ten-year sentence to a major who waterboarded a prisoner during the Spanish American War. After World War II, the Allies executed eight Japanese officers for waterboarding British prisoners. Another officer was sentenced to fifteen years for waterboarding a US civilian. On October 31, 2007, Republican senators John McCain (AZ) and Lindsey Graham (SC) sent a letter to attorney general–nominee Michael Mukasey stating that "water boarding under any circumstances, represents a clear violation of US law." The attorney general, presumably acting under orders from the White House, refused to enforce this law.

After the horror and disgust in the worldwide public reaction to the abuses of the American-controlled prisons in Iraq at Abu Ghraib, Congress passed a renewed prohibition of torture, authored by, and promoted vigorously by, Republican senator John McCain. President Bush, however, stated that he would interpret the law in a way that would not restrict his power to continue to torture. Here was the signing statement:

> The executive branch shall construe [the law] in a manner consistent with the constitutional authority of the President...as Commander in Chief...[This approach] will assist in achieving the shared objective of the Congress and the President...of protecting the American people from further terrorist attacks.[20]

The new statute curbing torture was designed by Congress specifically for the international conditions at the time, including the war on terror. The act even anticipated an attempt by the president to ignore it. The president did not disappoint: he told them he would do just that. The Bush White House, on its own initiative, simply nullified Amendment 8 of the Constitution, which was intended to give protection to the unpopular, the less advantaged, and the unpropertied.

In the sequence of events that brought American democracy to the crossroads in 2008, first came the consolidation of powers in the executive branch, ignoring Articles I and III of the Constitution. The most blatant examples were those of the repeated signing statements, which effectively ignored the other two branches of government intended to create a counterweight to overzealous executives. Second came the specific override of habeas corpus, included in the body of the Constitution in order to preserve the balance of powers and especially the powers of the courts. Third came the train of abuses that were supposed to have been prevented by the Bill of Rights, the protection against abuses of search and seizure, cruel and unusual punishment, and the right to be safe in one's home. All these assertions of executive power were claimed under apparently unlimited war powers. These were powers claimed even though that war had not been declared by Congress, was declared only by the then-sitting chief executive, and could last forever.

The war on terror, as the Bush administration named it and Justice Scalia sees it, is produced by radical Islam. According to this view, religious fury breeds irrationality and takes the matter out of criminal courts and into the realm of foreign policy, a matter only for presidents. The chief executive should have the power to pursue dangers, especially dangers fueled by religion, without restraint. It seems likely, further, that the Roberts-led Court—possessed of a young and healthy majority—will adhere to this view in decisions presented to them in years to come. It will be reminiscent of intolerant views heard through history. In the sixteenth century, Catholic Queen Mary burned Protestants because of the supposed danger they posed to the realm. In the seventeenth century, her Protestant descendants deposed Catholic King James II because he posed a danger to the realm.

Now, Justices Scalia and Roberts will apparently approve unlimited powers to pen up Islamists as long as they remain radical and therefore a danger to the country. If these expanded presidential powers are to last that long, without limitation of Congress or restraint of courts, the balance of powers that was so important to James Madison and John Adams will have been lost for that long too.

13

THE LAW OF NATIONS IGNORED

*International law, natural law, German law, any law at all
was to these men simply a propaganda device
to be invoked when it helped and to be ignored
when it would condemn what they wanted to do...
[These men] cannot show that they ever relied upon
international law in any state or paid it the slightest regard.*

—American Justice Robert H. Jackson in his opening statement as prosecutor of
German defendants before the Nuremberg war crimes tribunal[1]

Through the course of the twentieth century, following the chaos
and destruction of two global wars and in an attempt to prevent
such catastrophes from ever recurring, the United States has
been on the forefront of the development of rules of international
behavior, rules of war, rules of protection for civilian populations caught in war, rules for protection of prisoners, rules of self-
defense, laws of the sea and, increasingly, laws governing trade
and pollution. From President Franklin Roosevelt through Harry
Truman, John Kennedy, Lyndon Johnson, Richard Nixon, Gerald
Ford, Jimmy Carter, Ronald Reagan, George H. W. Bush, and Bill
Clinton, the US government has continuously signaled its intention to strengthen this body of law. All this began most vigorously
with the formation of the United Nations in 1945 and was pursued through the Nuremberg war crimes trials and the adoption
of the Geneva Conventions in the late forties. Throughout these

years the United States pioneered and forcefully advanced the claim that there is, indeed, a law of nations and a law of war. After World War II, men were hung for violations of that law as a result of trials that we fostered in Nuremberg and Tokyo. In recent years, the United States has also pursued United Nations resolutions and sanctions against countries thought to be violating the nuclear nonproliferation treaties, and over three recent administrations we continuously excoriated Saddam Hussein for his violation of that international law.

When, however, international laws might be applied to the United States, George W. Bush unilaterally elected to ignore them. He ignored the United Nations Charter Article 52, which restrains the right of countries to go to war, limiting such right to acts of self-defense. The charter is a treaty formally ratified by the US Congress, and according to Article VI of our Constitution, such a treaty is a part of "the supreme law of the land." President Bush, however, treated Article 52 of the UN Charter and Article VI of the US Constitution as if they were no law at all.

In the autumn of 2002, the Bush administration presented to the UN Security Council Resolution 1441 iterating a series of violations by Saddam Hussein of Security Council resolutions, most of which had been passed years before, during the Clinton administration. These resolutions had demanded that Iraq cease its nuclear and biological weapons programs and that it authorize inspections to make compliance visible. The iteration in Resolution 1441 did not, however, include concrete or specific evidence of a new weapons program in Iraq, or under construction in Iraq, or uncovered by the most recent years of UN inspections in Iraq. Nor did 1441 present specific evidence of current Iraqi threats to regional, global, or local peace other than subjective suppositions that Hussein continued "to intend" to develop such weapons at some time in the future. Iraq under Saddam Hussein would be a danger to the peace of the world at some unknown time, in some unknown place, in some unknown circumstance because of actions to be committed in an unknown manner by unknown persons. These suppositions were based upon violations of UN resolutions as far back as twelve years and without evidence of current violations. The Bush administration nevertheless proposed preemptive military action with all its attendant killing and destruction and inevitable catastrophic consequences to the civilians of that country and justified such catastrophic consequences on the basis of an allegation of the imagined or supposed intention of one of their number.

Unlike a standard prosecution for criminal conspiracy, the allegations in 1441 therefore contained no specific evidence of actual weapons, or intended time of any attack, or intended location of attack, or intended perpetrator of such an attack. The crime to be prevented was therefore wholly and entirely speculative in time, place, means, and the identity of the perpetrator. Such speculation was based upon the supposed ability of the Bush team to evaluate the psychology and motives, prospective madness and cruelty of Saddam Hussein. Probably no criminal code in any civilized country in the world authorizes preemptive killing and destruction of a supposed future criminal on such evidence. But this is how it went forward.

While promoting support for Resolution 1441 on numerous television programs, the president, vice president, and National Security Advisor Condoleezza Rice repeated the warnings to the country that Hussein probably did—or would soon—possess nuclear weapons. They warned that the United States "could not let the smoking gun become a mushroom cloud."[2] The premise of US preemptive action therefore would be the need to avoid a nuclear attack upon the United States by Saddam Hussein. The only way that Hussein might avoid preventive action by the United States would be to prove the nonexistence of weapons of mass destruction (WMD) in Iraq.

Proof of an absence is, unfortunately for Hussein or anyone else, not practically possible. One can never prove the nonexistence of anything because every place in the universe, or, in this case, every sand mound or every suitcase in Iraq, was a possible location for the storage of WMD. In addition to requesting proof of the impossible, the test of the proof was to be weighed by the White House and the White House alone. This was no different from Queen Elizabeth I deciding for herself that poor Mr. Penry intended to commit treason based upon papers found in his pocket.

On February 5, 2003, Secretary of State Colin Powell addressed the UN Security Council and offered evidence of supposed mobile labs for making biological weapons and possible underground facilities for perpetuation of Iraq's nuclear program. As it turned out, the administration would stand by this evidence and neither seek nor accept anything further. A month later, on March 6, 2003, in a nationally televised news conference, President Bush told the nation that Saddam Hussein, not he, controlled the decision for war. Hussein could stop the war by satisfactorily proving to the president the nonexistence of WMD; that is, if he could prove the negative. There would be no other way.

The next day, March 7, 2003, UN weapons inspectors Hans Blix and Mohamed ElBaradei reported findings from their inspections of the preceding three months, since the passage of Resolution 1441 and the intensification of these inspections. Each reported that the inspections had been proceeding with incomplete, but substantial, cooperation from the Iraqi government. ElBaradei reported:

> The IAEA [International Atomic Energy Agency] has now conducted a total of 218 nuclear inspections at 141 sites, including 21 that have not been inspected before. In addition, the agency experts have taken part in many joint...inspections with [Blix's UN team.][3]

Air, water, and soil samples had been gathered, the radiation team had covered some two thousand kilometers over the preceding three weeks, and seventy-five facilities had been surveyed. Interviews had been conducted with numerous relevant Iraqi personnel, both upon spontaneous and prearranged visits. The allegations of supplies of nuclear materials from Niger had been examined and determined to be "inauthentic." In conclusion, therefore, thirteen days before the US invasion and a day after the president called for more evidence, the International Atomic Energy Agency reported to the Security Council that "there is no indication of resumed nuclear activities," further that "there is no indication that Iraq has attempted to import uranium since 1990," and finally, "after three months of intrusive inspections, we have to date found no evidence or plausible indication of the revival of a nuclear weapon program in Iraq."[4]

A similar report was submitted to the Security Council on that same day by Hans Blix, who came to similar conclusions about the lack of evidence of any active Iraqi program to create biological weapons.[5] Ten days later Vice President Cheney totally ignored these findings and declared to the nation that he knew the opposite to be true:

> We know [Hussein] has, in fact, developed these kinds of capabilities, chemical and biological weapons...We know he's reconstituted these programs since the Gulf War. We know he's out trying once again to produce nuclear weapons.[6]

In US civil law, "intentional misrepresentation" is generally defined as the representation of a material fact made by one person to another knowing that that fact is false. Fraud may also include intentional failure to state material contrary facts, knowing that those omitted facts would correct a misapprehension. Or fraud may include speaking with reckless disregard for the truth or falsity of the statement made, or reckless disregard for the effects of omitting the correcting information.[7]

When Vice President Cheney said three days before the Iraq invasion that "we know" that Hussein "has reconstituted" nuclear weapons programs, he intentionally led the public to ignore the two widely publicized UN inspection reports that held to the contrary. Cheney knew, at the very least, that he was speaking with reckless disregard for those UN reports. His statement and conscious omissions fit the textbook definitions of fraud. His statement and those made in the preceding weeks by the president and National Security Advisor Condoleezza Rice induced the American public to accept a war. The war has damaged millions of dollars in property and taken hundreds of thousands of lives, and it is based upon representations that in a domestic civil suit would constitute actionable fraud. Under international law the violation was more than of civil law; it was criminal.

The administration had tried in the preceding autumn to gain Security Council consent for outright permission to go to war. In the end, the final paragraph of Resolution 1441 had, however, merely warned Iraq that that country would face "serious consequences" as a result of its *continued violations* of its obligations. By March, no new evidence of continued violations had been found, but it was clear that Bush and Cheney intended to invade Iraq in any case, with or without the evidence. Such "serious consequences" could now not be practically avoided. UN inspectors had scoured Iraq thoroughly for some years without finding such weapons. In the autumn of 2002, Hussein had produced more than twelve thousand pages of documents attempting to prove that no WMD program existed any longer. The president and the vice president, however, belittled the submission, saying that so much documentation was an obvious smoke screen for evil intentions that lay undisclosed. Then, in mid-March 2003, and before Blix and ElBaradei had completed their inspections, President Bush demanded that they and their teams leave Iraq. The last hope for fulfillment of the conditions by which Hussein might have avoided war was therefore rendered impossible.

During the negotiation of the UN resolution, it was reported that Secretary of State Powell promised to the nation's attendant in the Security Council that if Iraq did *not* comply with inspection requirements set forth in the resolution, the US *would return* to the UN for an additional authorization permitting the use of military force. Powell therefore obtained international consent for Resolution 1441 by agreeing that this resolution was not yet an authorization for the use of military force. His promise to return for an additional resolution was not, however, honored. President Bush ignored Powell's promise and contended that the "serious consequences" that had been authorized by 1441 could happen at any time. Given the steady buildup of forces on the borders of Iraq for more than twelve months preceding the invasion, it was clear to most observers that war was guaranteed. Hussein's failures to provide even more evidence would simply become the pretext. The UN and the International Atomic Energy Agency's showings that no current evidence of any present danger, or even any prospective WMD program, had been found would be ignored.

An invasion would take place, and it would not only be based upon fraudulent misrepresentations; it would be a war crime.

A showing of "imminent danger" has been customarily required by international law as a prerequisite to offensive military action under Article 52 of the UN Charter. In the event, however, Iraq's failure to prove the negative (a practical impossibility) was used by President Bush as the excuse for the invasion, and detailed proof of imminent danger was never proffered. When asked by journalist Diane Sawyer in an interview in December 2003 whether such imminent danger had actually existed in the form of nuclear weapons or had simply been a prospective threat that might exist sometime in the future—and therefore was not imminent—Bush responded "So what's the difference?" International law was either unknown to him or he did not care. In either case, he violated it.[8]

Justice Robert Jackson, who had been attorney general of the United States and was, in 1945, a sitting justice of the Supreme Court, argued in his opening remarks at the Trial of the Major War Criminals before the International Military Tribunal in Nuremberg that an "aggressor" is that state that is the first to commit any of the following actions:

1. Declaration of war upon another State;

2. Invasion by its armed forces, with or without a declaration of war, of the territory of another State;

3. Attack by its land, naval, or air forces, with or without a declaration of war, on the territory, vessels, or aircraft of another State;

4. Provision of support to armed bands formed in the territory of another State, or refusal, notwithstanding the request of the invaded State, to take in its own territory, all the measures in its power to deprive those bands of all assistance or protection.

Each of Justice Jackson's first three tests of aggression was violated by the Bush administration when it invaded Iraq on March 20, 2003.

Justice Jackson then said:

And I further suggest that it is the general view that no political, military, economic or other considerations shall serve as an excuse or justification for such actions.[9]

The justice further added that it can be justifiable self-defense to stop someone else's aggression. He did not, however, say that it can be self-defense to *imagine* someone else's aggression. Disrespecting the legal requirement for a showing of self-defense or imminent danger, President Bush and Vice President Cheney planned, promoted, and carried out crimes of aggression as Jackson had defined that crime and as the world community had come to understand it. Further, in the course of such aggression, by bombing schools, bridges, and hospitals, and by authorizing systematic and detailed programs for torture,[10] they also violated the Geneva Conventions, to which the United States is legally bound.[11] The Bush justice department declared that these Geneva Conventions' ban on "outrages against personal dignity" may be applied selectively, or, that is, according to the whims of leadership at any given time and in any particular circumstance.[12]

Crimes of aggression, destruction of civilian properties, intimidation of civilians, infliction of undue suffering upon them, and torture of prisoners are war crimes. A 2006 *Lancet* survey estimated 631,000 civilian deaths resulting from the war. Thirteen percent of these were from air strikes, a cause that could only come from the Americans and not from the civil war between the Iraqis themselves.[13] This would lead to a *minimum* figure of more than 80,000 civilians killed as a result of the Bush administration's decision to eliminate WMD that were not there and for which there had been no current evidence.

To conduct an invasion upon a fraudulent excuse, resulting in the loss of civilian lives in numbers ranging from 80,000 to over 1 million,[14] is to return to the methods and devices of tyranny. It is to fly in the face of the lessons from history, that democracy is rooted in nonviolence and only makes sense as a replacement for violence. It is all this, and, without the excuse of self-defense or imminent danger, it is also a war crime.

Whether President Obama will reverse this course is uncertain. One could hope that as a former teacher of constitutional law, he would be less willing to tread upon and ignore the limitations of executive power (those included within the first ten constitutional amendments). One could also reasonably hope that he would not ignore the balance of powers issues raised by George W. Bush's rejection of habeas corpus and disdain for the rights amendments regarding search and seizure, safety in one's home, trial by jury, and cruel and unusual punishment. On the other hand, the current president's prosecution of the undeclared war in Afghanistan raises doubts about his willingness to respect the framers' original intention that wars not be declared by executive order alone. Further, it was not only George W. Bush who abused the practice of signing statements. Bill Clinton and other presidents before him also used such statements from time to time. The practice was simply expanded or rendered systematic and comprehensive under Bush. The decisions made by this current president, and the restraint required of the president by both Congress and an observant people, will have much to do with whether, at the crossroads, the road taken will be back in the direction of the Republic or further toward the return of feudalism.

14

WHILE CONGRESS SLEPT

In these three decades when money became so
important in Washington, Congress lost much of its
effectiveness as a governing institution.
Running for re-election became more important
than running the country, or keeping an eye on the exercise
of executive power—the roles the founders envisioned
for the House and Senate. The quality of governance in the
United States had declined palpably in these years.

—Robert G. Kaiser, *So Damn Much Money*

When in 1628 King Charles I of England first threw people into prison, Parliament resisted. Sir Edward Coke and those most prominent members who protested did so at risk to their lives.

When in 1636 Charles attempted to collect ship-money as if it were a tax and John Hampden declared to the king that he would not pay, he did so at the risk of his life.

When, two kings later, James II sought to dispense with existing law governing religion, Parliament rose up to declare his override illegal. Then they threw him out.

When, by contrast, in 2003, three hundred years later, the president of the United States made war upon the barest pretext, in the face of international opinion that declared that such an invasion would be a war crime, the United States Congress bowed to his will and passed an authorization for the use of military force.

When the president of the United States declared that he would pay for such wars "off budget," through emergency and supplemental appropriations, and such expenditures exploded into the billions of dollars, Congress passed the appropriations, making no move to control him or to remind him of the balance of powers or his place in a constitutional system, but instead allowed him to use the national defense as an excuse for plenary powers.

When the same president of the United States violated the Foreign Intelligence Surveillance Act by conducting wholesale searches of e-mails and phone calls without a warrant, Congress abandoned that existing law and moved to ratify the president's action and give to him that power retroactively.

When the president of the United States justified waterboarding, a form of "enhanced interrogation" that the body of international law considers to be torture, and when the president admitted that he and his top cabinet advisors had approved such conduct, Congress passed a new law prohibiting waterboarding; but when the president vetoed the new law, Congress did nothing.

When the president of the United States challenged hundreds of legislative provisions, announcing to Congress that he would only enforce any law that that body imposed upon him to the degree that he wanted to do so, Congress duly passed new legislation requiring him to do as he was told, but when the president ignored that law as well, Congress did nothing.

When a congressional judiciary committee under the leadership of Representative John Conyers and with the assistance of Representative Dennis Kucinich assembled chapter and verse details concerning those violations of national and international law that should serve as the basis for impeachment of the president of the United States, the Speaker of the House of Representatives refused to bring the matter to a vote or to let committees hold hearings on the subject or to use the subpoena power to investigate the subject, and Congress did nothing.

Sir Edward Coke, a member of Parliament in 1628, risked his life to rally the houses for habeas corpus. John Cooke, the lawyer acting on behalf of Parliament in 1649, risked his life to rid the kingdom of a tyrant and eventually, when the monarchy was restored, was hung, drawn and quartered.[1] Sir Algernon Sidney, a former member of Parliament, gave his life in 1683 because he had written that power comes from the people and not the king. Thomas Paine, Thomas Jefferson, John Adams, George Washington, and the other founders of the American Republic pledged their lives, their fortunes, and their sacred honor so that a future Congress might restrain a king. In spite of these precedents, from 2001 to 2008, while a president assumed powers alike unto a king, the United States Congress did nothing.

The actions of the Bush administration demonstrate unequivocally that more is required for the rule of law than simply the Constitution or the statutes of the United States. Were these alone sufficient, the attorney general might have said, "Mr. President, you cannot do these things; they are illegal." Were these sufficient, Congress might have said, "Mr. President, we will not fund these things." Were these sufficient, the people might have said, "When we see tyranny we will impeach it; when we see treason, we will prosecute it." None of these occurred. The law, alone, is evidently not enough. When the mind of feudalism is present, or when it reemerges, the law by itself cannot contain it.

15

TODAY'S TUG-OF-WAR

As we cannot, without the risk of evils
from which the imagination recoils,
employ physical force as a check on misgovernment,
[we must]...watch with jealousy the first beginnings
of encroachment,...never to suffer irregularities,
even when harmless in themselves, to pass unchallenged,
lest they acquire the force of precedents.

—Lord Thomas Babington Macaulay, *History of England*

The rule of President George W. Bush and the reign of King James II were in some ways identical. Each man attempted to suspend troublesome laws or dispense with broad areas of law, to organize courts to do his bidding, or to confine criminals whom he himself—or his minions—would personally identify. Each acted on his own unilateral initiative to assume powers never formally granted in legal history. Each assumed philosophically that power creates its own rights and that he with the most power has the most rights. The major difference between the president and the king was the end result: Parliament threw the king out. Congress, on the other hand, acted more like a Roman senate happy to praise a Caesar for his foreign victories. James II stirred up a revolution. George W. Bush paved the way for more Caesars and our current tug-of-war between rival philosophical factions. Some factions today seek to protect the Republic while others push back, seeking to restore powers akin to those of a feudal monarch.

Violence and the attempt to assert moral authority based upon power were at the heart of the Bush-Cheney doctrine of preemptive war. These were no different values than those asserted by kings John I or Charles I when they each invaded France. Misrepresenting to Congress his lack of intention to go to war in Iraq long after that intention was clearly formed; overstating the dangers from al Qaeda as if they were based in Iraq; claiming solid intelligence that revealed WMD in Iraq when at best such evidence was speculative, uncertain, and contested; claiming not to torture when such torture had been authorized at the highest levels of the Department of Defense and given a green light by White House Counsel; and disclaiming facts concerning global warming and eliminating such facts from scientific reports for political purposes were among an avalanche of attempts by the Bush administration to assume that honesty is irrelevant to governance. In a democracy, the opposite is true. Democracy cannot survive without assuming the truth as the foundation for decisions both economic and political.

And if truth was not the standard, neither was competence. When, so as to protect political allies of the president, White House minions struck from Environmental Protection Agency reports scientific conclusions developed by the experts at that agency; when massive spending contracts for reconstruction were awarded without competitive bidding; when Harriett Miers, the president's longtime friend but desperately unqualified lawyer, was nominated to serve on the US Supreme Court; when Attorney General Alberto Gonzales fired eight US attorneys without regard to their stellar records; when hiring practices at the Department of Justice favored appointments of ideologically conservative new lawyers rather than seasoned prosecutors or legal researchers; when the Office of Legal Counsel was used to construe executive powers beyond the boundaries of widely held legal opinion; when the history of the evolution of the rule of law, the centuries-long struggle, was ignored; and when signing statements were used to undermine the fragile balance of powers won by that struggle, it was clear that historical or legal competence was not this administration's standard.

No American leader before had tried, as Vice President Cheney would do, to justify torture because it was effective. Until the Bush administration, it had been assumed that whether effective or not, it was sufficient to know that torture was illegal under the statutes of the United States, under the Uniform Code of Military Justice, and under the Geneva Conventions. "Effective" was no excuse and was legally irrelevant. In a series of television interviews in May 2009, however, Dick Cheney continued to excoriate those who, including now-president Obama, sought to restrain what he euphemistically called "enhanced interrogation," or what the rest of the world calls waterboarding. Cheney launched an attack against the rule of law with as much energy as any aristocrat defending the right of Charles II to behead Algernon Sidney.

The tug-of-war over the meaning of democracy is now more serious because of Bush's appointments to the Supreme Court and the leadership of the new chief justice, John Roberts. These appointments, and particularly that of the young chief justice, make the return to the principles of balanced democracy even more problematic. It is true, as we have seen, that despite Justice Roberts's objections, the Court has recently upheld habeas corpus and limited the Bush administration's flagrant disregard for the rights of prisoners. But one can take little comfort from the fact that George W. Bush leaves Roberts behind as the likely head of the Court for at least a generation to come. Jeffrey Toobin, writing in *The New Yorker* in the late spring of 2009, reviewed the Roberts record. He noted that while Roberts was humble and deferential in his respect for Congress during his confirmation hearings, his opinions from the high bench have not been humble:

> The kind of humility that Roberts favors reflects a view that the Court should almost always defer to the existing power relationships in society. In every major case since he became the nation's seventeenth Chief Justice, Roberts has sided with

the prosecution over the defendant, the state over the condemned, the executive branch over the legislative, and the corporate defendant over the individual plaintiff. Even more than Scalia, who has embodied judicial conservatism during a generation of service on the Supreme Court, Roberts has served the interests, and reflected the values, of the contemporary Republican Party.[1]

From the perspective of the history recounted in previous chapters, or, that is, the ongoing effort to balance executive power with that of the legislature or the parliament, the Roberts mind is royalist. He is rather like Archbishop William Laud, who did the bidding of Charles I, approving and implementing special prosecutions in Star Chamber and approving the torture of prisoners in the Tower of London. Laud's positions were meant to cement the royal prerogative and, therefore, in the words of Jeffrey Toobin, the "existing power relationships in society."[2] Roberts has not yet justified cutting off anyone's ears, as did Laud, but he has voted to continue military commissions and trials like those of the old days in Star Chamber, where a man like William Prynne had no protection in rules of evidence or common law standards that usually govern trials for sedition. In a process reminiscent of Star Chamber, the label "enemy combatant" has served to preclude any man brought before the military commissions the right to confront his accusers, know the evidence against him, or be protected against hearsay. Laud supported this streamlining of judicial process to the advantage of Charles I. Roberts supports streamlining to the advantage of whomever is president. When, therefore, waterboarding eventually reaches the Supreme Court, there is little evidence upon which to base hope that the new chief justice will value established law on torture above the Cheney principle that torture is, or may be, effective.

Even beyond the issue of torture, the record does not support the hope that Chief Justice John Roberts will value the rule of law for any other purpose than to support the established order. In this he will be acting in the same manner and to the same end not only as did Archbishop Laud in the 1630s, but even as did John of Gaunt, Duke of Lancaster, in stamping out England's first independent Parliament. Wat Tyler and those peasants and tradesmen who in 1381 marched on London chanting "kill all the lawyers" (because the law served only those in power) would today be sympathetic to those who seek to balance executive powers, not to increase them. Wat Tyler and his murderous mates went after the lord chief justice, found him in London, and killed him. Then they killed the archbishop of Canterbury. Those two dignitaries, thinking they were aiding stability, had simply used law to confirm established society, like Roberts has done. Today's attempt to approve the consolidation of executive power is also intended to increase security and stability. Unfortunately, a study of history suggests that just as in the 1300s, this kind of conservatism ultimately renders power less stable, the absolute opposite of the result Cheney and Roberts intend.

Perhaps even more desperate in its implications for the rule of law, it only takes a quick look at the Obama administration to see how little is understood, even with a different and far more enlightened president, of the roots and mind of true democracy.

War creates appeal and excuse not only for Bush, Cheney, and Roberts, but also for Barack Obama. Since his election, the new president has announced his intention to suspend habeas corpus in alien detainee cases and to continue the practice of indefinite or "prolonged" detentions. While at first he announced an intention to discontinue Bush's military commissions, within three months he reversed his stance and now intends to continue military courts designed to prosecute terrorist suspects. He has, it is true, eliminated the fateful "enemy combatant" label that was so effective in destroying all rights of these detainees, but will nevertheless detain suspects indefinitely if they are believed to "substantially support" al Qaeda. He will require some evidence in court but will still admit hearsay if it is "reliable." This is a huge flaw. Any trial lawyer will report that "reliable hearsay" is a contradiction in terms; hearsay is by definition unreliable. There are exceptions according to which it is sometimes admitted, but the exceptions require proof of particular circumstances that augur for authenticity. A hearsay statement might, for example, be admitted into evidence if it is an admission against the interest of the person speaking. There are other exceptions. But over the centuries these exceptions have been narrowly defined. In the Obama military commissions there is still no assurance that those traditional narrow exceptions will be adhered to. That means that some statement by, say, a tribal rival made in the middle of the night to an American soldier in Afghanistan, saying, "Go down there; the man in the house [his rival] is Taliban," could never be tested in a military commission for accuracy. The statement is hearsay; it is out of court, but it could keep the suspect in prison for life.

President Obama will also not require that all the evidence against a suspected terrorist be made known to that defendant, and this too will violate one of the oldest principles of US criminal law. Although Obama discards the propaganda term "the war on terror," he has nevertheless elected to treat terrorism as war and not crime, to continue renditions of suspected criminals to foreign prisons, and he continues to monitor domestic telecommunications on a massive scale.[3] To lay the blame where it appropriately belongs, the president is caught between two opposing principles of democracy. On the one hand, he is probably more aware than any president before him (who has not been a law teacher) of the origins and necessity for habeas corpus, common law courts, and protections against unreasonable search and seizure or cruel and unusual punishment. These are foundational in our republic. On the other hand, it is no doubt also true that the large majority of the American public supports a president if he does whatever he needs to do to prevent another terrorist attack like 9/11. The public is generally not as protective of the Constitution as are civil rights advocates and law professors. If the president is to follow this second premise in a democracy—that he abide by and serve the will of the people—he is caught between these two opposing values. The current crisis of democracy is deepened by the likelihood that ultimately the will of the people may trump and therefore evade, override, and even destroy the rule of law.

To his shame, Barack Obama is allowing himself to forget Wat Tyler, Sir Edward Coke, John Hampden, John Cooke, and Sir Algernon Sidney, all of whom stood up to royal power, and is even forgetting James Madison and his colleagues, who sought to bind that power to the rule of law forever. To Obama's credit, on the other hand, there is one significant difference between him and his predecessor: the current president is attempting to forge a policy on detention that binds the practice to democratic legal tradition instead of to inherent powers of the commander in chief. That is important. Obama attempts to bind his courts to democratic rather than monarchical principles. For Bush and Cheney, the main justification for presidential power was no different than it had been for princes three centuries before. Charles I said he could put people in prison because of his inherent powers as king. George W. Bush said he could do so because he had inherent powers as commander in chief. Both claimed to derive their authority from God. Both were content to thumb their noses at the legislative and judicial branches.

The Obama administration, in contrast, is making a serious effort to tie detention to law, that is, to contain it inside the democratic tradition. The briefs of Obama's prosecutors now cite congressional authorization, case law from the US Supreme Court, and the UN Charter.[4] This is probably more than window dressing. The current president may end up doing the same thing as his predecessors, but not in open neglect of, or defiance of, the law so much as in (attempted) consonance with it. At least under the current president the rule of law is regarded as a legitimate restraint on presidential power. Better that than to dismiss the rule of law altogether. Put another way, if Obama makes the case that he is honoring Congress, the Supreme Court, and the United Nations, while at the same time respecting and attending to the will of the people, he is at least attempting to reconcile the ideals of democracy, even though they cut in two different directions.

This navigation between traditional law that restrains him and the fears of the electorate that they may be blown up by another terrorist (this time one with a nuclear bomb in a suitcase) may serve the current president in the short run. But in the long run, it's clear that not only presidents must be educated as to the true roots and values of democracy, but so too must populations be educated. The long-term salvation of democracy, the hope to retain this small island of freedom in a globally hostile sea, depends upon the widespread understanding of values deeper than law, not just by leaders, but also by the general public. It requires a more penetrating analysis of democracy than simply of its codes and constitutions. Unless the values, intentions, or assumptions that these codifications are intended to protect are understood, law by itself is no barrier against tyranny. Those values—by contrast to the legal forms such as due process or habeas corpus—have received almost no attention in public discourse. And yet, as we shall see later, they are even more important than the law; they are the soil in which law must take root or be ineffective, a meaningless sham.

AMERICAN VALUES
DEEPER THAN CAPITALISM,
DEEPER THAN LAW

16

BEYOND THE ETERNAL ORDER OF LYING

Lord, Lord, how this world is given to lying.

—William Shakespeare, *Henry IV*, part 1, act 5, scene 4

In the evolution of human society, beyond the natural tendency toward lying, there is the possibility of honesty. Beyond trial by combat, there is the possibility of negotiation and exchange. Beyond self-interest and greed, there is the possibility of community. Beyond personal connections sealed by corruption and cheating, there can be recognition of superior competence. With all these, there may be democracy. Without these, there is the form only, and no real change from the traditions of kings.

Very often during the course of twenty years working back and forth across the boundaries of still feudal and Western democratic cultures, I have accompanied US teams of lawyers and various kinds of experts. We have been sent by well-meaning foundations and governments attempting to create the codes and designs, restraints and elections that might generate civil or democratic society.[1] Gradually, in the course of such work, however, I have become aware that the problem is not being met, or understood, at its deepest levels. Something unstated, some set of assumptions or values, or, perhaps most profoundly, some set of understandings characterizes democratic, or civil, society, and these understandings are seldom, if ever, stated. Something about democratic society remains unsaid.

It has to do with our intentions. The failure to describe these bedrock intentions has impeded all our conversations and often rendered the work of American experts irrelevant and off point. Americans and Kazakhs, or Americans and Armenians, or Americans and Russians are very often simply not meeting. In as many ambassadors' offices as I have been, or as many United Nations discussions as I have heard, the fundamental difference between democratic and feudal intentions is rarely, in my experience, articulated. The built-in cultural intentions are different in Peoria than they are on the streets of St. Petersburg, Russia. And now, following eight years of an American administration that also did not understand these democratic foundations but rather saw them as more cosmetic than important, it is necessary to examine them explicitly.

The Preamble to the US Constitution opens with an intention to promote the "*common* defence," "the *general* Welfare," and the blessings of liberty "to ourselves and our Posterity" (emphasis added). The phrase reflects the first intention of a civic culture. The goal is not just the welfare of the Rutledges or the Hancocks, the Washingtons or the Randolphs. The Revolution was not intended to serve only some individual power seekers or their prosperous plantations. The Preamble thus sets an intention for posterity. Henceforth, it will not be enough to know the family name or the status of the signers in order to know whether or not the Constitution applies, and it will not be enough to expect any individual to benefit, by himself, alone. It will also not, therefore, be enough to apply the law to the benefit of a single petitioner without the court taking into account the general interest. Law, contract, and civil rights will not any longer exist to serve only property owners, or only farmers or bankers, but to serve them all, equally. All will exist in the container of the common defense and the general welfare, and if the good of the whole is not preserved, it is assumed that the good of the individual will be sacrificed as well.

A second intention in functioning democracies is that the common good be achieved by nonviolent means. Parliaments at first arose to resolve conflicts between the king and his subjects, who would have to pay his taxes. Parliamentary debate, it was obvious, would provide a more effective means of conflict resolution, better than extermination of one's nobles, because extermination was not in the end likely to produce royal revenues. Dead nobles don't pay taxes. A parliament was therefore not so much a democratic concept but rather a way to bring into the same building and into one conversation landed gentry and the professions, the aristocracy and lawyers, the rich and the merchant class, all of whom, if they were not inside talking might be outside training knights and doing battle in the streets and on the farms. Parliaments satisfied the need for alternative, nonmilitary processes simply because—as King John and the nobles found out—prolonged civil wars had bled the country white.

Similarly, after the Magna Carta, courts too were expected to replace the king's sword or his knights in arms. Courts and parliaments, seen together, therefore, were subversive to the feudal principle that power determines righteousness. To the contrary, they were intended to provide a substitute for solutions dictated solely by the sword. Even though courts may be slow, boring, clumsy, or maddeningly mediocre, as a method of conflict resolution they are to be preferred because the alternative is popular riot, rebellion, and wars between the lords.[2]

A third intention is to base decisions upon truth, or some approximation of truth, rather than upon family loyalty, the needs of patriarchy, or power. Contrary to feudal cultures, in a democracy truth-telling is not naive but promotes reliability and is critical to commerce, the protection of property, stable personal relations, and most important of all, the function of government. Without truth on the floor of Congress, truth in reporting statistics, or truth in reporting profits and taxes, free government is a meaningless chimera. Commerce, when based upon false numbers or false claims, also grinds to a halt.[3] In sum, both the individual and common good, both politics and business are more advanced by integrity than by deception. This too is a rejection of the feudal principle.

A fourth intention of democratic society—one that as we have seen arises from the dictates of international commerce—is that even strangers can be told the truth. This is a total and complete reversal of the feudal principle. Strangers can be treated the same as those inside the clan, the aristocracy, or what the Russians today might call the "vodka circle." Obligations are not simply determined by kinship, religious affiliation, friendship, or power. Those outside the existing power structure can be accorded equal access to the law, the courts, and therefore to justice, and all this is to everyone's benefit. This too stands feudalism on its head.

The democratic assumption is that social stability results when diversity is peacefully accommodated rather than forcefully eliminated. Diversity and equality of opportunity produce creativity, new markets, fresh ideas, and cultural enrichment, and are therefore positives rather than negatives. Contrast the ongoing battles between Catholics and Protestants, Crusaders and Muslims, Shias and Sunnis down through time, all of which were intended to eliminate diversity. Democratic institutions intend to encourage a variety of contributors rather than to eliminate the unwashed, the irreligious, or the dark skinned. This in turn leads to spreading power more widely and deeply rather than creating hierarchies that concentrate power at the top. Telling the truth to strangers is required to make diversity work.

A fifth intention is to honor competence rather than class, hierarchy, or the moral authority that is assumed to come from raw power. In democracies, competence matters. In medieval feudal transactions, competence did not play a primary role in allocation of King John's favors, the granting of estates, and trading or assignment of the barons' daughters. Protection of the Plantagenets was far more the issue. Competence today in, say, Kazakhstan or Azerbaijan was not (in my negotiations from 1985 through 1998) the determining factor in whether a treaty would be negotiated and signed. An American negotiator could spend months or years determining who was most competent to generate water or power only to find that the deal would be made according to some other standard, perhaps clan connections or connections established through friendships or bribery. Or, in another example common within the former Soviet Union, reports of agricultural production would be doctored to reflect the desires of the regional commissar or the manager of the collective farm but would not reflect actual production, or, that is, actual competence. Indeed, when an industrial plant produced in excess of its yearly quota, it would be likely to disguise that success because there was no reward for efficiency. The rewards were for staying within the good graces of the planning bureaucracy, a completely different road to safety than being competent. In feudalism, quality and efficiency are not the path to security unless they can be used to gain access to power.

Because these five democratic intentions, or five civic virtues, had not yet taken root in England, the republic proclaimed by Parliament in 1649 (after they killed Charles I) did not last. Indeed, beheading Charles was itself a brutal solution that sowed the seeds for revenge and the eventual fall of his successors. With brutality rather than parliamentary discussion as the primary arbiter of righteousness, Lord Protector Cromwell ruled with the same iron hand as had his predecessor. This was still the feudal approach that might makes right. Protestants became the new tyrants. Due process was not accorded to Levellers, radicals, or other dissidents. The good of the whole did not include Catholics, and they were persecuted. When Cromwell died, the country breathed a sigh of relief and gladly slid back into the restoration of the monarchy of Charles II. Without the five intentions that are foundational to civil society, the institutions of democracy had no chance.

Similarly, since the collapse of the Soviet Union in 1991, after first adopting the legal shell of democracy, the Russians have returned once again to street shootings, corrupted courts, and the rubber-stamp Duma of Medvedev and Putin.[4] And, finally, as these five civic assumptions erode in the land of Jefferson and Lincoln, the US government itself shows signs of edging toward militarism, personal rule, centralization of power rather than decentralization. Without the five intentions, the institutions of democracy become masks of deception, purporting to offer stability, justice, and opportunity while in fact shielding the rich and powerful from the competitions of competence and creativity that might guarantee the general welfare.

17

BEYOND PURE SELF-INTEREST

After she read the Antifederalist letters,
[Catharine Macaulay] became skeptical of the American
Constitution the more so as she worried about the expansion
of luxury, consumption, and avarice in the American states.

—Vera Nünning, *A Revolution in Sentiments, Manners, and Moral Opinions*[1]

Make more loans? We're not going to change
our business model or our credit policies
to accommodate the needs of the public sector
as they see it to have us make more loans.

—John C. Hope III, chairman of Whitney National Bank in New Orleans,
in November 2008, explaining his bank's intended use of its
$300 million in federal bailout money[2]

Across the gamut of global culture, from codes for marriage to those for securities and derivatives, from families to hedge funds, from canon law to common law, the world has plunged into an age of moral ambiguity. The changes originated in the capitalist West, but more than economics has gone global: so too has deceit. Politicians propose and claim the power to deliver more than they possibly are able; ordinary carmakers and modest neighborhood restaurants claim to be legendary; manufacturers describe old products as "all new"; financiers and ratings agencies put the stamp of analytic approval on instruments that they have not analyzed. Our ancestors in the creation of civil society, men like Hampden,

Cooke, Sidney, or, later, Adams and Washington, would at the very least be surprised. More likely, they would be appalled.

Roger Williams, who, in the seventeenth century, founded the state of Rhode Island and was America's first real political philosopher, explained the turmoil of his century as a search for legitimate sovereignty, sorting out what belonged to God and what to kings and what to the people. He came down straight for the people, the whole of the people, not just some few who owned property. He wrote that the sole end and purpose for which government existed was for the furtherance of the *communal* well-being, the well-being of all. Williams's preaching was like the leaven in the loaf of early American thought; it was Williams who laid the groundwork for Jefferson and Madison a century later.

In the century after Williams, conversations among English radicals such as Catharine Macaulay and Joseph Priestly reveal men and women intensely concerned with virtue. They sought to do the moral thing, not just for their own gain or that of their families but for the good of all of society.[3] They sought the "civil" in civilization as they knew it, and during those centuries in England and the colonies, moral purpose was apt to be taken for granted as a requirement for public service.

This tide of radical writers in eighteenth-century England often addressed the problem of great wealth. Richard Sheridan was one of these writers, penning the opinion that "it will be granted that without liberty we can not be either a great or a flourishing people. It will be granted, that liberty cannot subsist without virtue, and…virtue is necessarily destroyed by luxury."[4]

Sheridan was among a significant gaggle of radical writers in that time who created the atmosphere of change in which, across the Atlantic, the American revolutionaries also flourished. Thomas Paine picked up the cry: "A pretty business indeed for a man [King George III] to be allowed eight hundred thousand sterling a year…and [to be] worshipped into the bargain!"[5]

The English radicals were aware that Parliament had won over the kings in 1689 but had unhappily remained controlled by a great landed gentry. They were aware too that vast inequalities persisted within the population and that these inequalities in turn endangered the peace of the realm. Luxury was opposed to virtue, as they saw it, and virtue was threatened by extreme possessions and excess consumption. They pointed to ancient Rome and the decline of that republic. Great wealth had undermined virtue, and despotism was the result. "Roman Virtue and Roman Liberty expired together" was a phrase they extracted from Cato.[6] Edward Gibbon's *Decline and Fall* contained the tale of the unfortunate Pertinax, whom we saw was a victim of the luxuried military class. The civic tradition, by contrast, held the public weal to be paramount, even greater than wealth or prosperity and more at the heart of the mind that maintained liberty. Civic tradition was traced back along with the evolution of the rule of law, but it was not just law, it was also virtue, and the great destroyer of such virtue was excess, and especially excess opulence. Virtue was a state of mind beyond clan and beyond self-interest, an identification with the good of the whole community.

"Opulence confessedly, with luxury and selfishness its concomitants, are the most obvious causes of the decay of patriotism in Britain," wrote Henry Home, Lord Kames.[7] It is here in this writing of the eighteenth century that we find a substantial discourse about those states of mind that must underlie the law and truly democratic institutions. The US Constitution was not framed in an intellectual wasteland of self-interest, but rather in the midst of an intense debate on both sides of the Atlantic over the mind and heart of a free people, and luxury was among the greatest dangers to that mind and heart. Luxury was the summary description for corruption, at first of the spirit and then of the public good.

It was a part of this concern that led men like Thomas Jefferson to highly esteem the value of small farmers and landsmen, persons more bound to the country than commercial people from the cities who might do business, he thought, with foreign interests and who might profit from war. Jefferson was probably wrong about this. Landsmen in the eighteenth century were wealthy too. Jefferson himself and Washington were far richer than, say, John Adams. But the overall concern that luxury would eat at the heart of public virtue echoes forward to the present day.

George Washington's Farewell Address speaks importantly to the search for the common good, as opposed to mere private interest. The outgoing president warns the nation of the division wrought by political parties, or those who do not hold the common good above local advancement:

> Let me now...warn you in the most solemn manner against the baneful effects of the spirit of party generally...It serves always to distract the public councils and enfeeble the public administration. It agitates the community with ill-founded jealousies and false alarms; kindles the animosity of one part against another; foments occasionally riot and insurrection.[8]

Earlier, in his defense of the new US Constitution, James Madison had argued that the provision for three branches of government and a representative republic (rather than a direct democracy) would provide security against the splintering and plundering of the public good by angry or self-interested factions. "Factious combinations are less to be dreaded" in a balanced republic than in a country in which fractious majorities may override the welfare of the minority, he argued.[9]

This preoccupation with the common good among the politically active who were to give birth to civil society in eighteenth-century England (and in the United States) is the more remarkable because such concerns are not so clearly evident elsewhere in the early history of Europe. Such goals do not characterize, for example, the earlier Renaissance republics in Italy, where one was less apt to find a dedication to the public good than to the maintenance of some family's political and propertied dominance. The first goal of true democracy or of civil society, the goal to provide for the welfare of *the whole* of the body politic, was not at all number one in these republics. Great families like the Medicis were far more interested in preservation of Medici estates, manipulation of allies and popes to preserve Medici banking interests, and insulation from competition from those who were not Medicis than they were in the general welfare of peasants, artisans, and shopkeepers or even of the republic as a whole. In 1466, when he was about to die and was given at last to truthfulness, Piero de Medici is said by Niccolo Machiavelli to have chastised his wealthy colleagues:

> I know now how greatly I have deceived myself as one who knew little of the natural ambition of all men and less [of] yours...You despoil your neighbor of his goods, you sell justice, you escape civil judgments, you oppress peaceful men and exalt the insolent.[10]

This was in the so-called republic of Florence. Nothing in Machiavelli suggests that Piero de Medici was wrong.

A commandment from conscience or from God to do the public good was given lip service throughout the Middle Ages, and all over Europe sovereigns like Queen Elizabeth were even cautioned to govern wisely and well or be punished by God. Mary Sidney, the Countess of Pembroke, wrote to Elizabeth to be careful, that she would one day have to answer to God. But there was never any idea that Elizabeth would put the advancement of her people above her hold on her crown.[11] Counselors of Siena were similarly urged toward good government by a famous mural in city hall, but none of these exhortations in any way trumped the feudal values of power, hierarchy, and hostility toward those who must be classified as outside the family circle, or, simply, toward those who must be treated as strangers. The noble ideal of public service for its own sake is lacking in the mind of feudalism or in any western European government before the Reformation. Indeed, something about the nature of Martin Luther's reform, the waves of conscience that swept Europe after the Medicis and after the Reformation, seems to have deepened an individual's responsibility for his own soul and his own moral conduct. And in some small part, the birth of civil society is a result of that. Or perhaps it is some much larger part.[12]

Before Luther, in fifteenth-century Italy, the city-state of Florence claimed to be a republic. Its leaders were well-schooled in the classics, familiar with the literature of ancient Greece and Rome. Elites in social clubs debated Aristotle, Plato, and Virgil. Elections were held annually, and important positions selected by lot. It had institutions of government that most people would consider to have given voice to the people. It also had great respect for the arts. Leaders such as Lorenzo de Medici brought to the city art and sculpture of great quality and encouraged trade with the other principalities of Italy. The city was generally prosperous, at least in terms of the Renaissance. On its face the republic could and did claim superiority to all the despots of the rest of Italy. They could claim to be responsive to the people and dedicated to the public welfare. The trappings of good government were all on display.

And yet the Florentine republic was rotten at the core. Piero de Medici's rant tells it all: "You despoil your neighbor of his goods, you sell justice, you escape civil judgments, you oppress peaceful men and exalt the insolent." Beneath the superficial trappings of republican government, the city was ruled entirely by a handful of families who vied for control, lied, cheated, and stole their way to power, manipulated the elections and selections by lot, and engaged in political murder and intercity warfare for their own ends. All this they did to the detriment of the greater population of Florence.

The Medicis were bankers, above all. They were wondrously rich, loaning money all over Italy, forming political and military alliances with popes and dukes, the Venetians, the Milanese, all in a constant effort to gain the upper hand against rivals within the city of Florence itself. They used their wealth for political ends even more than for personal aggrandizement and would spend great sums to entertain foreign dignitaries for the purpose of demonstrating power and intimidating local rivals. It was in the context of these games that Machiavelli wrote his famous advice about how to shift and turn, lie and be honest, deceive and condemn deception.[13]

Although they lived within a so-called republic, neither Machiavelli nor the Medicis had discarded the primary assumptions of feudalism. Violence was never excluded as a tactic and was employed when necessary. Wars between principalities were constant. The law was a nonviolent tool to be used by the elites when its outcomes were assured, but when the law did not serve those in power, violence was necessary. At one point when Piero de Medici's power was deemed by his rivals to be too great, they did not try to unelect him or prosecute him in court. They laid wait for him in ambush, meaning to surprise and kill him. Florentines said they lived in a republic, but reliance upon violence is feudal. According to the morality of the times, those who succeed in grasping power are righteous by definition.

In a similarly feudal vein, the Odysseus Principle of crafty dealing was the prevailing ethic among all except those within the family. One ought to give the appearance of honesty, but true honesty would be as naive as Odysseus telling truth to Penelope's suitors. The ideas of fairness, equality, or rewards simply based upon competence were maintained within the Medici family, or, in feudal terms, within the clan, but such qualities were honored in the breach when dealing with those outside the family.

All this brings to the surface the disturbing conclusion that trade and commerce, a thousand transactions with a thousand unknowns, are not by themselves sufficient to create and support the five intentions necessary to establish the rule of law or democracy. When the Odysseus Principle is combined with feudal ethics, lying, cheating, and stealing may yet persist. And the one feudal ethic most significant of all—that overrides all else—is allegiance to family. In fifteenth-century Florence, family names reached back for generations and sometimes for centuries. In spite of the patina of republic, loyalty to family was as important to the clans of Florence as it had been to the descendants of Abraham, the Plantagenets of England, or the Bourbons of France. An essentially feudal value had been translated into a new urban culture, but it had not been erased.

Today in the United States, a mere 1 percent of the population owns 33 percent of the wealth, and the top 10 percent have 85 to 90 percent of stock, bonds, trust funds, and business equity and more than 75 percent of nonhome real estate.[14] Jefferson and Catharine Macaulay, Richard Sheridan and Henry Home would be most alarmed.

But it is not the disproportion, only, that has the greatest impact on the Republic, not so much the fact that some are wealthier than others, or even a great deal wealthier, that was the worry at the time of the founding of the American Republic. It is true that, as conservatives correctly note, it takes great wealth to capitalize an automobile company or to create a steel company or to drill for oil. It was not the potential existence of such wealth, per se, that troubled those writers of the eighteenth century whose opinion shaped the American Revolution. They were concerned about inequality, certainly, and its effects on stability, certainly, but they were also concerned about the effects of such wealth on virtue.

Virtue, in the sense of those eighteenth-century writers, was the recognition of community responsibility, civic conscience. It was the loss of civic conscience as the inevitable result of extreme wealth that worried these radicals the most. It was the loss of conscience that they might have predicted in such now notorious firms as Enron and Tyco; the triumph of greed over responsibility at Moody's and Standard and Poors, which gave AAA ratings to debt obligations that they did not understand; or even, perhaps most blindly, the statement by a New Orleans banker who, after receiving a promise of $300 million in bailout funds from the federal government, rejected the concept that such funds would be infected with a public interest.

> Make more loans? We're not going to change our business model or our credit policies to accommodate the needs of the public sector as they see it to have us make more loans.

It was, in the same vein, twenty years of lack of care for massive evidence of global warming that led America's big three automakers to ignore such evidence but instead to blame SUVs and Hummers on "consumers' choices." It was the potential for the private jet flights to Washington, DC, by CEOs of those same companies, cup in hand, seeking handouts from the government, utterly insensible to the contradiction inherent within their conduct that would have confirmed the very worst fears of Macaulay, Home, and Sheridan.

Our ancestors feared plutocracy for good reason. And yet today there is an even deeper danger. If plutocrats are corrupted by excess wealth, ordinary citizens may be corrupted by the same thing, if only to a lesser degree. Materialism run rampant among the general population also eats away at the general public virtue. And while economic success creates the opportunity for virtue, it does not guarantee virtue and certainly does not guarantee civic values. If economic progress alone were sufficient to produce democracy, then China and Russia would today be democratic, or at least on their way to being so. The contrary is apparently true. Oil money in Russia and something akin to villenage labor in China have produced great economic gains and very little in the way of democracy, human rights, fairness, or social equality. Without these values, any progress toward civil society and human dignity is unlikely.

Modern America is an example of the paradox that economic prosperity—capitalism run to great extremes—does not by itself produce or protect the five intentions that underlie democratic society. Capitalism seems to have been the original spawning ground for the rule of law but does not yet offer all the necessary conditions to keep the law alive. Indeed, to the contrary, economic prosperity may, when it reaches a certain stage, undermine the very rule of law that it originally promoted.

Prosperity certainly gives us things to eat and places to live, cars to drive, separate rooms and computers and televisions for each child. Prosperity allows everyone his or her own domain names and separate identity. Americans rename themselves, over and over, from "bluetapdancer" to "cocoloverface" to "sternbythewater," until eventually they may find an identity they like. But the more individual we become, it seems also the more alienated we become and the more we may withdraw from common or communal efforts.

The collapse of the politics of compassion in the United States is therefore not due solely to the failures of progressive leadership, or the lack of inspiration at the top, or the absence of the rule of law. It seems equally to be a decline of civic virtue at the bottom, and that decline tracks fairly well with the growth through the years of suburbia, car sales, TV sales, cell phones, iPods, computers, and all the paraphernalia of individual taste. Each of us watches different programs on TV and reads different books. The progression toward all this separateness tracks very neatly with the fact that at the same time we resist state and local taxes for community projects. Compared to a hundred years ago, we contribute less and less to community days out on the irrigation ditch, or shoring up the levee on the river, or joining with neighbors to bring cattle down the mountain, or whatever else we used to do that bound our daily lives together.[15] We feel as if our destinies are separate now; we pay therapists to help us find our own individual stories and create our own songs and our own narratives to announce how independent and unique we all are. We like it this way. We would not have it any other way.[16]

And yet we may not have found the formula for happiness. We have a part of it, but not the whole, and there is nothing in the contemplation of Jefferson and Adams and Washington at the founding of the Republic that addresses this seeming contradiction between individual freedom and the need to have a strong public center: nothing to address the problem that we love this freedom and yet it may be the very thing that is doing us in. Milk may be good for us, but if we drink only milk, it will do us in. We need vegetables too. Strawberries are good for us, but a diet of only strawberries will not sustain us. We need protein too. Freedom is good for us, but if we only pursue freedom, independence, and individuality, we will not survive. We have now, at this stage in our national or cultural development, reached the point where we are happy, indeed ecstatic, with our own life schedules, our own time off, our own reading lists, and yet are these any different from a diet of pure strawberries? Can we survive on this diet?

If individuality and unlimited freedom make us stronger and more secure and better able to handle our lives, why, when a ragged cabal of nineteen terrorists flew their planes into our tallest towers, and when the steel and plastic came crashing down, did we not act as if we have it together and respond realistically? It was nineteen terrorists. It was not a foreign invasion. It was a cell of fewer than a thousand people around the world. It was not a collapse of capitalism. It was a band of religious fanatics fueled by hatred, an approach that our religions tell us does not work, cannot work, never works. It was not a collapse of Christianity and Judaism.

And yet we responded in fear, as a collective, and rushed off in panic to foreign lands to kill the fear, to stamp out the fear, to drive fear from our hearts. All our freedom and individuality had not prepared us; we were more lonely and more worried and more disconnected from the world than we realized, and we acted in desperation.

Was it because Republicans controlled the White House and Congress? Perhaps. More likely, it was deeper than that. Republicans controlled the White House in 1958 when President Eisenhower sent troops to Lebanon and when we feared a takeover of the world by communists. But our culture was different then. Eisenhower went simultaneously to the United Nations— acted as a part of the world collective—and promised to get out of Lebanon as soon as appropriate collective measures were taken. We went into Lebanon in July and came out in October. The

United States was also not as prosperous then, was not as individual, not as afraid, even though we have so much more wealth today. Or maybe we were not as afraid precisely because we did not then have the same great wealth, and with that wealth the great loneliness, the great insecurity that we have today.

The more cars, the more houses, computers, iPhones, iPods, vacations, cosmetics, candies, and cookies of capitalism, also the greater the unease, it seems. The greater the hunger for goods, the greater the dissatisfaction with those very goods. The greater the status, the less the sense of belonging to the whole. Prosperity seems to have bred individualism, and that is good, but it has also bred a greater consciousness of being alone, which is not so good. Being alone translates into me versus them. Prosperity, individuality, and freedom don't yet answer the eternal questions about inner peace.[17]

The pursuit of habeas corpus, free speech, and due process has afforded to US citizens a weapon against government, but these things do not by themselves create community or a sense of allegiance to the public good. Tyrants used to herd us into the common corral, terrorize and brutalize, but in that condition we at least knew who our friends were, who our neighbors were, and we could hang together against the common foe. Today we are more free but less together.

Democracy is today teetering between individual liberty and economic freedom on the one hand, and common purpose, communal responsibility, and a sense of shared destiny on the other. Economic freedom is only one half of the equation and has been achieved by many in the United States. The other half, a sense of togetherness and mutual interdependence, is declining. Without this intention to do the right thing for the whole, one of the key assumptions of civil society, for democracy, is missing. When one of the foundation assumptions is missing, the whole structure is in danger.

18

BEYOND THE SWORD

I think that no more absurd scheme could be invented for
settling national difficulties than the one we are engaged in—
killing each other to find out who is in the right.

—Major Robert Anderson, during the Mexican War, later in command of the Union
garrison at Fort Sumter, 1860, at the beginning of the Civil War

Although no balloting had occurred,
the English [in 1689] had chosen their political future freely,
and they would continue, in greater and greater measure,
to do so from then on. The [contract] basis for the creation
of a government that was to become, after a long
development, the liberal democratic rule we know today was,
in fact, a nonviolent revolution.

—Jonathan Shell, *The Unconquerable World*

A hundred years after the English Bill of Rights of 1689, the US
Constitution was also framed against a backdrop of potential
violence and dissolution of public order. It had been more than
ten years since the war for independence began and four years
after formal peace with the British was established. Nevertheless,
debtors' riots were spreading across towns in Massachusetts led
by farmers who could not pay their taxes and who intended to
shut down the courts to protect themselves against foreclosure.
From August 1786 through February 1787, a Revolutionary War
veteran by the name of Daniel Shays led an armed uprising in

Massachusetts. Shays is said to have owed money to as many as ten different creditors. He and thousands of angry debtors assembled to march on the Springfield Arsenal, which held cannon, muskets, bayonets, and thousands of barrels of powder. The mob planned to seize all this and lead a general rebellion against the Commonwealth of Massachusetts and, if necessary, against the new confederation of American states. They were not successful. Shays was turned back at the arsenal with little actual fighting. But the rioting and uproar was fresh in the minds of those men who three months later assembled in Philadelphia, in May 1787, for what would become known as the Constitutional Convention. The cost of failure of their discussions would be more public unrest and the possible unraveling of all that they had won in the Revolution. They had meant to establish an alternative to patriarchy and feudalism. They had won the battle but might now lose the war. European, especially British, observers sat on the sidelines and could not wait for the chance to march back in and reclaim the empire.

Southerners and those in the western territories of Kentucky and Tennessee had been for some time engaged in conversations with the Spanish.[1] They sought ways to guarantee the slave trade and open markets for rice and indigo, upon which the southern economy depended. When the delegates from those states came to Philadelphia, it was not clear whether their future lay with an American union or in an alliance with Spain or Britain. Thirteen completely separate countries was a possible outcome.

The heat in Philadelphia that summer was unbearable. Delegates sweated through days of endless wrangling. At night, boardinghouses were full and some delegates were forced to share a bed. Hanging over their heads was the certainty that if they failed to create a new union, they would all in their various ways face chaos, continued unrest, involvement of foreign powers, and, again, probably war.

As the Convention unfolded—moving into June and July of 1787—debates over continuation of the slave trade occupied center stage. Slavery was the linchpin of the southern economy and was highest priority for important southern leaders like John Rutledge of South Carolina. In the month of July, Rutledge maneuvered to have himself appointed to head a committee to create a first draft of the new constitution. That draft subsequently included the provision that the new Congress of the United States should never, in perpetuity, have power to outlaw the slave trade. That recommendation then became the fulcrum upon which agreement to form the new nation turned. If the slave trade could not be guaranteed, the southern states would never join the union, said Rutledge, backed by delegates from Georgia, North Carolina, and Connecticut. Delegates from Pennsylvania and Massachusetts viewed slavery with horror and disgust and said they could never abide—and would never recommend joining—a union that guaranteed slavery for all time. The Convention nearly came unraveled. They could stop or they could go on. The prospect of more rebellions like Shays's and more disunion, bloodshed, and suffering lay within recent memory. With war as the probable alternative, they pushed on.

It was under these conditions that the drafters of the US Constitution, not unlike the drafters of the Magna Carta five hundred years before, declared for a balance of powers between the small states with little population, like Delaware and Maryland, and the larger states, like Pennsylvania and Virginia. It was a balance between those who abhorred slavery and those whose lives and fortunes depended upon slavery. It was a balance between those with an interest in powerful central government and those with a dread of kings and fear of aristocracy. It was a balance of those who wanted common people to elect the new office of president and those who thought that the masses had too little learning and too little sophistication to allow them to participate in any meaningful way. The result was a series of compromises and trade-offs that had motives both holy and unholy. We know now that the compromise over slavery proved disastrous in the long run, merely postponing for eighty years the most awful war in our history. But at the same time we also know that the founding purpose of those at the Convention was to avoid just such dissolution and chaos.

The government they established created institutions through which all those disparate interests could be balanced, over and over. It was not a God-given formula for good government or the perpetuation of virtue. It was not the final revelation about how governments should divide jurisdictions or territory. It was, more fundamentally, a way to force conversation between opponents, to require debate before resorting to arms, to force compromise between the landed and the urban, the artisan and the philosopher, the militant and the religious. It was not an unconditional victory for any one of them. The Republic was, in the end, simply a means to substitute deliberation and votes for gunfire. In this sense it was born of the same need as that of the nobles at Runnymede who had confronted King John.

The reforms that ensued in succeeding centuries in the United States were also in some sense necessary to preserve civil discourse and avoid widespread unrest. These included regulatory commissions like the Interstate Commerce Commission, the Security and Exchange Commission, and at the local level, planning commissions—design review commissions or hospital commissions—all of which typically provide for public participation. People who have a right to speak at the lectern are less likely to gather angrily in the streets.

Among the loudest and most troublesome to establishment male leadership of the first part of the twentieth century were women publicly parading in the streets, demanding the right to vote, to be fully human in a system that claimed to honor humanity. The Nineteenth Amendment, granting women that right to vote (1920), was in some sense a measure to regain peace in the streets. Next would come African Americans demanding their own equal protection. That opening was created in a school case decided by the Supreme Court, *Brown v. Board of Education* (1954), holding segregation by local law to be a violation of the federal Constitution. After that, attempts to integrate universities in the South were met with solid white resistance, confrontations arose in the streets of Mississippi and Alabama, and the nation was witness to beatings by police and bombings of black churches. Civil rights workers who went south to aid in the struggle mysteriously disappeared. Riots then broke out in the inner cities of Los Angeles, Detroit, and Washington, DC. A decade of violence swept away President John F. Kennedy and then Martin Luther King Jr. and Senator Robert F. Kennedy. After President Kennedy's death and in this climate of crumbling social peace, Congress passed the historic Civil Rights Act of 1964, opening up public places to racial integration. By 1973 the Supreme Court weighed in again, deciding *Keyes v. School District No. 1*, integrating a northern school district for the first time, even though the segregation had been covert and disguised.[2] Courts and legislation were the nonviolent response to the obvious violent potential in an unsatisfied population.

In recent times, these reforms have included public input for environmentally sensitive federal decisions, tax regulations, tax courts, commercial laws, antitrust reforms, and a multitude of open processes. All these processes are end products of a tradition that begins with the nobles and Robin Hood complaining about their taxes. And of course it is these latter developments rather than any military successes that have earned the claim that this republic brought about the end of feudalism.

The women's rights movements of the nineteenth and twentieth centuries and the civil rights movement of the 1960s were accomplished by those working on the first assumption of a society governed by law: that nonviolence is to be preferred over violence. Elizabeth Cady Stanton and Martin Luther King Jr. understood that history was slowly moving in the direction of forceful but rational, passionate but nonviolent resolution of social conflict. The combined forces of commerce and law had gradually been undermining patriarchy, patrimony, and privilege, and while appearing to be ahead of their times, these movements were actually capturing a wave that had been rising over the previous seven hundred years.

Shortly after World War II, the governments of France, Italy, Germany, and Spain were in constant chaos, and the persistent subject of conversation among intellectuals in Europe was whether these countries had the appetite or the mind for democracy.[3] The question was put as if it were a choice of philosophies, or political science. As it has turned out, however, the choice was not philosophic so much as practical. The twentieth-century wars of Europe had been devastating to economies on a scale unprecedented in human history. The toll in lives and capital assets, in treasure and to the collective psyche had been more tragic than glorious, even for the victors. "Victory" was survival, simply, for France and England, for Scandinavia, Australia, and the Philippines, but not anything grand or wonderful and did not result in the acquisition of riches as in days of old. As the post-war decades unfolded, democracy was simply a rational choice because armed conflict was clearly obsolete.

Fifty years after the war, democracy in Germany, Italy, and France was assumed and the Spanish electorate in the first decade of the new century used an election to respond to terrorist violence. Governments all across the former Eastern Bloc of Soviet power are now also experimenting with elections and all the trappings of democracy. Latin America is making a gradual transition in the same direction. In Venezuela, in Bolivia, in Mexico, governments are emerging that are more in touch with the masses and less controlled by oligarchies of great wealth. From 1949 until fifteen years ago, China was under the rule of unrestrained violence. Today, it is reluctantly opening up to the processes of capitalism, which simply cannot function on a battlefield and are necessarily and persistently nonviolent.

War is now unthinkable between France and Germany, but these countries considered constant war more or less inevitable from at least Napoleon in 1812 to 1945, or more likely all the way back to Frederick Barbarossa in the twelfth century.

War between France and England is now also unthinkable, although war was a staple between these two peoples from at least the Battle of Hastings in 1066 until 1814, for nearly seven hundred years.

War between the capitalist West and the Russians was considered by Lenin a commandment of history, and Lenin's followers in Russia maintained the inevitability of war between communist and capitalist powers for seventy years. Today the projection of war's inevitability is the idea that is in the dustbin of history. War between the two systems was not, and is not, inevitable after all.

Today, the United States would find it useless to attack communist China, because business needs China's economy intact and China needs the US economy intact. The same holds true with Japan and the United States, even though it has only been sixty years since we were at war. Business has trumped political conflict. The corporate world has great difficulty functioning in a country that has been leveled—like Iraq—without law or courts or reliable contracts.

The tragic experience of the Bush administration in Iraq was that war to gain territory for oil exploitation destroyed the very territory and infrastructure upon which those oil corporations would depend after the invasion. The United States intended to destroy the regime of Saddam Hussein and did that. It also destroyed billions of dollars of essential infrastructure—schools, hospitals, roads, and shops—in the process, making it far too dangerous for any corporation to safely do business in that country. The planners of this invasion simply had no grasp of the limitations of force in our current commercial world. It might have been possible to create a country through military conquest in King John's thirteenth-century Europe, but after eight hundred years of commerce and communication involving masses and whole cultures, it is not possible today, not in Europe and not in Iraq.

These changes in the global mind are not happening according to the feudal principle, dictated by the force of arms. They are happening because of a revolution of consciousness that armies can neither provide nor contain, a revolution of consciousness that peaceful, nonviolent processes facilitate. People do not renounce armed revolution because they love the Magna Carta or Thomas Jefferson; they do so because democracy is cheaper, safer, and more likely to protect them than governments imposed by force.

In the 1980s in Leningrad, in the former Soviet Union, a handful of courageous people were secretly creating and passing around newspapers that they had typed up themselves. These hand-typed broadsides were called samizdats, meaning "self-made," and they had become a major source of information for liberals and dissenters of Soviet power. In them, one could read real information about plane crashes, or earthquakes, or the fates of other dissidents, none of which the government ever reported. Samizdat information was generally regarded as more reliable and more interesting than that offered by official television or government newspapers such as *Pravda* or *Izvestia*. On the one hand, then, were the official publicity organs of the Central Committee of the Communist Party of the Soviet Union—TV and newspapers were totally within control of the feudal hierarchy. On the other hand were the secret reports contained in the samizdats, spread throughout the empire by hand, their writers like termites eating at the borders of Soviet propaganda. On the one hand were tanks and missiles and nuclear weapons of the Red Army, which was allied with the KGB to listen and track down dissidents in their homes and at work. On the other hand was the magnetic attraction of truth, spreading at great risk, but spreading nevertheless. Bolshevism had been imposed throughout the twentieth century, brutally and ruthlessly. In the end, however, that violent, autocratic regime could not hold. All those concentration camps and all that killing—estimates now number 20 million suspected dissidents killed—were not enough to silence the little circles of equality and moral purpose, the men and women who were passing around their own secret newspapers, undermining Soviet thought control and therefore Soviet power. The typewriter (they did not yet have computers) had become more powerful than fear or terror.

In August 1991, a coup d'état was under way in Moscow. A group calling itself the State Emergency Committee detained President Gorbachev at his dacha in southern Russia and began issuing orders to close down newspapers and take over television throughout the country. Confusion reigned all over the Soviet Union while competing sides issued orders and dictates in city after city, attempting to bring the population either to the side of dictatorship or democracy. The KGB was ordered to take control of Moscow, and tanks rolled into the central city and halted in front of the so-called White House, the home of the Supreme Soviet of the Russian Federation. Boris Yeltsin crouched inside, issuing decrees, declaring the coup leaders treasonous. Urged on by the State Emergency Committee, tanks fired at the Russian White House, sending rounds directly into Yeltsin's refuge.

At the same time, another division of tanks approached the city of Leningrad. In the year preceding, that city had been the most outspoken source of liberal discontent anywhere in the Soviet Union. The coup leaders would therefore have to take Leningrad at the same time as Moscow. But at a critical moment the generals halted outside the town, apparently uncertain whether to go in, guns blazing. Before them lay the queen city of Russia, founded by Peter the Great, with its golden onion domes, chandeliered palaces, and rich museums. Within these confines, so-called democrats had been meeting in the newly elected Lensoviet, or city council, for almost a year. And there these democrats met even as the tanks were poised to attack, in the Mariinsky Palace in the center of town, opposite St. Isaac's Cathedral, near the world-famous Winter Palace of Catherine the Great. Thousands of Leningrad's citizens poured out of their apartments to surround Mariinsky Palace. The coup leaders would have to take out the Lensoviet over the dead bodies of the population, risking destruction of the historic city, the cathedral, the Winter Palace, the narrow bridges where Pushkin had wooed and died.

For hours the tanks stalled on the outskirts of town, engines rumbling, filling the air with black smoke. Citizens slowly began to drift out from the city along the main road toward where the tanks were parked. They carried leaflets in their hands and began to climb up onto the tanks, dropping papers down to the soldiers inside. Samizdat typewriters had been working through the night; their leaflets were going to the tankers. One of them, translated into English on the day after these events, read as follows, and was e-mailed to sympathizers all around the world:

To All All All

The coordinating council of the Democratic Russia movement reports that a group of top-ranking plotters removed Gorbachev and also Yeltsin and lawful authorities across the country from power and attempted a military coup...

We ask to avoid actions in such forms that would give the dictatorship direct pretexts for using violence. We appeal to officers and men of all arms of the service to depose commanders who abide by the mutineers' unlawful orders.

Generals and officers loyal to the oath, take initiative into your hands. Democrats, set up civil resistance committees everywhere.

Party apparatchiks and generals, who staged a terrible adventure, hope to preserve power and privileges which are slipping from their hands. The peoples of Russia and other republics will stymie their plans.[4]

For three days the Red Army's tanks did not move. A great massed phalanx of steel and armor was held up by the written pleadings of those who had for years secretly been writing samizdat leaflets. At last, after three days, the coup collapsed and the tanks withdrew. The typewriters had won. Within a short time the empire that was the Soviet Union also dissolved without violence. The culture of czars and commissars had been pried open to confront, at least temporarily, the idea of the rule of law, an idea completely at odds with the rule of tanks. The confrontation, nonviolent as it was, would change that country's history and that of the rest of the world.

19

BEYOND THE EASY LIE

Just tell them yes, and don't do anything.

—Fyodor Burlatsky to the author during Soviet-American negotiations, 1989

Despite the victory of typewriters against Bolshevism, the world would soon see that nonviolence alone does not create the rule of law.

In December 2008 the head of a distinguished Moscow institute, Igor Yurgens, proudly proclaimed that his country is governed by friends. "We do not have laws in this country, but we have a lot of friendships, and friendship is more important than laws," he said.[1] For a country flirting with democracy, this was a stunning remark. He could have been quoting from Homer. What he did not say was that in a society ruled by friendships, those who know each other personally, or those within the vodka circle, get the jobs, permits for business, and favor in the courts. Advancement comes through connections, family, ethnic preference, and not primarily through competence. Those outside the vodka circle must therefore cheat to stay in the game. But those inside the circle also have to cheat to compete against the genuinely competent. As a result, corruption is pandemic.

This culture of corruption, violence, and family connections replicates important themes of ancient feudalism. True, there are no medieval knights in armor, but the mentality of modern Russia is only slightly different from that of Ivan the Terrible. The type-writers and samizdats, Internet and movies have brought Russia into contact with commerce, trade, and law for the first time in a major way. But cultures do not transform overnight and feudal lords do not give up easily, even if they call themselves democrats.

In twelfth-century Europe, friendships and family deter-mined every advantage. Allegiances were hierarchal. Truth-telling between strangers outside the hierarchy or outside the family would have seemed naive. Rules to exclude outsiders—in different countries, different groups were outsiders—were brutally enforced. Violence and treachery were acceptable tools to main-tain the family, clan, or religious dominance of one's own. In 1170 King Henry II of England overcame his religious rival St. Thomas à Becket by having him murdered. In Russia today, Putin's sup-porters famously murder governmental critics such as Alexander Litvinenko, Anna Politkovskaya, or Natalya Estemirova.[2] In 1170 it was five knights in armor who did the deed. Today it is simi-lar enforcers who get rid of people who are not Putin's friends. Litvinenko was poisoned in London; Politkovskaya was shot in her apartment in Moscow; Estemirova was kidnapped and shot in Chechnya. Today, still, in Russia, law is used to serve the elite but not to serve those who contest power, are poor, or are politi-cally weak. All this is as old as the hills. All this is still feudal.

In his quote about friendship, Igor Yurgens did not only, however, describe the difference between Russia and the West. He put his finger on the single most profound difference between two worlds. One world is bound by law more than friendships and struggles to uphold the law even when the powerful are threat-ened. In this world corruption is seen as a danger to commerce and government and therefore also to peace and security. The other and larger part of the world sees corruption as the cement of personal connections, and therefore friendship is more important than law. This part of the world is not at all limited to Russia. In Jordan the word for Yurgens-style connections is *wasta*.[3] Without *wasta*, young people have no hope. Others who have studied Peru, the Philippines, Egypt, Haiti, and Mexico have identified the same systemic problem that is emblematic for much of the world.[4] Over a sixty-year period, I myself have been cheated by public officials in Lebanon, arrested for breaking the elite's rules in Damascus and Moscow, held up for bribes in Botswana, Georgia, Azerbaijan, Armenia, Kazakhstan, Kyrghistan, and Burma. Reports from those who travel to China, Latin America, Central America, and Indonesia repeat similar stories.

Even in today's world a few democracies are still surrounded—surviving as islands—in a sea of governments abiding by the persistent feudal principle of personal rule. The principle may seem benign to Igor Yurgens or those who are on the inside or at the top, just as it seemed benign to kings and bishops and the lords and ladies of eight hundred years ago. But for those not among the elite, the rule of "friendships" is a rule of rigid hierarchies solidified by horrific violence and widespread deceit. The boundary between our two worlds is not, of course, absolute. Each influences the other. Much of what occurs in US politics is also based upon personal connections and is sometimes corrupt. The rule of law may be said to have been under siege here too, especially during the years of Bush and Cheney. One might ask after that eight years whether the United States is regressing, becoming more like feudal societies, or are feudal societies becoming more like the democracies? Which way is the evolution going today? Can islands of law survive in a feudal sea?

Most people—not all, but most—know when they are telling the truth. Most expect to tell the truth to their friends and family, perhaps to their close business associates. This is the case everywhere. Almost every human has that inner governor. When negotiating in the Caucasus, however, or in Russia, or in Central Asia, I found that most people consider truth-telling between strangers to be optional, or worse, naive. The key word is *strangers*. Foreigners, persons not known or inside the vodka circle, persons outside the clan, Jewish persons if one is not Jewish, or Armenians if one is Azeri, or persons not from Nakhichivan if one is part of the ruling elite of Azerbaijan, and so on are all "strangers" to whom the truth is not owed. Persons whom one might meet only once are strangers; persons in a customs line whom the agent will never see again, persons stopping by the road to purchase a bottle of petrol are all persons to whom truth is not owed and from whom truth is not expected.

I have spent days attempting to explain to high-level government negotiators, ministers, heads of water departments and public utilities, journalists, and lawyers that telling the truth in a negotiation is *not* naive and is in fact at the heart of a civil law culture. It may be the most important foundation of both democracy and capitalism and the secret to the success of these two institutions in Western history. It may be absolutely critical to the development of what is civil in civilization as opposed to what is militant or brutal. And it may be the watershed that divides east and west. But when I have asked ministers around a bargaining table to detail *for themselves* the true costs of a deal, they have resisted. When asked to reveal the costs of failure to make a deal—the financial, social, and health costs of not getting a deal—they are apt to refuse. They are impeded from such analysis because someone may be sitting in the room, even a room of their own national colleagues, who is not of the insider's clan, not within the vodka circle, not a friend by marriage, and to whom the truth is not owed.

To understand within one's own delegation the true costs of failure is a standard tactic in interest-based negotiation. It is axiomatic that knowing the cost of failure is a predicate to knowing how much one can afford to pay to make a deal. If the deal does not go through, for example, a country might expect to lose, say, $100 million in cotton revenue. That country should therefore be willing to pay any amount less than $100 million because this will be a gain over what would be lost if the deal does not go through. This is common sense in the Western world of interest-based negotiation. But discussing failure requires open examination by the delegation of the true facts. And if one's colleagues are not all of the same clan, the truth will most often not be put upon the table. Even in the intimacy of a private caucus, when I have asked ministers to detail the costs of failure and therefore the amounts up to which they might go to make a deal, they have stared back at me, awed by my naivete. Such truths are not to be shared except to those within their vodka circle. That circle would not, of course, include an American outsider. That is the Odysseus Principle in practice.

Some have argued that Ronald Reagan's military expansionism and threat to build a missile defense (Star Wars) is what brought down the Soviet Union. Some say it was financial collapse. These may be part of the explanation. But the failures in space and in the economy and the ultimate collapse were only what was happening on the surface. More deeply and more pervasively, the cause of the collapse was the culture of violence, lying, personal versus public good, and the rejection of competence as the arbiter of commercial transactions. The Soviet culture retained the old feudal values, and these hamstrung every effort, including the effort to get into space and to revitalize, or to perestroika-ize, the economy. Soviet feudalism simply could not keep up with emerging economies in Europe, Japan, South Korea, or even Southeast Asia. It was bound together by webs of interlocking personal allegiances, accustomed to treachery between factions and horrific persecution intended to silence those outside these personal networks. Secrecy, violence, corruption, and intolerance of diversity were hallmarks of leaders from Stalin to Khrushchev, to Bulganin, Brezhnev, Andropov, and finally even to Gorbachev. Gorbachev was the first of all these to have had a college education, and it was no doubt that education that exposed him to the value of diversity and openness. He later would call it *glasnost*. When he announced glasnost in the spring of 1985, the very idea immediately began to threaten all the personal networks of power and privilege in the Soviet Union. But rather than creating a new collaborative society, as Gorbachev intended, glasnost had the practical effect of unleashing all those personal networks against each other. When city elections were finally held in Leningrad in 1990, hundreds of newly elected delegates gathered in Mariinsky Palace, huddling in dozens of rooms, shouting epithets and accusations, maneuvering for position. Having no history of cohesion around any ideal except opposition to the communist government, they also had no reason to gather in coalitions except for personal benefit. No ideology, no policy of economics or human rights united them, and every group of one kind of friends set out to defeat every other group. Chaos marked those first sessions of the Lensoviet in 1990. I was present. I walked around from room to room with a press pass, totally overwhelmed by the shouting. Only the communists had a principle larger than themselves, but they were so completely discredited by seventy years of feudalism that everyone else was against them too.

In the end, the decline and fall of the Soviet Union has to be explained by the complete absence over the preceding four hundred years of legal and commercial values other than feudal values. They did not know the meaning of compromise for the public good, or nonviolence, or diversity, or equality, or openness. They knew only the rules of power. They had had an election. Now they sought to translate the results into power based upon personality, allegiance, and hierarchy, and of course they failed.

Russian culture never developed the five assumptions of democratic society and therefore was then and is still constantly breeding treacheries between and among leaders and followers. In the Soviet Union most transactions moved with the speed of cold molasses, encumbered by the unwillingness to deal with truth except between friends and family. Glasnost would have required a revolution, not only of the law but, more fundamentally, of culture. That is why it failed. The Soviet people did not ever understand the magnitude of the challenge and would most certainly have rejected that change had it been made clear. They did not, and do not today, believe that truth-telling between strangers is required when it is not in one's self-interest.

This is not just a question of politics. Commerce, building and construction, transportation, and education all depend upon the reliability of promises, including promises between strangers. Reliability of contract depends upon people doing what they say they will do. Millions of transactions occur every day, too numerous or too detailed to be enforced by courts. Courts are not equipped to handle any but the occasional or most egregious disputes. On the whole, in a commercial society disputes are not enforced in court but are more likely avoided by persons or corporations doing what they say they will do. Not only is civil society endangered by cynical willingness to distort the truth to aid the rich and deprive the poor—or by the justification that power must be exercised to be maintained—but so too is capitalism also endangered by a lack of truth-telling. Transactions that are held up by the required meetings to pay bribes or that are derailed because they are attempted outside the clan or that do not aid one's friends are transactions delayed and very often killed. Transactions that must be enforced by force of arms, as in the parking lot killings common in the last ten years in Moscow, or that are enforced by clans loyal to clan leaders, as in Iraq or Afghanistan, are more the basis of feudalism than capitalism. Capitalism cannot function in a brutal, dishonest, and therefore wholly undependable environment. The sword can be no arbiter of the complexity of modern contracts.

To tell the true story of capitalism and democracy is to tell a grand, relatively new narrative, historically speaking. The idea that truth is the foundation of reliability and enforceability of contract—and is, further, the essential precondition for honest bargaining in the halls of any legislative body—is an idea raised from the soil of western Europe over only a seven-hundred-year period. It is not a given of human relations. It is a product of a certain set of conditions that may or may not be repeated. Those conditions are now under extreme pressure as the global economy engulfs the old European trading economies of the past. But while it is true that a nation riven by corruption and personal deals is one that turns its people against each other, the opposite is equally true. A government that abides by the rule of law, that brings justice and fairness, notice and cooperation to the population as highest values, is a government that relieves the tensions of difference through nonviolent processes and unites its people and gives them hope. This is a story too, and one more remarkable for its relative lack of historic precedent. Truth-telling is profoundly woven into the texture of a successful civil society, one in which the rule of law predominates and in which personal rule is not the governing principle.

I have seen a high-level Jew from Tajikistan excluded from internal strategy sessions of his own countrymen; I have been invited to private sharing of vodka and fish while he complained to me about his exclusion by his own countrymen. He was excluded even though he held the highest responsibilities for Tajikistan and had the most competence in the subject of the international negotiation. He was excluded because he was not part of the accepted insider network; he did not drink with the ministers. This man would sit in bargaining sessions with the most relevant information and be unable to put it on the table because he was not in the vodka circle. In Moscow it would be common for bargainers to refuse to say what they were willing to give for an agreement because some Jewish staff person was present who was not an insider. I, the foreigner, would argue the need for accurate facts and the importance of truth-telling in order to determine the best alternative to a negotiated settlement. Heads would nod, eyes would drop, and I could see that they thought that the foreigner was inexperienced in the ways of the real world. They were right: I was inexperienced and lacked the connections to be effective in a clan-based world. But they were wrong if they thought that feudal values could make them successful in a democratic world.

20

BEYOND BRIBERY

Going after big fish hasn't worked.
The fish won't fry themselves.

—John Githongo, former chief of anticorruption prosecutions in Kenya[1]

The renowned Peruvian economist Hernando de Soto has described the failure of capitalism in developing countries and the extent to which business competence is simply irrelevant. Having conducted studies in Peru, Egypt, Haiti, Mexico, and the Philippines, he found that it is nearly impossible for people who are not established or part of the power structure to accumulate capital. The touchstone of the problem, he believes, is the absence of a formal, dependable system for registration of property titles. Without defensible titles, borrowers cannot get credit. Without credit, they cannot create new business. Without new business, local economies stagnate and capitalism is clogged by corruption and alternate, usually illegal, economies.

> Imagine a country where nobody can identify who owns what, addresses cannot be easily verified, people cannot be made to pay their debts, resources cannot conveniently be turned into money, ownership cannot be divided into shares, descriptions of assets are not standardized and cannot be easily compared, and the rules that govern property vary from neighborhood to

neighborhood or even from street to street. You have just put yourself into the life of a developing country or former communist nation; more precisely, you have imagined life for 80 percent of its population, which is marked off as sharply from its Westernized elite as black and white South Africans were once separated by apartheid.[2]

De Soto documents in detail a modern feudal system. In Peru, according to his investigators, it took six years and eleven months and 207 administrative steps in fifty-two government offices to obtain legal authorization to build a house on state-owned land. To obtain legal title to the same land took 728 steps. In Egypt, a similar attempt took 77 bureaucratic procedures at thirty-one public and private agencies, a process that could take between five and fourteen years. In Haiti and the Philippines it was the same. This is also the situation, says de Soto, in formerly communist countries.[3] And I agree with that observation because that has been my experience over a period of more than twenty years in those formerly communist countries. Then de Soto points to the problem of dealings between strangers:

> Whereas all manner of anonymous business transactions are widespread in advanced countries, the migrants [strangers] in the developing world can deal only with people they know and trust. Such informal, ad hoc business arrangements do not work very well…A legal failure that prevents enterprising people from negotiating with strangers defeats the division of labor and fastens would-be entrepreneurs to smaller circles of specialization and low productivity.[4]

De Soto is right that the absence of enforceable titles inhibits or completely destroys the ability of small entrepreneurs to get credit, and this lack of an adequate property legal system is a failure persistent throughout the developing world and former communist countries. But de Soto does not adequately recognize that when power is the dominant arbiter of right and wrong, and hierarchy rather than equality is the expected norm, and when violence and terror are accepted tools of enforcement, the problem is not simply legal title. When clan or family is more important than the general welfare or the law that is intended to protect the general welfare, then for the man who seeks a building permit or business license, competence does not enter into the equation. Neither quality of the legal title, nor preparedness, nor the quality of the product, nor the careful business plan will be relevant.

De Soto has vividly described the delays and frustration, the injustice and the resulting "alternate" illegal economy that develops when the mentality of feudalism lingers into the present day. Further, when a population is itself wholly engaged by the ancient feudal norms, it expects these conditions, indeed, even counts upon them, and is therefore complicit in their continuation. Just as Wat Tyler cried out to kill all the lawyers in the fourteenth century, or as Algernon Sidney found when courts were controlled by King Charles II, the masses in developing and former communist worlds believe that the elite jurists will not ever rule in their favor. Bribes are therefore necessary and natural, might does make right, and if there is a word in the language for "fairness," it is preempted as a slogan of the oppressors to mute the expectations of the oppressed. Expecting all this, the masses play the system as it is, not as Europeans or Americans claim that it might be, and the population ends up substantially supporting and participating in corruption.

It is illustrative that after seventy years of communist brutalization, the inhabitants of the former Soviet Union still do not expect their courts to become open to dissenters or fair to the weak or less powerful. They do not expect hierarchy to suddenly disappear. They do not expect bribery to stop. They (most of them) do not trust that any place exists in the world where the feudal mentality does not rule. Russian emigrants who come to the United States and who may have been here for years still are apt to expect that our elections and courts will be fixed. Many of them would not think of going to court to enforce a contract, because they assume that these courts, like those in the old country, will enforce the law in favor of established elites, or, that is, American citizens.[5] They hide their competence under a bushel for fear of retribution by authorities whom they do not know and do not trust. I once gave legal advice to a Russian businessman doing business on the East Coast, telling him that he should follow the applicable local law. I could tell from his tone that he had called me to gain advice to the contrary, that is, about how to avoid the law in the United States. He was at first incredulous that he had been directed to a lawyer who did not understand how to game the system. When he realized his mistake, he hung up.

Russian emigrants to this country know in their bones that bureaucracy does not operate to facilitate change but, to the contrary, it operates to maintain the status quo. Agencies should provide the *appearance* of reward for competence, but their real purpose is to block newcomers, to say no. Doors are opened not by competence, but by reinforcing patronage, by payoffs made at every level from the highest officials to the lowest, with much more required at the upper end, in the ministries. Modern feudalism is therefore a system that holds out the appearance of building permits, housing sales, apartment permissions as if it were a modern commercial state. But at every level these appearances are fraudulent. Whether it is Egypt or Russia, Zimbabwe or Pakistan, Armenia or Kazakhstan, the poison of distrust then overflows into all the crevices of society. Bribes must be paid at airports, at customs, to obtain tickets for concerts, to arrange a bed in the hospital, to enter a child in school, to get a doctor for his care. Listed prices, listed qualifications for exams, for universities, or for jobs are fraudulent. They are used to defend against outsider applicants and to reward members of the vodka circle or its equivalent.

But the problem is not just in developing or former communist countries. Feudalism hangs on tenaciously even in the West. Piero de Medici's condemnation of his rivals in fifteenth-century Florence was this: "You despoil your neighbor of his goods, you sell justice, you escape civil judgments, you oppress peaceful men and exalt the insolent." Six hundred years later, a writer for *The New York Times* noted that Italian prime minister Silvio Berlusconi was regularly accused of bribery, self-interest, improper use of public funds, and the use of his TV stations and great wealth to manipulate allies and control popular opinion. Neither Berlusconi, however, nor apparently the rest of Italy saw anything unusual. Berlusconi, even while under public attack for corruption, has been continually reelected. So too were the Medicis of Renaissance Florence, even when faced with the same charges. In the summer of 2009, *The New York Times* commented—as one might also have done in the fifteenth century—that in Italy, "abuse of office is something of a foreign concept." To them, why else have the office if not to use it for personal gain?

Earlier in 2009, *The New York Times* had also carried a story critical of Berlusconi. After that story, the author of the piece was quietly contacted by an Italian magistrate asking if the paper was attempting to serve as an agent of New York's Mayor Bloomberg (who also has a strong media empire). The American journalist asked for clarification. What was the Italian magistrate really trying to say?

Well, came the reply, was the *Times* not trying to bring down Berlusconi's media empire? And that, commented Rachel Donadio, the writer for *The New York Times*, is the Italian way of seeing the world. Everything is personal, and law enforcement and modern media are seen as simply one way of cementing personal power. In feudalism, empires of personal interest are the reality of politics, and these empires are always in collision. Corruption, manipulation, and contest between fiefdoms are the order of the day. "The real issue...is that Italy is not a meritocracy," wrote Donadio. "It is a highly evolved feudal society in which everyone is seen as—and inevitably is—the product of a system or a patron."[6] It is therefore not only in the United States that democracy is at a crossroads. Even in a place as noteworthy as Italy, it has not fully arrived. Not, at least, if we count concern for the common good, truth-telling, and competence as foundational.

The Odysseus Principle is therefore a contagion. It lives like a parasite in the bowels of the economy. The population as a whole comes to accept fraud and deception as normal. To say one thing and mean another is normal. To say "yes" and mean "no" is normal. To say "tomorrow" and mean "never" is normal. During a difficult negotiation that had lasted for several days, I was once approached by a prominent Russian journalist, himself formerly a speechwriter for Nikita Khrushchev, who advised me to "just say yes, and don't do anything."

Most common and perhaps most characteristic is for the applicant or petitioner to ask a straightforward question and receive a complicated answer. At first the applicant searches the response for a yes or a no. The response, if oral, is apt to go on and on, dwelling on many things that seem inapplicable. Details in the response are blandly and maddeningly irrelevant. The nonresponsive answer is then the appearance of response but without any definite—or dangerous—clarity of a firm yes or no. Through all this process, through the hundreds of steps that de Soto describes, competence, the quality of the expected performance, is of the *least* relevance. The point is this: for the bureaucracy, maintaining the status quo amongst the already powerful is paramount. This feudal mentality is far more important, therefore, than property titles. Such titles will be no more useful than any other laws of Parliament or rules of court. So long as the feudal culture controls like a straitjacket top to bottom, the rules are irrelevant.

How then do cooperation, capitalism, and good government evolve? Robert Axelrod's groundbreaking work in the early 1980s suggests an answer.[7] He found that there is another dynamic, one that is working against the Odysseus Principle and in favor of competence. His formula was, and is, that clusters of cooperation are the natural outcome of multiple transactions with repeated contacts and an expectation of a shared future.

Axelrod suggested that the reality of modern commerce is that people who cooperate and do what they say tend to seek each other out while at the same time avoiding those who in previous transactions had cheated. Truth-telling therefore aids in the formation of successful clusters of cooperation and the gathering of competence. This would be true whether in business or in government. As competent and honest cooperators come to find one another, their clusters gradually grow larger. A corporation is simply one of these large clusters, and it seeks to find other large clusters with which to exchange. The greater the reliability between clusters—the greater degree to which they do what they say they will do—the greater the success of both entities. Honesty, the production of reliable numbers and reports, budgets and cash flow sheets that are accurate, is therefore key to the formation of large-scale cooperative enterprise, which is to say that truth-telling is essential, in the long haul, to the success of corporate capitalism. It is through honesty that competence becomes relevant.[8]

Axelrod predicted that those who do *not* cooperate will find themselves increasingly isolated over time. They will pay a price for cheating. If cooperation is limited to a narrow circle of fellow cheaters, creative input is limited, the product is likely to be less a result of multiple minds and talents, of lesser quality. This describes exactly the production of everything from cars to watches in the former Soviet Union. Competence is always reduced when the clusters of information exchange are limited. In the Soviet Union, these exchanges were very limited indeed.[9]

The internal contradiction in the feudal mentality is that it may eventually be self-defeating. In the long run, it may be doomed by the operation of the same nonviolent incentives that led the bourgeoisie of Paris to leave the ranks of knighthood and become merchants. Those merchants had found that encouraging collaboration and even relations with strangers in the markets was an easier way to make money and stay alive than the life of pillage and plunder. As long as one is more successful dealing with other truth-tellers, the circles of cheaters will correspondingly shrink. One would think therefore that cheating and hierarchy, power for its own sake, law as a fraud, and diversity as an enemy are feudal values that cannot survive in the modern world.

The problem with this conclusion, however, is that when governments are themselves tyrannical, when they generalize the encouragement of cheating, bribery, and violence throughout the whole society, then that norm overtakes the natural ability of noncheaters to find allies. Honest people are swamped, themselves isolated and unable to develop even the smallest clusters of cooperation. This explains why even after some years of advancing capitalism, norms have not yet changed in developing or former communist countries.

In my work, I have found that within the family, or within circles of trusted friends (perhaps friends even closer than family), truthful reporting and honest acknowledgment of the facts is common. Humans seem to understand that they cannot lie all the time, and we are aware that transactions based upon falsehoods are insecure. In every culture, probably everywhere in the world, there is a respect for honesty in these certain situations. No one, and no culture, can be ruled out. In my experience, however, when it comes to truth-telling to *strangers*, the ethic is often apt to change. When ministers were unwilling to share the true facts about the costs of failure to make an international agreement, they were unable to make that agreement at all. Negotiations would be stalled until some connection could be made between unknown parties at an undisclosed time and place. Bribes, deals, and payoffs would have to be arranged.

Corruption in the West probably has the same consequences. If the annual reports of a corporation are inflated or false, that can lead to corporate disaster, as in the Savings and Loan scandal of the 1980s, or the Enron case in 2001, or Madoff's Ponzi scheme in 2008. Reliability of information is central to market analysis, investment, and evaluation of stocks and resources. If the ethic of truth-telling is replaced by the ethic of personal transactions, or transactions within the vodka circle, then the taint of unreliability is apt to spread throughout relations with third parties. If objective numbers are not to be trusted, then transactions can only be reliable if guaranteed by some form of personal connection, or, even worse, some form of personal payment or bribe. For a transaction to be reliable, on the other hand, truth in speech must be matched by truth in numbers, truth in projections, truth in annual reports, and truth in pricing. A false report obscures incompetence, and competence becomes irrelevant.

The rule of law is the rule to make truth and competence relevant. It makes it more relevant than political or economic power, status, or the will of the lord of the manor, the minister, or the corporate CEO. For this to be the case, the law must work to protect the common good, be a substitute for violence, operate as a search for truth, protect fairness, equality of opportunity, openness, and diversity, and have as its goal the promotion of competence or quality. It must protect democracy's five assumptions.

AN AGE ENDS

21

FINDING DIRECTION IN A TIME OF CHAOS

> Empty as a conch shell by the waters cast
> The metaphor still sounds but cannot tell,
> And we, like parasite crabs, put on the shell
> And drag it at the sea's edge up and down…
> This is the destiny we say we own.
>
> —Archibald MacLeish, "Hypocrite Auteur"

"A world ends when its metaphor has died," wrote the poet Archibald MacLeish near the middle of the last century.[1] He meant to suggest that when the images of old metaphors no longer have meaning or no longer teach, then the age is over.

Today, the web of beliefs that we have held dear in the United States is being shredded and torn by new realities. Several old myths that have supported the three pillars of American faith—capitalism, militarism, and dualism—are now diluted, weak, and unpersuasive. Capitalism without the burden of a public conscience patently does not foster equality, diversity, truth-telling, and the public good. Sometimes it does not even foster competence. Foreign policy premised upon raw militarism betrays democracy's central purpose of nonviolence, especially if the rule of law is based upon ignorance of the law. Finally, the exclusionary view of feudalism, a view that protects those on the inside but condemns those outside the clan, is not sufficiently variegated to explain our increasingly complex world, therefore placing us philosophically at the end of simplistic dualism. The metaphors of these three pillars are now empty as conch shells that we drag at the sea's edge up and down.

The tendency to allow financial markets to go unregulated; to turn a blind regulatory eye toward Fannie Mae and Freddie Mac; to assume that the public good will be achieved by personal greed running to plutocracy; to allow multiple cabinet members to leave the cabinet and then enlist with private lobbying firms, as if the purpose of government service were ultimately to secure private enrichment, all belie the triumph of an ethic that does not regard the public good as paramount. The financial collapse of 2008 and 2009 underscored how terribly important it is that capitalism be contained within a public purpose, that it be culturally understood that it's not enough to be free, or for markets to be free if they are not also harnessed to the production of real wealth, real work that produces something of real value. Truth in marketing must be the coin of the realm.

It is now clear that raw economic self-interest does not establish public morality. According to a *New York Times* report, the salary of just one chief executive in the United States for the year 2007 exceeded $83.7 million.[2] That's just base pay. That does not include stock options that added billions. Bonuses, which are neither salaries nor stock options, added more. For employees of the failed financial companies in New York, bonuses totaled $329 billion in 2007, and even though the companies were by then on the rocks, bonuses climbed to $18.4 billion more at the end of 2008.[3] Such excess in the face of rising desperation among the world's middle classes and poverty and hunger among its poor is the opposite of moral. Such excess and disconnection from the rest of the society is profoundly immoral; it is very close to obscene. Such self-congratulation came at a time when many of the corporations these CEOs led were sitting on assets of uncertain value, with only gamblers' prospects for survival.

Further, in spite of the $700 billion bailout enacted by Congress in October 2008, the Toxic Assets Relief Program, bankers were not quick to loan to other bankers. Credit still remained tight. That meant that the most elevated practitioners of capitalism did not trust the judgment of other bankers to whom they might lend, or, that is, did not trust the judgment of the other most elevated practitioners of capitalism.

Altogether, in 2008 and 2009 the country was experiencing a collapse of confidence in the free market, a system upon which Americans have feasted without doubt, reservation, or regulation for thirty years, since the commendation of greed ushered in by Ronald Reagan. Further, without a conceptual explanation for how we got into this mess or how we get out, no one in either party has had a star to steer by. The 2001 Bush prescription, urging everyone to go shopping, was a formula that brought us all a great deal of superficial prosperity that we cannot now pay for. It turned out to be a formula for grief, and perhaps bankruptcy. Capitalism as a religion of consumption based upon credit is now demonstrably flawed. It does not explain the real world, in which debts must be paid, eventually by the production of new real wealth. Contrary to the orthodoxy of the last thirty years, credit as the source of commercial and industrial growth only works if there is, as a result, a return to the economy of additional real commercial value. Derivatives do not do that. Hedge funds do not do that. Credit default swaps do not do that. They are only gambles. Gambles cannot be the basis of new real wealth.

But if capitalists have discredited capitalism, so have socialists discredited socialism (in the last seventy years), and to say that any presidential advisor knew or now knows a new formula, a slogan, or an economic ideology to guide us out of this confusion is to be hopeful beyond evidence. It is not just Alan Greenspan who did not know; no one else yet knows how this will turn out.

When it comes to commerce and trade, the United States, Europe, and all the developing nations are today adrift, tossed on a sea of ideological contradictions. Capitalism may be partly good and partly not so good, but it is not the whole good.

Since World War II, a second pillar of American policy has been reliance upon military strength to keep us safe. No president has been immune from this ideology, and yet none has proven its profound weakness until George W. Bush. We now see that raw militarism does not work for three reasons. One, it does not work because tanks and guns do not protect against ideas. Two, it does not work because tanks and guns destroy cities that we need to keep whole and undestroyed. And three, tanks and guns do not stop global warming, rebuild infrastructure, provide reasonably priced healthcare, or fix any of the other more serious problems that now endanger our survival.

The biggest fear of many Americans is Islamic terrorism. But Islamic terrorism feeds on martyrdom and, therefore, on *defeat*. Conversations in mud huts, at the water hole, or around the poppy field feed on the deaths of heroes. Islamic terrorism's yearning for justice is fed by defeat. Its sense of purpose is fed by defeat. Its identification of good and evil is fed by defeat. To go out and defeat Islamic terrorism with tanks and guns is therefore to go out and promote terrorism. Military defeat creates martyrs, heroes, and propaganda and demonstrates the need for the eternal struggle. No Westerner in his right mind would go around claiming that the West "won" the Crusades. There would be no surer way to fuel the fury of millions of Islamists. To plan to win the war on terror with military force is equally delusional.

This means that a way of seeing the world that might have been appropriate against Charles V of Spain in the sixteenth century, or Napoleon Bonaparte in the nineteenth, or the Hun or even Hitler in the twentieth will no longer lead to success against the threat we face in the twenty-first century. The seasons of civilization change, and not just with the weather.

Militarism is obsolete because it tends to destroy territory rather than preserve it, and preserve it we must if we are to expand markets. With Toyota building cars in the United States and Canadians owning Chrysler and Wal-Mart creating labor camps in China, and in turn with China having $5 billion of investment in Sudanese oil and owning more than $300 billion in US Treasury Bills, with India telephoning computer repair advice to New Mexico, Venezuela making oil compacts with Russians, and Dubai looking more like New York than New York looks like New York, victory in the old sense of conquest of territory is insane. Conquest is no more appropriate to today's competition with China and Russia or Germany and Japan than bows and arrows. Victory in the modern era will be when all the parts of the global economic and political machine run smoothly together, complementing each other, not when one of the parts runs by itself. The steering wheel of a car may be very important, but it is useless without the tires, the spark plugs, and the fuel injector. Bush and Cheney thought the steering wheel could go it alone. They explicitly went for US control. They were wrong. The result was that the whole wide world of finance came grinding to a halt.

The old view of military victory is the same as the illusion of victory in the Crusades. That victory, if there was such a thing, fueled continued tension and competition and hatred and nationalism that has persisted continuously through these last nine hundred years. To claim victory in an interdependent world is to take a slogan from the *Iliad* or from Caesar's wars or from El Cid or Charlemagne as a strategy for modern foreign policy, and that is, frankly, also delusional.

Finally, militarism does not solve our most pressing problems. The ice caps are shrinking. Seas are rising. Deserts are heating up. Populations are exploding. Water and food are in short supply, and famine is spreading. The very rich stay rich, but the poor are sinking under. There is no one to shoot, no land to conquer, no nuclear threat to dismantle that will stop the ice from melting, the water from rising, populations from exploding, or oligarchs and plutocrats from destroying democracy.

We are at a crossroads in global civilization for which traditional military power does not offer a solution. Nuclear weapons, stealth bombers, infrared night sensors, and body armor do not serve us to design a response to global warming, to the contradictions of free trade and fair labor, to the issues of population growth, to the alarming increase in the number of failing states, from Pakistan to Zimbabwe, to the stupendous gap between the incomes of those who run corporations and those who work for them, to the disproportionate influence of big money on politics, or to the independent (practically autonomous) governments of giant multilateral corporations. In the years to come, strength will not be defined by victory militarily so much as by innovations culturally, diplomatically, and, most significantly, innovations that wean us from carbon fuels.

Which brings us to our third major ideological precipice, the even larger transition that is upon us, beyond capitalism's failings and beyond militarism's obsolescence, to a world too complex for a dualistic approach.

From the wars of the Athenians against King Minos of Crete through the wars of the Romans against Cleopatra, through the wars of popes against the Cathars and eventually even the Templars all the way to the wars of George Bush and Dick Cheney and their attempt to extend US empire to the deserts of Iraq, the Western world has been dominated by a dualistic view. This is the view that won out in Athens in 500 BC when they celebrated the victory of Athena over Poseidon. It has remained in our mythology ever since. It is not, however, a true view of the real world. It is not true, because it is too simple. It attempts to explain a diverse and multisided world, a multipolar world, as if it were either good or bad, and in the simplification it misses the chances for solutions that do not fit formulas of capitalism, empire, or us versus them.

In the first three chapters of Genesis, written in about 1000 BC, we were told that man has dominion over the earth, that survival comes from power against the forces of nature, that men shall rule women, and that this hierarchy was to protect those who are good from those who are evil. We were told to choose sides.

In the last thousand years, Christianity, Judaism, and Islam have all three been doing just that. They have been choosing sides, and each has fostered the view that there are two worlds: one good (us) and one less good (everyone else). Each of the three religions has promoted the idea of two, of someone on the other side of its religious confession, or outside the chosen people, or on the other side of some moral fence.

The values expressed in that earliest biblical literature are similar to those in Greek mythology of the same period: hierarchy, dominion, subordination of the weak, disconnection from the earth, rejection of intuition, and the supreme centrality of patriarchal property. Those who agreed were Greeks; those who did not were barbarians.

This dualistic view is tribal—King Solomon against the Moabites, the Ammonites, the Edomites, and the Hittites—but the world is no longer tribal. Not only are we beyond tribes, we are beyond the simple construct of the nation-state. The nation-state is a sixteenth- and seventeenth-century ideology that came to us on the heels of feudalism. France, we would then say, was different from Spain; China was different from Italy, and that is who we were, French or Chinese. But today, with China making goods for Italy, and Indians watching American movies, and Georgians speaking Russian, and Russians eating Georgian oranges, those boundaries drawn largely from military experiences generations past are no longer a true reflection of the real economic, political, or cultural world. The nation-state, like the tribe before it, is a concept dissolving beneath our feet.

To survive in today's world, we must address a challenge that is not outside the fence. It is not some "them." It is not in those cultures that originally gave rise to Judaism, Christianity, and Islam. It is not the Trojans bedeviling the ancient Greeks, or the Babylonians holding the Israelites, or the Moors invading Spain, or Huguenots undermining French Catholicism, or the papists undermining English Protestants; it is not the Hun against democracy or the communists against freedom, or even today the fundamentalists of all stripes screaming words of hate and terror. It is none of those threats that in the past led us to believe that we could divide the world in two. The problem is not someone outside the fence. It is all of us, inside and outside the fence. In a sense, the purpose of feudalism was to create a protection against strangers or visitors. Now, within every city and every country we are all visitors to someone and must now at last adopt the rules of conduct that are necessary in that situation. We must all develop rules of truth-telling, respect for diversity and equality and competence. Democratic institutions provide the crucible within which that could happen. The crossroads question is whether we will use these institutions for that purpose.

This ideal way of thinking is now dangerously obsolete, though that is not just the result of George W. Bush, even though it is most profoundly expressed in the neoconservative movement that supported him and in the seemingly irresistible urge to attack and vilify, demonize and view the world with disdain. It was the way of 2008 campaign attacks on Obama as someone not like us, or someone who associates with terrorists. It was the theme of town hall meetings and conservative "tea parties" in the summer and fall of 2009, at which people were apt to scream epithets of "Hitler!" and "Stalin!" or carry placards showing President Obama in black face, or generally to describe any opinions with which they disagreed as "lies." Those attacks were primitive. But more than this, they probably reflect the way we as a nation thought after World War II, facing communism, or the way we think in democracies facing totalitarianism. It is the way we think of danger, altogether, as if it came from the outside. As if the world were divided into two parts. As if we could wall danger out. But of course we cannot wall *us* out, and it is our own energy use and our own profligate consumption, our own denial of the larger community of needs, our own denial of our responsibility to pay taxes or even to discipline children, and our own obscene waste on weapons (which are totally irrelevant to resolving these threats); it is all these things that puts us all, globally, inside the fence.

The revolution that is before us in the season of the Obama administration is therefore not just about electing a black man, or regaining wages for the working poor, or expanding health insurance. The greater reality is that, unlike in the aftermath of any election in our history, the world is ideologically chaotic because it is unexplained and the future is uncharted. We are left spinning into an age of ideological confusion because the three pillars of our prior understanding of our recent civilization have toppled. Classic economic doctrines lauding raw self-interest are collapsing around us, and there's no sensible concept of socialism to replace capitalism. Militarism, the mainstay of our foreign policy for fifty years, which fuels rather than diminishes terrorism, is now irrelevant to conquer or influence the trading habits of other developing countries and is irrelevant to address global warming. And finally, after three millennia, a dualistic way of seeing the world, with one part good, the other evil, is nothing less than delusional. Our earliest Greek philosophy and its dependent religions have prepared us for a world no longer extant.

All this creates a space. The emptiness and uncertainty could be a time of terror or it could be a time of rebirth. It could be a time of resignation and despair or it could be a time of struggle against the odds, the imagination of possibility and competence. Something about our frontier experience, pulling boulders out of fields in Vermont, bringing water down from the mountains in Colorado, planting villages in the woods of Indiana where none had been planted before, augurs well.

22

DEMOCRACY AT THE CROSSROADS

It is rather for us to be here dedicated
to the great task remaining before us...
that we here highly resolve that the dead
shall not have died in vain—
that this nation, under God,
shall have a new birth of freedom—
and that government of the people,
by the people, and for the people,
shall not perish from the earth.

—President Abraham Lincoln, Gettysburg Address[1]

If, instead of red states and blue states in the United States, the whole world could be painted with red and blue to denote feudal states and civil states, the globe would still seem dominated by red. A great many more, of course, claim to be civil, or democratic, than actually are. A great many conduct elections and maintain parliaments. That is true, for example, in Somalia or Azerbaijan or Zimbabwe, even in Russia and China. But as we have seen in these pages, the superstructure of elections, parliaments, constitutions, and codes, even the appearance of courts ruled by law, is not at all a sufficient test. The test is whether the *essence* of democracy is there. The test is whether the *culture* remains feudal—whether the basis for transactions is power, hierarchy, personal connections, and a willingness to discard the truth. The democratic institutions can be completely deceptive if, underneath the superstructure, the culture has not adopted the values or intentions of civil society. Further, the appearance of democracy is not entirely benign. In Azerbaijan or Somalia or even in Russia, the appearance is intended to lull people, including the local populations and foreign observers, into thinking that rules of fair play and equal justice apply when the actual mentality is precisely the opposite.

If, therefore, one were to draw a map of red and blue countries representing each hundred years all the way back to Abraham and Odysseus, say 350 such maps, including civilizations in China, India, Japan, Africa, Latin America, and North American Indian cultures, one would see that personal government, government stitched together by kinship connections, or what Igor Yurgens in Russia calls "friendships," has been the dominant culture for most of recorded history. One would see a little uptick in blue in fifth-century-BC Athens and again in Rome before the Caesars, a similar uptick in Florence and Venice in the early Renaissance, but in truth, with the exception of Athens, in each case these regimes were more red than blue. One would not see a blossoming of blue in any substantial form until the seventeenth century, predominantly in England, largely due to the lives of those we have sketched here. Of course, there was great civility between the clans and within the tribes of the native cultures of the Americas and Africa and the Middle East. But the extension of principles of due process and justice to strangers outside one's culture; the requirement of truth-telling in commerce, including to persons outside the circle of known friends; the extension of the law to the king himself, the subordination of the most powerful to the same codes as are applied to those who are less powerful; the expectation that courts will do the will of the law rather than the will of the powerful—this is a late-blooming phenomenon.

It is the emergence of this phenomenon that is symbolized by the speech of John Cook at the trial of Charles I in 1649. In the subsequent three hundred years the principle enunciated on that day has burst across the stage of world politics with extraordinary rapidity so that one can indeed speak today of a clash of civilizations. The clash is not, as it has been sometimes argued, between Muslims on the one hand and Christians and Jews on the other so much as it is between feudalism and civil society, or between societies that require civic virtue and those that consider such virtue to be naive. This would be the clash between those cultures that, because of their allegiance to these primary civic virtues, actually enforce rules for protection of outsiders and those that parade those rules only for show, between those that pry open the hierarchies of privilege to allow access to strangers without the advantage of caste, clan, or religious preference and those that still arm the barricades against all outsiders. Perhaps most significantly, the difference would be between those cultures that follow the norm that might makes right and those that follow the ideal that justice and fairness make right. It is of course the search for justice and fairness in which, in the words of Abraham Lincoln, so many people have given the last full measure of devotion.

For sixty years, since World War II, Americans have operated under the assumption that the global sphere of democracy—or, in our metaphor, blue states—was expanding. Elections have been happening in new countries every year, from Bolivia to Ukraine. Parliaments meet and grumble in Pakistan, Kazakhstan, and Russia. Courts try the former dictator Pinochet in Chile. But when one examines the detail, when one watches how governments actually govern in China, Venezuela, Libya, or Azerbaijan, it is apparent that a contrary riptide has also appeared. This riptide is now swelling with gradually increasing deadly force, pulling along just beneath the surface of so-called global democratization, threatening the survival of civic virtue altogether. The riptide is threatening to take it all back down; threatening to reintroduce the Odysseus Principle, to mimic civil society but not actually adopt it, threatening to reestablish rule by friends, allowable corruption, and endorsed violence. In Somalia, Zimbabwe, Pakistan, Liberia, Sudan, Belorussia, Tajikistan, Burma, Mexico,

Panama, Syria, Iraq, Saudi Arabia...the list goes on and on, this is true. In all these places personal rule is in contest with the new principles of civil society, and in all these places the outcome is in doubt.

I have singled out and especially emphasized examples of modern feudalism in the former Soviet Union and today's Russia. It is wise to do this because after the Russian entry of tanks across the border of the Republic of Georgia in 2008 and their conspicuous rumbling back and forth over the Baku-to-Turkey oil pipeline, it is clear that Prime Minister Putin is embarking again on a campaign to reassert Russia's influence in global politics. His further manipulation of gas deliveries to Ukraine in 2009 sent a similar message. Two things are now clear from these examples and the other elements of Russian society that we have noted in these pages: (1) Vladimir Putin intends to reestablish Russian global influence, and (2) he is not a democrat. Putin is not a man in search of justice or patient for the awkward processes of representative government. He is not a man to allow the law, or a contract, or a treaty to get in his way. He has not yet had the comeuppance of Charles I or James II. He is a man caught even yet in the feudal mind that says that power is the arbiter of what is right. In January 2009 another journalist of the independent *Novaya Gazeta* was shot down in Moscow. Anna Baburova was twenty-five, a cub reporter. She was shot along with Stanislav Markelov, a human rights lawyer whom she was apparently interviewing. Markelov had specialized in representing Chechens, environmentalists, and human rights activists. Today there is terror among liberals and progressives in Putin's Moscow, and his government stands as a useful symbol of the riptide that still tugs at the world.

At the same time, the collapse of Western ideologies of raw capitalism, militarism, and dualism now creates a yawning hole in America's self-confidence. The doubt began with the loss of the Vietnam War, and the first cracks in capitalism followed soon thereafter, when inflation and stagnation all happened at once in the 1970s. Jimmy Carter cried out for a change in direction and reorientation of national purpose, but Ronald Reagan strode onto the stage, redoubled our military budget, railed against Russia as if to deny the Vietnam defeat, and told Americans to stand tall. In order to overcome the stain of Vietnam, military pride was revived and militarism restored. Reagan cast US survival in terms of capitalism versus communism and proclaimed capitalism the winner. And well it was. Communism as it was practiced in the Soviet Union was feudal to the core. The Soviet Union was brutal, violent, corrupt, and criminal. But the attack should have been against the brutality, violence, and criminality. Instead, it was against the idea of government as a friend of the common man. In the nineteenth century, Karl Marx had been a determined foe of feudalism and personal government. By attacking communism rather than criminality, Reagan was unwittingly attacking the more significant values of equal opportunity and protection of diversity, ethnic neutrality, and liberty for the masses. From Lenin in the 1920s to Brezhnev in the 1980s, Soviet leaders had replicated the very feudal ideas that Marx deplored. But instead of attacking feudalism's criminality, Reagan attacked government as an institution, and not just in Russia. "The scariest words in the English language," Reagan is supposed to have said, "are 'I am here from the government and I am here to help.'"

But Reagan was an actor, not a historian. In pursuit of the common good, and therefore in a complete reversal of the feudal mentality, the US government, at both federal and state levels, has in the previous hundred years fostered fairness for small business, broken up monopolies, resisted gerrymandering, and passed laws securing the rights of women and African Americans. In pursuit of the common good, government has fostered Social Security and Medicare and Medicaid. When government took steps to control air and water pollution and to protect the tidelands and wetlands and the national forests, it set the quality of life for the whole of the country against the advantages of a few. The evil of government in the Soviet Union had been to claim to work for the common good when in reality it feathered the nests of the elite. The evil was in the fraud, not in the statement of intentions. The evil was in the complete and total disregard for truth-telling, the fear of strangers, the neglect of competence, the return to feudalism. The Reagan failure was to not attack that; his blindness was to attack all government instead.

The Reagan attack on government also turned inward against our own courts. When it did so, it ignored the role of nonviolence as one of democracy's intentions. When courts ensured equal protection of the laws, gave rights to African Americans to go to school, protected free speech, they were creating alternatives to riots in the streets. After labor unrest in Haymarket Square in Chicago (1876) and massacres of miners at Ludlow, Colorado (1910), government's protection of the right to organize had become absolutely essential to keep the peace. Reagan's attacks on government as an institution therefore reinforced the feudal reliance upon hierarchy and privilege, inequality and mass unrest.

When government opened world markets to US agriculture and industry, it was promoting markets for goods of high quality and therefore promoting competence. When government pioneered science at the Centers for Disease Control and research in space, it was promoting competence. These are the details of civil society, the implementation in a thousand, thousand ways of the civic virtues, protections against government by oligarchy or friendship, subjecting them all to the good of the whole as the king had once been subjected to the law. Many of these were initiated as reforms protecting against plutocracy so great that it would create yawning gulfs of inequality and rampant instability. All these were, of course, complicated and complex, and the solutions were often clumsy and hard to understand. All these misunderstandings and the resistance to complexity was the basis for the ignorant statement that the scariest words in the English language are "I am here from the government and I am here to help."

In fairness, something more than ignorance was involved. Here also was a cry from the heart of those who wished that the world could be as simple as it had been in days of our rural past. It was a cry for common sense rather than bureaucratic complexity. At its core, Reagan's voice was a cry for civic virtue as it might once have existed, and the desperate belief that civic virtue could be implemented without government mediation. That cry was in this sense natural and understandable, and it met with a great upwelling of popular support. The wave of deregulation that has occurred in the last thirty years has been borne on that tide. This tide was not composed of conservatives seeking to avoid virtue, but rather more likely their attempt to reestablish virtue. But, unfortunately, by thinking that virtue could be established by way of feudal values, the forfeiture of the public purpose in government, the choice of violence in foreign policy, the disregard for truth-telling and equality of opportunity or diversity, and the neglect of science and therefore competence, conservatives had embraced a contradiction in terms. They had unknowingly relinquished the very democratic values that lay as the bedrock to the American Revolution. The collapse in 2008 of markets, the failure of the military to establish real civic virtue or democracy in Iraq or Afghanistan, and the failure of a dualistic view of the world to produce comity among nations has been the result.

Reagan, who led the crusade for simplicity, was not well equipped with knowledge of history, or the law, or even the deeper reasons why the Soviet Union was evil. He appeared essentially ignorant of the sources of law and capitalism and the absolute necessity of limitations on militarism, military spending, and the bankruptcy of empires. The conservative movement that he spawned was perhaps understandable and well intended, rooted in values even, but it was also dismissive of the necessary foundations of democracy. With these flaws, it swept the country toward unregulated credit default swaps and collateralized debt obligations, empire in the Middle East, torture, and ignorance of international law. It was a tide that swept us in the direction of the very government that Reagan had identified as evil.

The crossroads for Americans comes from two choices. We

might decide to drift further along the road toward plutocracy, back toward personal government in order to match and run abreast with the manipulations of China and Russia. We might ignore the significance of honesty, reward incompetence, treat outsiders and the less fortunate with indifference, and respond to dissent with violent oppression. The world understands these values and no doubt beckons us to rejoin them. When, at the Republican National Convention in August 2008, radio journalist Amy Goodman and her camera crew were arrested attempting to cover a demonstration, and when Goodman's press badge was ripped from her chest by angry law officers determined to suppress not only dissent but the coverage of dissent, it was clear that some in the United States are willing to go down that road. These exercises in violence and suppression signaled a greater allegiance to order through power than to order through empowerment. They signaled two governments, one local and one national, willing to exercise power in the tradition of kings rather than the tradition of democratic nonviolence, or truth-telling.

On the other hand, in some ways this is the perfect condition for the rise of democracy. Its natural origin and historic justification is, after all, a substitute for the inadequacies and cruelties, the clumsiness and failures of feudalism. We might therefore decide to ignore the siren's call. We might revive the civic virtues and the nobler intentions of that long line of courageous men and women who produced what was then the jewel of Western civilization. Ahead, down the road in this direction, lies that new order of the ages pioneered by Coke and Hampden, Sidney and Macaulay, Paine, Madison, Jefferson, and Adams. The dream of the new order is not yet fulfilled, its promise not yet complete, and there is work to be done.

During the course of many years of informal negotiations between Armenians and Azerbaijanis, and while they were at war, I enjoyed the company of a counterpart in Baku with the marvelous name of Zardusht Ali Zadeh. He worked alongside a generous, compassionate woman named Arzu Abdulaeva. Arzu had a heart bigger than the world, worked for refugees and children, and was once awarded the Olaf Palme Peace Prize for her efforts to settle the war with the Armenians. They were a considerable pair, Zardusht and Arzu. He had once run for president of Azerbaijan and for his troubles had been attacked, beaten, and left bleeding on the streets. They both knew what democracy could mean for Azerbaijan and that it was not yet established. The three of us became friends, and we would regularly head out into the day to take on issues of poor refugees, violence, deceit, corruption, and unbridled tyranny. In spite of these conditions, the two of them were among the most civilized people I've ever known. They knew the United States' history and my Colorado rural roots and my love for the rule of law. On those days, heading off to some difficult negotiation, Zardusht and Arzu would drive by in their old gray car, and Zardusht would lean his head out the window and shout to the sidewalk, "Craig! Saddle up!"

The last time I saw them, in 2007, Zardusht and Arzu were planning a press release to contest a new presidential decree intended by the Azerbaijan government to grind journalists down, to stamp out dissent of any kind. Some of their journalist friends were already in jail. Still, after years of struggle, their courage had never flagged. They sat in a small circle, planning to speak out, saddling up for the next encounter with tyranny.

When the extraordinary story of the emergence of the rule of law is fully written, it will, I hope, include the names of men and women such as William Marshal, Wat Tyler, Mary Sidney, John Hampden, John Cooke, Algernon Sidney, and Catharine Macaulay. But now it may also include a whole new array, a thousand new heroes, devotees of nonviolence, honesty, equality of opportunity, and competence, enforced by the rule of law. Perhaps these numbers will also include men and women like Zardusht Ali Zadeh and Arzu Abdulaeva. Intelligence, courage, and enthusiasm for civic virtue is still alive in the world. With men and women like these scattered here and there across the globe, there is hope. The noble inheritance of the rule of law may yet gain a permanent foothold.

Prologue: John Cooke Indicts His Majesty the King

1. The tale of this trial and the life of John Cooke are marvelously told in Geoffrey Robertson's *The Tyrannicide Brief* (New York: Anchor Books, 2007). This incident is at 154–55.

1: The Long Life of Lying

1. When Epimenides, a Cretan, says that all Cretans are liars, he himself is lying, in which case all Cretans are not liars. This phrase has provided a paradox for philosophers for some considerable time. But to note the paradox for philosophical purposes reveals a much later preoccupation than that which no doubt occupied Epimenides, who was equally likely to be describing the real world as he had experienced it, giving practical advice rather than creating some Socratic conundrum.

2. Homer's writing does not occur until much later, about 750 BC, and reflects values of the Mycenaeans. The poet idealizes and hopes to generalize these values for emerging Greek civilization. See Craig Barnes, *In Search of the Lost Feminine* (Golden, CO: Fulcrum Publishing, 2006).

3. The most detailed and informative parsing of these myths is still found in Robert Graves, *Greek Myths*, 2 vols. (New York: Penguin, 1960). For the killing of Clytemnestra's children see, e.g., vol. 2, 52.

4. The Romans studied Homer indirectly, through the poet Virgil, who derived his *Aeneid* directly from Homer.

2: The Short Life of an Honest Man in Rome

1. Edward Gibbon, *The Decline and Fall of the Roman Empire*, abr. ed. (New York: Dell, 1963), 82.

2. Ibid., 87.

3: The Miserable Life of a Feudal King

1. Barry Nicholas, *An Introduction to Roman Law* (Oxford: Clarendon Press, 1962), 17.

2. Winston S. Churchill, *The Birth of Britain* (New York: Dodd, Mead & Co., 1958), 253–54.

3. Magna Carta, par. 14 (emphasis added). The text of the Magna Carta is available on multiple websites. A reader-friendly copy is provided by the Avalon Project of the Yale Law School.

4. Ibid., par. 39.

5. Ibid., par. 40.

6. Ibid., par. 45.

7. Ibid., par. 63.

8. "Self-restraint and compromise were the cornerstones of all Marshal's policies. Both before and after the peace of 1217, [when] he reissued the Magna Carta." William Marshal, from David Nash Ford's Royal Berkshire History website.

4: The Half-life of Feudalism and the Birth of Law

1. Quoted in Barbara Tuchman, *A Distant Mirror* (New York: Ballantine, 1978), 157.

2. Looking back from the perspective of the eighteenth century, Henry Home, Lord Kames, a leader of the Scottish enlightenment, would write: "In the social state under regular discipline law ripens gradually with the human faculties, and by ripeness of discernment and delicacy of sentiment, many duties formerly neglected are found to be binding on conscience." Duties are forced to catch up with the new attitudes and, said Kames, "such duties can no longer be neglected by courts of law." Cited in Arthur Herman, *How the Scots Invented the Modern World* (New York: Three Rivers Press, 2001), 97.

3. In my personal experience, I have been urged to disguise the truth in political negotiations in Moscow, water negotiations in Central Asia, and commercial negotiations in the Caucasus, and I have been approached for bribes in Russia, Armenia, Azerbaijan, Georgia, Botswana, Kazakhstan, and Kyrgyzstan.

4. This is what is happening in the ongoing negotiations and demands between Russia and Ukraine over the transport and sale of natural gas. The prime minister of Russia changes his mind, sees himself in new difficulty domestically, and changes the deal with Ukraine. This is not a new deal based upon the existing terms of contract; this is a deal enforced by the power that Russia has because it controls the switch.

5. This has been amply illustrated in the last twenty years in Russia. For a time, under Boris Yeltsin, entrepreneurs were encouraged to develop the country's natural resources and its television industries, and many enterprising young people became billionaires. But then Yeltsin left the scene and was replaced by Vladimir Putin. Whereas Yeltsin's hierarchy of personal loyalties had been among an emerging class of liberals and progressives, Putin's was within the KGB. The ripple effect was immediate throughout the whole system. One prime example was Mikhail Khodorkovsky. He had relied on Yeltsin and his encouragement of entrepreneurship, but now, with Yeltsin gone, all deals were off. Khodorkovsky was prosecuted, lost his television enterprises, and was forced out of his ownership of Yukos Oil. Putin's courts sent him to the labor camps. Khodorkovsky's story is merely one, albeit a very public one, of many examples that still today in Russia no deal is permanent, no contract protects against the changing tides of personal favor.

5: Poets as Midwives

1. For a complete and marvelous retelling of the trials of this century, see Barbara Tuchman, *A Distant Mirror* (New York: Ballantine, 1978), and for the rising of the Estates General in 1356–57, see ch. 7.

2. Ibid., 374.

3. Ibid.

4. Ibid., 376.

5. David Hume, *History of England* (Philadelphia: Porter & Coates, n.d.), 4:357.

6. Margaret P. Hannay, *Philip's Phoenix: Mary Sidney, Countess of Pembroke* (New York: Oxford Univ. Press, 1990), 128.

7. For the best presentation of the Sidney case, see Robin P. Williams, *Sweet Swan of Avon* (Berkeley, CA: Wilton Circle Press, 2006).

6: The Cradle Century

1. This quote was traditionally related as "Magna Carta is such a fellow, that he will have no sovereign," which is an accurate interpretation of its meaning if not its actual wording. Coke meant to say that the king cannot carve out, or "save," an exception to Magna Carta

for his royal prerogative and in that sense the king was not sovereign above the ancient charter. See Jeffrey D. Goldsworthy, *The Sovereignty of Parliament: History and Philosophy* (Oxford: Oxford Univ. Press, 1999), 114.

2. After the Magna Carta in 1215, the councils called for in that document consisted entirely of nobles and prelates. But in the latter half of that century, when Edward I needed more sources of income for his wars, he began to call knights and burgesses to his meetings as well. This was no great honor, since those called would have to go home and raise more money from their constituents. Still, successive kings continued the practice until, in 1431, the knights and burgesses were of such a number that, when called, they met separately from the lords and prelates. By the sixteenth century, this latter group became known as the Commons and the upper house became the Lords. It was not until the era ushered in by Sir Edward Coke and John Hampden that the Commons began to rise to the levels of power of the Lords.

3. The order to Charles's commissioners was not unlike a plan of George W. Bush's Justice Department under Attorney General Ashcroft to have letter carriers, meter readers, and firemen watch out for suspicious activity, to become spies for the state. This was a proposed component program of the Citizen Corps to be known as Operation TIPS (Terrorism Information and Prevention System).

4. Catharine Macaulay, *The History of England from the Accession of James I to that of the Brunswick Line*, 8 vols. (London: Printed for J. Hours, Bookseller to his Majesty, in the Strand, 1763). The only volumes that I have been able to examine were in the Huntington Library in Pasadena, California.

5. Ibid., 1:359.

6. Ibid., 1:360–61.

7. Ibid., 1:363–64.

8. David Hume, *History of England* (Philadelphia: Porter & Coates, n.d.), 5:34.

9. Ibid., 5:32 (emphasis added). Lest one consider these battles over, in the United States in 1987 after the scandal involving presidential sponsorship of arms sales to the contras in Nicaragua, a select committee in the House of Representatives, headed by the future vice president Dick Cheney, issued a minority report in support of actions that the majority in Congress and the courts deemed illegal. Cheney's report asserted that a president "will on occasion feel duty bound to assert monarchical notions of prerogative that will permit him to exceed the laws." Jane Mayer, *The Dark Side* (New York: Doubleday, 2008), 60. In complete agreement with Charles I, Cheney was also after 9/11 willing to pursue his enemies with brutal force if necessary. Speaking of torture, he said, "We think it guarantees that we'll have the kind of treatment of these individuals that we believe they deserve." Ibid., 52.

10. Hume, *History of England*, 5:32.

11. Ibid., (emphasis added).

12. Macaulay, *History of England from the Accession*, 1:381.

13. Ibid., 1:383–84.

14. Ibid., 1:386.

15. These historic arguments are the foundation of habeas corpus and underlie today's arguments in the US Congress concerning the very same authority, not long ago claimed by President George W. Bush.

16. Macaulay, *History of England from the Accession*, 1:410–11.

17. Ibid., 1:413–15. Modern scholars say that the accurate recording is that the Magna Carta will have no saving, or that is no saving out of royal power exempt from the charter's provisions. The meaning is the same either way. Catharine Macaulay uses the older formulation.

7: A Rebel Even a King Would Save

1. John Adair, *A Life of John Hampden, The Patriot (1594–1643)* (London: Macdonald and Jane's, 1976), 243.

2. Ibid., 244–45.

3. "John Hampden's refusal to pay Ship-Money in 1635 took his name into every household and made it a byword for patriotism. Before that historic stand, wrote [the Earl of] Clarendon [a supporter of the king and opponent of Hampden's], 'he was rather of reputation in his own country than of public discourse or fame in the kingdom, but then he grew the argument of all tongues, every man inquiring who and what he was that durst at his own charge support the liberty and property of the kingdom, and rescue his country from being made a prey to the court.' Why did this wealthy man resist the demand for a mere twenty shillings assessed on his land in Stoke Mandeville? What principles underlay his opposition to Ship-Money?" Ibid., 107.

8: Unparalleled Courage, Fraud, and Revolution

1. If there were women in England in the underground of this struggle, I have not yet learned their names. The Massachusetts Bay Colony, however, was riven and desperately divided by the claim by Anne Hutchinson—an émigré from England—that a woman might have her own direct connection to God and need not search through the mediation of any man. She began to teach the Bible in her own home to large crowds of women and men and, as she developed an increasing popularity, became a threat to the Massachusetts patriarchy. She was branded a heretic and destructive to the peace of the colony and was banished from the colony. After settling in Rhode Island, she was killed by Native Americans in 1643. Ironically, she had been an advocate for better treatment of the Native peoples and for the right of women to speak for themselves.

2. He had made a commitment to the king of France to convert to Catholicism. In return, the French king secretly paid a stipend to Charles to help pay for Charles's wars against the Dutch. Resistance in England against Catholics was, however, overwhelming, and Charles was unable to actually, or openly, convert to Catholicism until upon his deathbed, in 1685.

3. In this he was strong in the Sidney family tradition. He was the grandnephew of Sir Philip Sidney and Mary Sidney, both poets of Queen Elizabeth's era. Mary Sidney, especially, in her writing had chastised the queen and warned her that even a monarch would one day be forced to answer to God for her deeds. Such warnings were life threatening if not disguised in poems or plays or other creative forms. The young Algernon Sidney may have thought such disguises no longer tolerable.

4. Article III, Section 3 of the US Constitution seems to have been drafted by those fully aware of the Sidney trial and the abuses of kings, because it provides that no person shall be convicted of treason except upon testimony of two witnesses to the overt act.

5. Alan Craig Houston, *Algernon Sidney and the Republican Heritage in England and America* (Princeton, NJ: Princeton Univ. Press, 1991), 5.

6. Samuel March Phillips, *State Trials, or the Most Interesting Trials Prior to the Revolution of 1688* (London: W. Walker, 1826), 100.

7. Ironically, it was Anglicans who at this time led the fight against tolerance. Although it was Anglican leadership in the House that eventually led to the Bill of Rights of 1689, the rights that they sought were to be protected against resurgent Catholicism. During the early years of Charles II's reign, they pushed hard to exclude Catholics from any role in government whatsoever, and while in the end they seemed to have laid the groundwork for civil rights in general, a groundwork upon which we rely even today, the roots of that effort grew from furious intolerance. This is a defining difference in motives when comparing the revolutionaries of 1689 and those of 1776. The latter were far more dependent upon a general tolerance and determined to give freedom of expression to all, not just to their own favored point of view.

8. David Hume, *History of England* (Philadelphia: Porter & Coates, n.d.), 6:204.

9. Ibid. Hume, while noting that the act is a pillar of English liberties, is not altogether sure that this "extreme" of liberty is a good thing.

10. Lord Macaulay, *History of England*, ed. Charles Harding Firth (1848. repr., London: Macmillan and Co., 1913), 2:998. Not to be confused with Catharine Macaulay, who published on the same subject in 1763.

11. Ibid., 2:1019.

12. Ibid., 2:1030.

13. It is clear that the opposition Whigs in England were aware of the gap between themselves and France, for example, which they considered to be "the seat of despotism and superstition;…a country where the last traces of liberty had disappeared; where the States General had ceased to meet; where parliament had long registered without one remonstrance the most oppressive edicts of the sovereign; where valour, genius, learning, seemed to exist only for the purpose of aggrandizing a single man [the king]." Lord Macaulay, *History of England*, 1:1269.

14. Emphasis added.

15. Magna Carta, par. 63.

9: The Birth of a Republic

1. This statement was in Cooke's prepared remarks for his closing but was never in fact delivered because the king chose not to present evidence and therefore no closing was required from the prosecution. Geoffrey Robertson, *The Tyrannicide Brief* (New York: Anchor Books, 2007), 191. Robertson interprets Cooke's meaning as follows: "All just power is now derived from and conferred by the people who consent and voluntarily submit to a form of government."

2. The opening paragraph of the Petition of Right of 1628 contains this language: "It is declared and enacted, that from thenceforth no person should be compelled to make any loans to the king against his will, because such loans were against reason and the franchise of the land; and by other laws of this realm it is provided, that none should be charged by any charge or imposition called a benevolence, nor by such like charge; by which statutes before mentioned, and other the good laws and statutes of this realm, your subjects have inherited this freedom, that they should not be compelled to contribute to any tax, tallage, aid, or other like charge not set by common consent, in parliament."

3. Catharine Macaulay, *The History of England from the Accession of James I to that of the Brunswick Line* (London: Printed for J. Hours, Bookseller to his Majesty, in the Strand, 1763), 1:vii.

4. Ibid., 1:x.

5. Ibid.

6. John Adams, *Diary and Autobiography of John Adams*, ed. Lyman H. Butterfield et al. (Cambridge, MA: Belknap Press, 1961), 1:360, entry for September 8, 1770, quoted in Vera Nünning, *A Revolution in Sentiments, Manners, and Moral Opinions* (Heidelberg: Universitätsverlag C. Winter, 1995), 48. In 1785, after the war but before the writing of the Constitution, Macaulay went to the new country and made the rounds of these leading lights of the Revolution. Among others she visited with George Washington for ten days, who thereafter wrote that Macaulay was "justly admired by the friends of liberty and of mankind."

7. Harvey J. Kaye, *Thomas Paine and the Promise of America* (New York: Hill and Wang, 2005), 39 et seq.

8. Ibid., 40 (emphasis in the original).

9. Ibid., 45.

10. Thomas Paine, *Common Sense* (New York: Penguin Classics, 1996), 76. Capitalization in the original.

11. Ibid., 81.

12. Ibid., 98 (capitalization and emphasis in the original).

13. Young Sidney, in turn, had been politically active and acquainted with Oliver Cromwell when on January 4, 1649, Parliament prepared to abolish both the monarchy and the House of Lords. On that date, Parliament issued this declaration: "The Commons of England assembled in Parliament declare that the people under God are the origin of all just power." Unfortunately, the intention to create a republic was short-lived, and after the restoration of the monarchy in 1660, Sidney would have to revive the issue again, to his mortal detriment. Not until Jefferson's time did the phrase that power resides in the people become sufficiently outside control of the great lords that it could take hold. For even earlier roots of the subversive theory that power comes from the people and not the monarch or from God through the clergy, Sidney and Cooke may in turn have relied upon George Buchanan's *The Law of Government among the Scots*, published in 1579. Buchanan may have been the first in Europe to open up the question to public examination. See Arthur Herman, *How the Scots Invented the Modern World* (New York: Three Rivers Press, 2001), 18 et seq.

14. "Thomas Jefferson spoke for many Americans when he wrote that the *Discourses on Government* [Algernon Sidney, London, 1698] was 'a rich treasure of republican principles' and 'probably the best elementary book of principles of government, as founded in natural right which has ever been published in any language." Alan Craig Houston, *Algernon Sidney and the Republican Heritage in England and America* (Princeton, NJ: Princeton Univ. Press, 1991), 8.

15. Luster Brinkley, *On This Hill:, A Narrative History of Hampden-Sydney College, 1774–1794* (Farmville, VA: Hampden-Sydney, 1994), 19. The college spelled it "Sidney" rather than "Sydney" until 1928.

16. Quoted in Houston, *Algernon Sidney and the Republican Heritage*, 244 (capitalization in the original). For Adams's knowledge of Sidney, see also William Alan Ryerson, "A John Adams Paradox" (paper delivered at a conference entitled John Adams & Thomas Jefferson: Libraries, Leadership, and Legacy, June 21–27, 2009), 13. Jefferson appears to have first obtained for his library a copy of Sidney's *Discourses on Government* in 1805. Given Sidney's martyrdom and fame, it is highly likely that Jefferson had read this important book of republican principles early in his career.

17. When I was a schoolboy in rural Colorado, it was a matter of pride that the small states were protected by their two senators. But the undemocratic consequences of this choice are not small. In the healthcare debate raging in the US Senate Finance Committee in the summer of 2009, it was six senators from states with less than 10 percent of the country's population who were said to be in control of the compromise legislation. The strikingly conservative result is that the majority of the country's citizens have not sufficient power in the Senate to create a response to the healthcare needs of a mostly urban population. The six state senators in this core negotiating team came from Montana, Iowa, New Mexico, Maine, North Dakota, and Wyoming.

10: To Suspend the Law, Again

1. For comparison, today's California constitution fills volumes, spreading over thousands of pages.

2. Arthur Herman, *How the Scots Invented the Modern World* (New York: Three Rivers Press, 2001), 258 et seq.

3. John Adams, *A Defence of the Constitutions of Government of the United States of America* (C. Dilly, London, 1787). Photographs of the first pages can be found at the website Reading Revolutions, http://hua.umf.maine.edu/Reading-Revolutions/Adams.html. Chapter titles photographically reproduced include Machiavelli, Sidney, and many others. The accompanying website texts, however, contain misprinting of dates, and the new text should be read with care.

4. Beth Prindle, "Thought, Care, and Money: John Adams Assembles His Library," 11–12. Available at www.adamsjefferson.com/papers/Thought_Care_Money_Prindle.pdf.

5. Based upon allegations of aggressive action by North Vietnam against the US naval fleet off the coast of Vietnam, President Johnson pressed upon Congress the Tonkin Bay Resolution, authorizing the expanded use of military force against North Vietnam. Later, one of those actually present at Tonkin Bay at the time of the alleged incident and responsible for intelligence reporting from the US Navy to the Pentagon reported that material details of the president's claims concerning North Vietnamese aggression had been untrue. (Personal communication to the author from Maj. Kenneth Mayers, USMC [ret.], who was stationed on the flagship of the fleet and as an intelligence officer participated in the first reporting of the "incident.")

6. *War Powers Resolution*. Public Law 93–148. *U.S. Statutes at Large* 555 (1973): 87, codified at *U.S. Code* 50, ch. 33, sec. 1541–48.

7. American Bar Association Task Force on Presidential Signing Statements and the Separation of Powers Doctrine Recommendation, 14. "He [George W. Bush] asserted constitutional objections to over 500 in his first term: 82 of these related to his theory of the 'unitary executive,' 77 to the President's exclusive power over foreign affairs, 48 to his power to withhold information required by Congress to protect national security, 37 to his Commander in Chief powers. Whereas President Clinton on occasion asked for memoranda from the Office of Legal Counsel on his authority to challenge or reject controversial provisions in bills presented to him, it is reported that in the Bush II Administration all bills are routed through Vice President Cheney's office to be searched for perceived threats to the 'unitary executive'—the theory that the President has the sole power to control the execution of powers delegated to him in the Constitution and encapsulated in his Commander in Chief powers and in his constitutional mandate to see that 'the laws are faithfully executed.'" Ibid., 14–15.

8. This is an edited transcript drawn from two interviews conducted by PBS's *Frontline* on July 10 and August 7, 2007. See www.pbs.org/wgbh/pages/frontline/cheney/etc/script.html.

9. Nor can it be said that the action is merely a struggle over principle. News accounts on February 22, 2008, state that "in late January, during the final days of Navy exercises using a type of sonar that has been linked to fatal injuries in whales and dolphins," a rare dolphin died on the beach of a navy island off the coast of Los Angeles, having suffered damage to its ears and ear canals. In effect, the president overrode the statute, the action continued, and rare dolphins died, rendering the legislative and court processes to that point irrelevant. Kenneth R. Weiss, "Death of Rare Dolphin Creates More Tension over Sonar Use," *Los Angeles Times*, February 22, 2008, A-8. Subsequent to this unilateral action by the president, however, upon appeal to the Supreme Court, the president's authority to override the statute was upheld. That is to say that later, after he had taken the bold step of asserting his broad authority over the act of Congress, his action was ratified by the Court. In effect, the president resisted the order of the lower court, gambled on the final outcome in the higher court, and won. The fact that Congress and lower courts had made his gamble illegal underscores the boldness of it.

10. Jesse McKinley, "Judge Reinstates Rules on Sonar, Criticizing Bush's Waiver for the Navy," *The New York Times*, February 5, 2008.

11. In November 2008, the Supreme Court declared that President Bush's assertion of prerogative was justified by the requirements of national defense and that therefore his suspension of the Coastal Zone Management Act was justified. See *Donald C. Winter, Secretary of the Navy, et al. Petitioners v. Natural Resources Defense Council, Inc., et al.* USSC, Slip Opinion, No. 07–1239, 518 F. 3d 658, decided November 12, 2008. It is perhaps fair to argue therefore that his willingness to override a lower court decision by executive order, as he did in January 2008, was eventually ratified. Such argument would, however, lead to the conclusion that a president might ignore any lower court order upon his own

judgment that a higher court will eventually vindicate such action. Since any lower court judgment could be resisted on these grounds, this position substantially nullifies the idea of the separation of powers, at least for so long as the president decides to wait for some other court to come to his rescue.

12. John Adair, *A Life of John Hampden, The Patriot (1594–1643)* (London: Macdonald and Jane's, 1976), 174–75.

13. Maps of Iraqi oil reserves, their locations, and lists of bidders for their extraction were provided by the Department of Energy to the vice president's Energy Policy Task Force in the spring of 2001, well before 9/11. These maps were subsequently supplied under a Freedom of Information Act request to Judicial Watch and thereafter made public. A map locating the first thirteen intended permanent bases can be obtained from CIA documents available on the Internet. When one map is laid upon the other, it is clear that the oil reserves and proposed location of permanent bases were largely coincident. For a dramatic presentation of the arguments surrounding these maps and the intentions of the George W. Bush administration, see the author's play *A Nation Deceived*.

14. The White House, "President Bush signs H.R. 4986, the National Defense Authorization Act for Fiscal Year 2008 into Law," news release, January 28, 2008.

15. Walter Alarkon, "House Overwhelmingly Rejects Signing Statement," *The Hill*, July 9, 2009.

16. Herman, *How the Scots*, 260.

11: Special Courts, Again

1. This was also true in the Middle Ages, when any lawyer who might come to the aid of a woman accused of witchcraft was likely himself to be accused of having been deluded by the witch and would then himself be persecuted. Defense was therefore an impossibility, practically speaking, and women like Jeanne d'Arc faced their judges entirely on their own. See Alan C. Kors and Edward Peters, eds., *Witchcraft in Europe: A Documentary History* (Philadelphia: Univ. of Pennsylvania Press, 1972), 160. For a narrative of the plight and trial of Jeanne d'Arc, see Craig Barnes, *In Search of the Lost Feminine* (Golden, CO: Fulcrum Publishing, 2006), 220.

2. In the former Soviet Union, it used to be true that if an American introduced himself to local professionals as a lawyer, faces in the room fell, secret smiles were shared, and the feeling was as if one had introduced himself as the Communist Party's chief executioner.

3. Relevant paragraphs of the Magna Carta, signed by King John at Runnymede on June 15, 1215, include these:

   (17) Ordinary lawsuits shall not follow the royal court around, but shall be held in a fixed place.

   (18) Inquests of *novel disseisin, mort d'ancestor,* and *darrein presentment* shall be taken only in their proper county court.

   (20) For a trivial offence, a free man shall be fined only in proportion to the degree of his offence, and for a serious offence correspondingly, but not so heavily as to deprive him of his livelihood. In the same way, a merchant shall be spared his merchandise, and a husbandman the implements of his husbandry, if they fall upon the mercy of a royal court. None of these fines shall be imposed except by the assessment on oath of reputable men of the neighbourhood.

   (34) The writ called *precipe* shall not in future be issued to anyone in respect of any holding of land, if a free man could thereby be deprived of the right of trial in his own lord's court.

   (38) In future no official shall place a man on trial upon his own unsupported statement, without producing credible witnesses to the truth of it.

   (39) No free man shall be seized or imprisoned, or stripped of his rights or possessions, or outlawed or exiled, or deprived of his standing in any other way, nor will we proceed with force against him, or send others to do so, except by the lawful judgment of his equals or by the law of the land.

(40) To no one will we sell, to no one deny or delay right or justice.

4. Barbara Tuchman, *A Distant Mirror* (New York: Ballantine, 1978), 373–74.

5. David Hume, *History of England* (Philadelphia: Porter & Coates, n.d.), 4:321.

6. Ibid., 4:326.

7. Essex was tried in Star Chamber before a jury of twenty-five peers, or, that is, lords of the House of Lords, who found him guilty and sentenced him to death.

8. "The Act of 1487 (3 Hen. VII.) created a court composed of seven persons, the Chancellor, the Treasurer, the Keeper of the Privy Seal, or any two of them, with a bishop, a temporal lord and the two chief justices, or in their absence two other justices. It was to deal with cases of 'unlawful maintainance, giving of licences, signs and tokens, great riots, unlawful assemblies'; in short with all offences against the law which were too serious to be dealt with by the ordinary courts." Luminarium: Encyclopedia Project, "The Court of Star Chamber," www.luminarium.org/encyclopedia/starchamber.htm.

9. Hume, *History of England*, 4:346.

10. William Prynne, from *Histrio-Mastix: The Player's Scourge; or, Actor's Tragedy*, at Norton Anthology of English Literature, Norton Topics Online, www.wwnorton.com/college/nael/17century/topic_3/prynne.htm.

11. *Hamdan v. Rumsfeld*, 548 S.D. 557, June 29, 2006.

12. Pub. L. No. 109–366, 120 Stat. 2600 (Oct. 17, 2006), enacting Chapter 47A of title 10 of the *U.S. Code* (as well as amending section 2241 of title 28).

12: War Privileges, Again

1. "In some cases, the administration simply used immigration law as a proxy for criminal law enforcement, circumventing constitutional safeguards. In others, the government seems to have acted out of political expediency, creating a false appearance of effectiveness without regard to the cost." Muzaffer A. Chishti, Doris Meissner, Demetrios G. Papademetriou, Jay Peterzell, Michael J. Wishnie, Stephen W. Yale-Loehr, *America's Challenge: Domestic Security, Civil Liberties, and National Unity after September 11* (Washington, DC: Migration Policy Institute, 2003), 7.

2. Amendments Five and Fourteen, guaranteeing due process, meaning at least a chance to know for what reason one is being held, and for equal protection, meaning that people of color may not be held for that reason alone.

3. American Civil Liberties Union, "Internal Justice Department Report Details 9/11 Detainee's Plight: Arab, Muslim, South Asian Immigrants Languished in Detention for Months," press release, June 2, 2003, www.aclu.org/safefree/general/17241prs20030602 .html. "Specific findings of the Inspector General's report include:

*   An official DOJ [Department of Justice] 'no bond' policy that prevented immigrants from accessing the justice system;

*   The government process for clearing immigrants of any connection to the terrorists attacks was understaffed and not given "sufficient priority;" clearance took an average of 80 days and in some instances took more than 200 days;

*   The OIG [Office of Inspector General of the US Department of Justice] report criticized the "indiscriminate and haphazard manner" in which immigrants 'who had no connection to terrorism' were labelled [*sic*] as possible suspects;

*   Early in the 9/11 crisis, hundreds of immigrants were held without being charged within the prescribed three-day window;

*   The Justice Department actively sought to limit detainees' access to attorneys, to other detainees and to family members; prison officials were told, 'don't be in a hurry' to assist immigrants in finding attorneys or contacting their consulates;

*   The OIG investigation was hampered by the destruction of hundreds of prison videotapes documenting what are thought to be harsh conditions of confinement and reported abuses of immigrants;

* Assistant Attorney General Michael Chertoff of DOJ's criminal division urged immigration officials to 'hold these people until we find out what's going on,' despite the fact that many had been swept up and detained on minor immigration charges." And see Jim Lobe, "Post-9/11 Immigrant Roundup Backfired—Report," www.commondreams .org/headlines03/0627-03.htm, June 27, 2003.

4. ACLU testimony at "Justice for All: A Nationwide Public Forum on Selective Enforcement After September 11, 2001," forum before Senators Edward M. Kennedy and Patty Murray, June 4, 2003, www.aclu.org/safefree/general/17238leg20030604.html.

5. *Hamdi v. Rumsfeld* (03-6696) 542 U.S. 507 (2004). Hamdi had been born in Louisiana and so had the rights of a US citizen. The issue would therefore be left open whether habeas corpus could also be applied to the benefit of a foreigner.

6. *Hamdan v. Rumsfeld*, 548 U.S., 2006.

7. Military Commissions Act of 2006 (MCA), 28 U.S.C.A. sec. 2241(e) (Supp. 2007).

8. Craig Houston, *Algernon Sidney and the Republican Heritage in England and America* (Princeton, NJ: Princeton Univ. Press, 1991), 71. In ancient Greek mythology, peace, order, and justice were also among the daughters of mighty Zeus. Royalists and conservatives on the Supreme Court might therefore have traced their ideology back to those who established governments on the Greek mainland in the first millennia BC. See Hesiod, *Theogony*, trans. Dorothea Wender (New York: Penguin Classics, 1973), 52.

9. *Boumediene, et al. v. Bush*, 553 U.S. ___ (2008)

10. Ibid.

11. Ibid.

12. Ibid.

13. I use the term *war on terror* with great reluctance. It is neither a war nor against all terror. It is targeted at certain terrorists of Muslim identity but does not include Irish terrorists nor Chechens nor Italian Mafia nor Tamil Tigers, etc. It is a political term used to raise funds and media interest and should therefore most likely always be considered by skeptics as a "war."

14. US Constitution, Fourth Amendment. Addresses search and seizure, warrants. Ratified December 15, 1791.

15. US Constitution, Eighth Amendment. Prohibits excessive bail and fines and cruel and unusual punishment. Ratified December 15, 1791.

16. Fourth Geneva Convention, part 4, sec. 1. art. 147. "Grave breaches to which the preceding Article relates shall be those involving any of the following acts, if committed against persons or property protected by the present Convention: wilful killing, torture or inhuman treatment,...wilfully causing great suffering or serious injury to body or health, unlawful deportation or transfer or unlawful confinement of a protected person,...or wilfully depriving a protected person of the rights of fair and regular trial prescribed in the present Convention. See also art. 37: "Protected persons who are confined pending proceedings or subject to a sentence involving loss of liberty, shall during their confinement be humanely treated." And art. 43: "Any protected person who has been interned or placed in assigned residence shall be entitled to have such action reconsidered as soon as possible by an appropriate court or administrative board designated by the Detaining Power for that purpose."

17. Scott Horton, "Justice After Bush: Prosecuting an Outlaw Administration," *Harper's Magazine*, December 2008, 50.

18. The author wrote and produced a play in 2006 in which, during early runs, a witness was overturned and waterboarded, water pouring into his mouth and nostrils. The effect on the audience was so horrifying that the dramatization was discontinued in future runs. A DVD of the play, *A Nation Deceived*, is available from the author, but without the waterboarding scene, which has been deleted.

19. Ayaz Nanji, "Report: 108 Have Died in US Custody," Associated Press, March 16, 2005.

"The figure 108 is based on information supplied by Army, Navy and other government officials. It includes deaths attributed to natural causes."
20. Charlie Savage, "Bush Could Bypass New Torture Ban," *The Boston Globe*, January 4, 2006.

15. The Law of Nations Ignored

1. "Second Day, Wednesday, 11/21/1945, Part 04," in *Trial of the Major War Criminals before the International Military Tribunal* (Nuremberg, Germany: International Military Tribunal, 1947), 2:98–102.
2. See, e.g., transcript of CNN interview with Condoleezza Rice, September 8, 2008, at http://transcripts.cnn.com/TRANSCRIPTS/0209/08/le.00.html: "The problem here is that there will always be some uncertainty about how quickly he can acquire nuclear weapons. But we don't want the smoking gun to be a mushroom cloud."
3. Transcript of ElBaradei's UN presentation, March 7, 2003, www.cnn.com/2003/US/03/07/sprj.irq.un.transcript.elbaradei/.
4. Ibid.
5. Transcript of Blix's UN presentation, March 7, 2003, www.cnn.com/2003/US/03/07/sprj.irq.un.transcript.blix.
6. Vice President Dick Cheney, *Meet the Press*, NBC News, March 16, 2003.
7. See, e.g., Eleventh Circuit, Pattern Jury Instructions, (Civil Cases), 2005, sec. 3.1 Intentional Fraud.
8. Richard W. Stevenson, "Remember 'Weapons of Mass Destruction'? For Bush, They Are a Nonissue," *The New York Times*, December 18, 2003.
9. Robert Jackson, on behalf of the Office of the United States Chief Counsel for Prosecution of Axis Criminality, "Nuremberg Trials: Opening Address for the United States," ch. 7 in *Nazi Conspiracy & Aggression*, vol. 1 (Washington, DC: US Government Printing Office, 1946), 166.
10. Helen Thomas, "Bush Admits He Approved Torture," Hearst Newspapers, May 1, 2008.
11. Fourth Geneva Convention, part 3, sec. I, art. 32: "The High Contracting Parties specifically agree that each of them is prohibited from taking any measure of such a character as to cause physical suffering or extermination of protected persons in their hands." Art. 33: "No protected person may be punished for an offence he or she has not personally committed. Collective penalties and likewise all measures of intimidation or terrorism are prohibited [compare in this regard especially the Bush bombing of Baghdad labeled as 'shock and awe']." Section 3, art. 53: "Any destruction by the Occupying Power of real or personal property belonging individually or collectively to private persons, or to the State, or to other public authorities, or to social or cooperative organizations, is prohibited, except where such destruction is rendered absolutely necessary by military operations." Art. 56: "To the fullest extent of the means available to it, the public Occupying Power has the duty of ensuring and maintaining, with the cooperation of national and local authorities, the medical and hospital establishments and services, public health and hygiene in the occupied territory, with particular reference to the adoption and application of the prophylactic and preventive measure necessary to combat the spread of contagious diseases and epidemics."
12. Joby Warrick, "Administration Says Particulars May Trump Geneva Protections," *The Washington Post*, April 27, 2008, A11. "The Geneva Conventions' ban on 'outrages against personal dignity' does not automatically apply to terrorism suspects in the custody of U.S. intelligence agencies, the Justice Department has suggested to Congress in recent letters that lay out the Bush administration's interpretation of the international treaty."
13. Gilbert Burnham, Riyadh Lafta, Shannon Doocy, and Les Roberts, "Mortality after the 2003 Invasion of Iraq: A Cross-sectional Cluster Sample Survey," *The Lancet*, October 11, 2006. Studies differ. Some put the number of civilian casualties from all causes at above 1 million. Others, perhaps the lowest, put the number at above 90,000. Taking a small proportion of the Lancet study yields a very conservative estimate.

14. Munqeth Daghir, *More Than 1,000,000 Iraqis Murdered* (London: Opinion Research Business, September 2007); Tina Susman, "Poll: Civilian Death Toll in Iraq May Top 1 Million," *Los Angeles Times*, September 14, 2007.

14: While Congress Slept

1. When the English monarchy was restored in 1660, poor Mr. Cooke was among a few of those who had been prominent in the trial of the new king's father. He was identified as a regicide and was not accorded even the legal procedures that had governed the trial of Charles I but was summarily condemned to death. As a commoner, he was not either accorded the more humane treatment of beheading but was subjected to the excruciating pain of death by degrees, being at first hung, then released, then while still alive, disembowled.

15: Today's Tug-of-War

1. Jeffrey Toobin, "No More Mr. Nice Guy," *The New Yorker*, May 25, 2009, 44.
2. Bishop Laud wrapped his authority in religious doctrine and ceremony and in extreme public display. Roberts cannot be accused of that conduct. There are, however, other similarities. In his famous *History of England* (well known to Jefferson, Adams, and Madison), David Hume wrote of Laud: "This man was virtuous...He was learned...He was disinterested...with unceasing industry...zeal...and unrelenting in the cause." David Hume, *History of England* (Philadelphia: Porter & Coates, n.d.), 5:68. The same might be said of Roberts. Laud was to use Star Chamber to advance his extremely conservative religious views. Roberts seems not to shrink from military commissions to advance his conservative political convictions. The founders, in 1789, having read Hume and often disputed his conservative views, agreed on this point: the Constitution must contain executive power. The founders might therefore have come to the conclusion that Chief Justice Roberts is far more like William Laud than, say, John Hampden or Algernon Sidney. They were intent to write a constitution to prevent the Lauds of the world from taking over. The rise of the Roberts Court would certainly have disappointed them.
3. For an extended review of the new administration's continuation of Bush policies, see Jack Goldsmith, "The Cheney Fallacy," *The New Republic*, May 8, 2009.
4. See, e.g., the brief of the Obama administration filed in the Guantanamo Bay Detainee Litigation: Respondents' Memorandum Regarding the Government's Detention Authority Relative to Detainees Held at Guantanamo Bay, In the United States District Court for the District of Columbia. Misc. No. 08-4442 (THF).

16: Beyond the Eternal Order of Lying

1. I use the terms *civil* and *civil society* because they point toward the goals and values of democracy, and, at an even deeper level, toward an intention to foster and enhance what is truly civil in society, or what is decent and contained, responsible and generous, or compassionate. I do not use the word *civil* to mean simply what is not military so much as in the sense of the values found in a "civil" debate or a "civil" conversation, meaning one in which violence plays no part. A civil, or a democratic, society is therefore profoundly different from one in which the leader takes over.
2. The concession by Al Gore to the highly suspect ruling of the Supreme Court in the matter of the 2000 election is a perfect example of the willingness of the American people to submit to a nonviolent process rather than overturn the government by resistance in the streets.
3. The collapse of the financial industry in 2008 and 2009 is an example of commercial enterprise failing because assertions of value were inflated, in some cases knowingly so. When the falsity of values became known, when the truth surfaced, the whole economy ground to a halt. This is a perfect example of the importance of real numbers, or truth, in commerce.
4. In January 2009, *The New York Times* reported that Sonja Kohn, an Austrian financier

who had solicited funds for the notorious Madoff Ponzi scheme, had gone underground. Kohn had apparently invested and lost substantial funds for Russian oligarchs. She has gone underground because it is feared that the Russian solution for this problem is not courts or law but execution. Nelson D. Schwartz and Julia Werdiger, "Austria's Woman on Wall Street and Madoff," *The New York Times*, January 6, 2009.

17: Beyond Pure Self-Interest

1. Author translation of text from Vera Nünning, '*A Revolution in Sentiments, Manners, and Moral Opinions': Catharine Macaulay und die politische Kultur des englischen Radikalismus, 1760–1790*, (Heidelberg: C. Winter, 1998), 49.

2. Mike McIntire, "Bailout Is a Windfall to Banks, If Not to Borrowers," *The New York Times*, January 17, 2009.

3. Vernon Louis Parrington, *Main Currents in American Thought* (New York: Harcourt Brace, 1927), 69.

4. Thomas Sheridan, *British Education: Or, the Source of the Disorders of Great Britain* (Dublin: George Faulkner, 1756), as reported in Nünning, '*A Revolution in Sentiments,*' 76.

5. Thomas Paine, *Common Sense* (New York: Penguin Classics, 1996), 81.

6. Sheridan, *British Education*, 75.

7. In *Loose Hints Upon Education, Chiefly Concerning the Culture of the Heart,* Ibid., 76.

8. Roger Butterfield, *The American Past* (New York: Simon and Schuster, 1947), 23.

9. Ibid., 12.

10. Miles J. Unger, *Magnifico, The Brilliant Life and Violent Times of Lorenzo De' Medici* (New York: Simon & Schuster, 2008), 164. Unger goes on to observe: "In the time-honored fashion of Florentine politics, one faction, having swept all opposition before it, used its authority to tax and spend to enrich friends and ruin enemies, thereby consolidating its hold on power."

11. To the contrary, it would have advanced the security of England had Elizabeth married and birthed an heir, but the queen showed over and over that she was fully aware that either a consort-king or a prince would have weakened her own hold on absolute power. In spite of years of urgings by her Parliament to marry Philip II or the Duke d'Anjou or *someone*, she refused, and her power remained uncontested to her last breath. She was apt to tell her people that whatever she did, she did for them, and they seemed to believe her. But when it came to this most important action that would have secured alliances but diluted her personal power, she put herself very much in first place.

12. "There was gunpowder packed away in Luther's doctrine of the priesthood of all believers, and the explosion that resulted made tremendous breaches in the walls of a seemingly impregnable feudalism." Parrington, *Main Currents in American Thought*, 6.

13. Unger's *Magnifico* provides a detailed and eminently readable account of Florence during this period.

14. G. William Domhoff, *Who Rules America?* http://sociology.ucsc.edu/whorulesamerica.

15. Robert Putnam's *Bowling Alone* dramatically details the dissolution of what he calls social capital in the United States over the last generation: "In 1992 three quarters of the U.S. workforce said that 'the breakdown of community' and 'selfishness' were 'serious' or 'extremely serious' problems in America. In 1996 only 8 percent of all Americans said that 'the honesty and integrity of the average American' were improving, as compared with 50 percent of us who thought we were becoming less trustworthy. Those of us who said that people had become less civil over the preceding ten years outnumbered those who thought people had become more civil, 80 percent to 12 percent. In several surveys in 1999 two-thirds of Americans said that America's civil life had weakened in recent years, that social and moral values were higher when they were growing up, and that our society was focused more on the individual than the community." (New York: Simon & Schuster, 2000), 25.

16. "A 1958 study under the auspices of the newly inaugurated Center for the Study of Leisure

at the University of Chicago fretted that 'the most dangerous threat hanging over American society is the threat of leisure.'" Ibid., 16.

17. "The story of wealth failing to translate into extra happiness is the story of the Western world. In almost every developed country, happiness levels have remained largely static over the past 50 years—despite huge increases in income. What the happiness research suggests is that once average incomes reach about £10,000 a year, extra money does not make a country any happier." Mark Easton, "Britain's happiness in decline," BBC News, May 2, 2006.

18: Beyond the Sword

1. A marvelous recounting of these times and the deliberations at the Convention can be found in David O. Stewart's *The Summer of 1787: The Men Who Invented the Constitution* (New York: Simon & Schuster, 2007). Much of the detail that follows here is told with the assistance of Stewart's tale of that summer.

2. The author was co-counsel for African American and Hispanic plaintiffs in this case.

3. As late as 1965 I attended a six-week program for the study of international law in Strasbourg, France, through the course of which the constant debate among Germans and Frenchmen was whether democracy was suited for Europe. My brilliant young German roommate was very skeptical.

4. Gleb Pavlovskii, "Three Days in August: August 19–21," *Postfactum News Agency and Interlegal Center Analytical Review*, no. 9 (August 22, 1991): 9. In possession of the author, having been received immediately after the coup failed.

19: Beyond the Easy Lie

1. Nicolas Kulish, "Germany Aims to Protect Its Interests by Guiding the West's Ties to Russia," *The New York Times*, December 2, 2008, A6.

2. The Committee to Protect Journalists (CPJ), an American group of journalists based in New York, reports that at least twenty-one journalists have been murdered in Russia since Putin came to power in 2000. While I cannot verify the accuracy of these reports, the list of names of those killed includes men and women from many of those outlets with which I was familiar in the late 1980s, which were at that time publishing the first progressive reports that contributed to the collapse of the Soviet Union. The list includes, according to CPJ, reporters from *Moscow News*, *Moskovskiy Komsomolets*, *Novaya Gazeta*, *Kommersant*, and a great many more, including some foreign reporters from well-known groups such as Reuters. For a recent report highlighting killings at *Novaya Gazeta*, see Mike Eckel, "Ghosts of Dead Journalists Linger over Newspaper," Associated Press, February 1, 2009. The murder of Estemirova was condemned by President Medvedev, which could suggest government disapproval or that the government was not behind it. But the leadership of Chechnya that Estemirova was investigating and reporting upon has been thoroughly backed by Prime Minister Vladimir Putin, who has shown no willingness until now to investigate the killings of other critical journalists.

3. Michael Slackman, "Generation Faithful: Jordanian Students Rebel, Embracing Conservative Islam," *The New York Times*, December 24, 2008.

4. Hernando de Soto, *The Mystery of Capital: Why Capitalism Triumphs in the West and Fails Everywhere Else* (New York: Basic Books, 2000).

20: Beyond Bribery

1. Celia W. Dugger, "Battle to Halt Graft Scourge in Africa Ebbs," *The New York Times*, June 9, 2009. Dugger's reporting finds evidence of increased corruption, payoffs, political murders, and blocking court prosecutions throughout sub-Saharan Africa, including, inter alia, Kenya, Congo, Zambia, South Africa, and Burundi. There is no apparent or demonstrable difference in political attitudes of those who control these sub-Saharan legal systems today and that of King John I in thirteenth-century England, or John of Gaunt, Duke of

Lancaster in the fourteenth century. Attitudes then and today are essentially feudal. More disturbingly, there is little daylight between corrupt officials in South Africa, Nigeria, and Kenya and Silvio Berlusconi, who embodies feudalism still dominant in modern Italy, and even less difference between them and the reign of Vladimir Putin in Russia.

2. Hernando de Soto, *The Mystery of Capital: Why Capitalism Triumphs in the West and Fails Everywhere Else* (New York: Basic Books, 2000), 15.

3. Ibid., 19–28.

4. Ibid., 71.

5. I have a Russian emigrant friend who, after years living in the United States, found himself being divorced by his American wife. He was amazed to experience an American judge of Hispanic descent who would give him equal visitation rights and order his American wife—who earned more money than he—to pay child support to him, the Russian emigrant who had absolutely no family connections to any Hispanics.

6. Rachel Donadio, "Questions Are from Enemies, and That's That," *The New York Times*, June 7, 2009, 3.

7. Robert Axelrod, *The Evolution of Cooperation* (New York: Basic Books, 1985).

8. "A society characterized by generalized reciprocity is more efficient than a distrustful society, for the same reason that money is more efficient than barter. If we don't have to balance every exchange instantly, we can get a lot more accomplished. Trustworthiness lubricates social life." Robert Putnam, *Bowling Alone* (New York: Simon & Schuster, 2000), 21.

9. Lynn Berry, "US Vice President Biden Hits Nerve in Russia," Associated Press, July 23, 2009. Biden predicted that the new Russia would not do any better than the old Soviet Union. He called the state "weak." That made the Russians very angry, and he was roundly excoriated in Russian papers. But Biden was probably right. Unless the mentality changes, in the long term any feudal country remains fundamentally dependent upon personal relationships, loses or punishes its most competent, corrodes truth, and gradually declines into mediocrity.

21: Finding Direction in a Time of Chaos

1. Archibald MacLeish, "Hypocrite Auteur," in *The New Pocket Anthology of American Verse*, ed. Oscar Williams (New York: Pocket Library, 1955), 294–95.

2. Claudia H. Deutsch, "Executive Pay: A Special Report, A Brighter Spotlight, Yet the Pay Rises," *The New York Times*, April 6, 2008, and also Deutsch, "Executive Pay: The Bottom Line for Those at the Top," *The New York Times*, April 5, 2008.

3. Ben White, "What Red Ink? Wall Street Paid Hefty Bonuses," *The New York Times*, January 29, 2009.

22: Democracy at the Crossroads

1. Garry Wills, *Lincoln at Gettysburg: The Words That Remade America* (New York: Simon & Schuster, 1992), 263. This is from the text that Wills describes as final, as compared to the spoken version. The differences are minor.

Index

© Sally Hayden von Conta

Craig A. Barnes started law practice in a large firm in Denver and then became a public interest lawyer trying cases dealing with school integration, women's rights, and natural resources. He has run for Congress, been a commentator on public radio, a columnist for the *Rocky Mountain News*, and a lecturer on three continents. In the 1980s he negotiated with the Soviet Academy of Sciences on nuclear issues and was executive editor of the first book since 1917 to be jointly published by the Soviet Academy and Western scientists. In the 1990s he facilitated informal bilateral talks in the Caucasus in the wars of ethnic cleansing between Armenia and Azerbaijan, and thereafter was employed by the US government to conduct multilateral negotiations in Central Asia on issues of water development. Barnes is the author of an Elizabethan trilogy of plays as well as a memoir, *Growing Up True*, and another social history, *In Search of the Lost Feminine*. Barnes and his wife, Mikaela, divide their time between their home in Santa Fe, New Mexico, and Lily Lake Ranch in Marble, Colorado. Visit his website at www.craig-barnes.com.

SPEAKER'S CORNER is a provocative series designed to stimulate, educate, and foster discussion on significant topics facing society. Written by experts in a variety of fields, these engaging books should be read by anyone interested in the trends and issues that shape our world.

The Brave New World of Health Care: What Every American Needs to Know about the Impending Health Care Crisis
Richard D. Lamm

Condition Critical: A New Moral Vision for Health Care
Richard D. Lamm and Robert H. Blank

Daddy On Board: Parenting Roles for the 21st Century
Dottie Lamm

The Enduring Wilderness: Protecting Our Natural Heritage through the Wilderness Act
Doug Scott

Ethics for a Finite World: An Essay Concerning a Sustainable Future
Herschel Elliott

God and Caesar in America: An Essay on Religion and Politics
Gary Hart

Iraq Uncensored: Perspectives
The American Security Project; Edited by James M. Ludes

Junk News: The Failure of the Media in the 21st Century
Tom Fenton

Last Chance: Preserving Life on Earth
Larry J. Schweiger

Names, Not Just Numbers: Facing Global Aids and World Hunger
Donald E. Messer

No Higher Calling, No Greater Responsibility: A Prosecutor Makes His Case
John W. Suthers

On the Clean Road Again: Biodiesel and the Future of the Family Farm
Willie Nelson

One Nation Under Guns: An Essay on an American Epidemic
Arnold Grossman

Parting Shots from My Brittle Bow: Reflections on American Politics and Life
Eugene J. McCarthy

Power of the People: America's New Electricity Choices
Carol Sue Tombari

Red Alert!: Saving the Planet with Indigenous Knowledge
Daniel R. Wildcat

A Return to Values: A Conservative Looks at His Party
Bob Beauprez

Social Security and the Golden Age: An Essay on the New American Demographic
George McGovern

A Solitary War: A Diplomat's Chronicle of the Iraq War and Its Lessons
Heraldo Muñoz

Stop Global Warming, Second Edition: The Solution Is You!
Laurie David

TABOR and Direct Democracy: An Essay on the End of the Republic
Bradley J. Young

Think for Yourself!: An Essay on Cutting through the Babble, the Bias, and the Hype
Steve Hindes

Two Wands, One Nation: An Essay on Race and Community in America
Richard D. Lamm

Under the Eagle's Wing: A National Security Strategy of the United States for 2009
Gary Hart

A Vision for 2012: Planning for Extraordinary Change
John L. Petersen

For a complete list of all titles in the Speaker's Corner series and to order a catalog of our books, please contact us at:

 **FULCRUM PUBLISHING**

4690 Table Mountain Drive, Suite 100
Golden, Colorado 80403
E-mail: info@fulcrumbooks.com
Toll-free: 800-992-2908
Fax: 800-726-7112
www.fulcrumbooks.com